About the Author

Kern R. Trembath is Assistant Chair of the Department of Theology at the University of Notre Dame.

DIVINE REVELATION

DIVINE REVELATION

Our Moral Relation with God

KERN ROBERT TREMBATH

New York   Oxford
OXFORD UNIVERSITY PRESS
1991

Oxford University Press

Oxford   New York   Toronto
Delhi   Bombay   Calcutta   Madras   Karachi
Petaling Jaya   Singapore   Hong Kong   Tokyo
Nairobi   Dar es Salaam   Cape Town
Melbourne   Auckland

and associated companies in
Berlin   Ibadan

Copyright © 1991 by Kern R. Trembath

Published by Oxford University Press, Inc.
200 Madison Avenue, New York, NY 10016

Oxford is a registered trademark of Oxford University Press

Library of Congress Cataloging-in-Publication Data
Trembath, Kern Robert.
Divine revelation : our moral relation with God / Kern Robert Trembath.
p. cm.   Includes bibliographical references and index.
ISBN 0-19-506937-4
1. Revelation.   I. Title.
BT127.2.T74   1991   231.7′4—dc20
90-24020

1 3 5 7 9 8 6 4 2

Printed in the United States of America
on acid-free paper

To my parents
Harry and Caroline Trembath

ACKNOWLEDGMENTS

It is surely the case that any book is the primary responsibility of its author. Just as surely, however, the very notion of *responsibility* itself invites us to think of the communitarian nature of our lives and work, for the word asks us to consider carefully those to whom we are responsible. I am especially pleased to mention the following persons as foremost among those whose thoughts and values contributed to the eventual shape of this book. (They are also hereby absolved of anything in it with which they might disagree.) In most instances, they did not know of my personal agenda and thus of the larger context to which their specific words contributed. It is hence a double pleasure to mention them here.

Father Charles Curran, who lectured at the University of Notre Dame on July 1, 1987, on methodological shifts in the Catholic social-ethics tradition. He suggested that "truth, justice, freedom, and love" form the axis around which critical and evolutionary ethical changes have been made in the Catholic church, especially progressive ones. Eventually, that axis became the "knowledge, love, hope, and community" of this book.

The Reverend Robert V. Bizzaro, dean of the Episcopal Cathedral of St. James in South Bend, Indiana, who preached the Trinity Sunday sermon on May 29, 1988, insisting that *Trinity* follows upon our experience of God and reflects back on it from the perspective of who we are, which gradually evolved into the structure of Chapters 3 and 4.

Professor Chris Menzel of the Department of Philosophy of Texas A&M University, who helped me to revise my thinking on the nature of human beings, especially the relationship between being a moral creature and being a material creature.

Professor Rita K. Hessley of the Department of Chemistry of Western Kentucky University, who read and constructively criticized an early draft of Chapter 3.

The Unitarian-Universalist Fellowship of Lafayette, Indiana, and especially its pastor, the Reverend Libbie Stoddard, who invited me to preach on February 12, 1989. The opportunity given me to step back from the "triadic" structures of Chapters 3 and 4 and reflect upon them in a more unified fashion resulted in a much stronger trinitarian expression.

The staff of St. Thomas Aquinas, the Catholic Center at Purdue University, from which I taught the University of Notre Dame Extension Program in Theology from 1988 until 1990, and especially the pastor, Father Patrick Click. The collective encouragement of the staff for me to finish this project reduced the time I could otherwise have devoted to them, and I am grateful for their generosity.

The Department of Theology of the University of Notre Dame, and especially its chairman, Father Richard P. McBrien. I would imagine that few American evangelicals owe so large a debt to Catholic systematic theology as I, and this book is but a small expression of my gratitude.

My wife, Sally M. Vance-Trembath, whose love of God and of the church continues to inspire me to wonder why she loves me as well. She and our children—Mark, Emily, Alex, and Calvin—are the greatest reasons for my disenchantment with many traditional evangelical (especially "propositional," that horrid word) theories of divine revelation and my search instead to explore the more theologically sensitive relational theories to which the present one belongs.

CONTENTS

DIVINE REVELATION

"Oh, Aslan," said she, "it was kind of you to come."

"I have been here all the time," said he, "but you have just made me visible."

"Aslan!" said Lucy almost a little reproachfully. "Don't make fun of me. As if anything *I* could do would make *you* visible!"

"It did," said Aslan. "Do you think I wouldn't obey my own rules?"

C. S. Lewis, *The Voyage of the "Dawn Treader"*

Introduction

This book is written with the intention of clarifying the Christian notion of revelation—that is, of saying what revelation is and what it is not. Thus, it is written as a contribution to a critical enterprise, critical in the classic sense of providing and outlining "criteria" by which one can better understand a particular notion within a given community. Implicit in this task is the need to identify why the concept of revelation arises as a Christian interest in the first place, and subsequently the need to identify the general criteria or judging mechanisms that are necessary to employ if we hope to be clear about our continuing use of revelation as Christians. In addition to meeting these two needs, I will also attempt to say what I believe the idea of revelation means.

So, our task is threefold. In the nature of the case, the third function is the most significant. This is because the criteria by which we assess the meaningfulness and adequacy of a given idea are themselves largely shaped by the idea itself. Granted, there are larger rules or canons by which to assess meaningfulness (such as the laws of logic), but since by definition these apply to all rational thinking, they cannot apply to this or that idea in particular. With respect to divine revelation, therefore, the canons of logic cannot be used to determine what the idea itself means but only whether a particular proposal of that idea makes sense with respect to the other things that Christians believe and hold.

That the notion of revelation has been important in the (Jewish and) Christian tradition can scarcely be challenged. There are various ways of specifying why this is so. In general, it seems to be because Christianity presumes a gap between what human beings are (sinful) and what they ought to be (perfect), with revelation serving as the content God supplies as the means to overcome the gap and be saved. Revelation thus has inescapably to do with divine intentions for human beings who, without those intentions, would not be able to become what God wants them to be.[1]

If this deliberately general and vague statement is true of all or most theories of Christian revelation, then what has traditionally accounted for the tremendous diversity among those theories are the ways specific authors and traditions attempt to make it more specific. Thus, the precise origin and nature of the "gap," the means of identifying God's intentions, the ways God communicates those intentions, and the precise ways in which those intentions actually overcome the gap are all features of the discussion that, variously interpreted, led to variety and disagreement among Christian traditions and theologians.

From the outset I shall argue that this procedure is wrongheaded. It is not wrongheaded because I reject the validity of those various features but instead because their mere mention presupposes something that is itself far more fundamental than any of the features themselves, and that is the possibility of a personal and intentional relationship between God and human beings in the first place. Many Christian theologians, for example, some of whom will be represented in Chapter 1, argue that the purpose of divine revelation is to overcome both the reality and the effects of human sinfulness. But *sin* is by definition a violation of an existing personal relationship whose precise meaning thus depends on the possibility and nature of that prior relationship. To say, then, that the purpose of divine revelation is (merely) to overcome human sin is to leave unaddressed the question of the shape of that prior relationship, an omission I believe is fatal. Why? Because both conceptually and ethically it does relatively little good for us to know that our sin has been overcome without knowing anything about the renewed relationship that is now ours by virtue of that overcoming. And if we do not know about it, then it will probably not much occupy our time and thoughts. And that which does not occupy our time and thoughts cannot be essential to human existence the way Christianity has usually claimed that divine revelation is.

I believe that divine revelation is crucial to human existence itself, in the most literal sense. That is, I believe that human existence as we experience it is itself the effect of divine revelation; such existence cannot ultimately be accounted for except by recourse to divine revelation. I shall postpone the specific steps of this claim until the final chapters of this book, but here I shall say only that if it is true, then of necessity there will be a methodological similarity between what we take *human existence* itself to mean on the one hand and the God who is revealed through divine revelation on the other. This suggests that revelation must first be considered with respect to the possibility and then the actuality of its reception by human beings, for unless we are clear about how it is received, we will not be able to say what it is that has been received with any confidence.[2]

To illustrate the need to approach the discussion of revelation in this manner, consider a keyhole.[3] The existence of a keyhole makes certain presuppositions about the kinds of things that could be successfully inserted into it; they must have certain kinds of shapes in order to get the lock to move. Thus, if all we have available to us is a keyhole, careful analysis of it will identify what kind of things will, and will not, fit it. But this presupposes the *possibility* of keys; from the existence of keyholes, we may conclude that keys exist, at least in principle. We may not conclude that a particular key exists; that is, from the possibility of keys, we cannot conclude the actual existence of *the* key needed to open *this* lock. But once having established the possibility, we can say what a particular key would have to be like in order to open a particular lock and then begin our search for it. Initially establishing the possibility not only establishes the reasonableness of our search but in addition greatly narrows down the field of objects that we may consider to resolve that search successfully.

Granted, we would all prefer the situation in which the key itself were in our possession, so that all we would have to do would be to use it. But this is precisely the situation that is not immediately or obviously available to us with respect to revelation. Initially, unless we are content simply to assert and insist upon an arbitrary definition,[4] we do not know what constitutes revelation. We do, however, know two helpful bits of information. The first is that some form of relationship is possible between God and human beings. This claim is difficult to establish except by recourse to warrants which are themselves fundamental features of religion (whether Christian or otherwise). In a book such as this one, however, whose beginning point is Christian and whose method is theological, taking such recourse is not fatally circular; all authors must assume certain things about their readers, and I can assume that mine do not reject either the possibility or the relationality of God out of hand.

Second, in principle we know enough about ourselves to know what that revelation would have to be like in order for it success-fully to account for the relationship with God. With these two fertile bits of information at our disposal, then, we may work backward to come to some reasonable conclusions about the actual shape of revelation itself. We would then be able to say that revela-tion must occur, a thought that sounds heretical to philosophical propositionalists because they refuse to accept the essentialness of God's relationality. That is, for propositionalist and other kinds of discontinuist theologians whom we shall meet in Chapter 1, it is entirely possible to conceive of a God who does not relate, a God for whom relationality is completely voluntary, a God who cannot meaningfully be described as essential to the existence of human beings. As I have already hinted, I take issue with this understand-ing of God because it is indistinguishable from atheism; a God whose existence may or may not be essential to human existence is not worthy of consideration. But if this is true, then revelation, understood as that which grounds the specific shape of human existence, must occur.

Michael Polanyi makes this same point in his discussion of what it means for something to be a tool. When we identify a certain object as a tool, he says, we can only do so because we already know its use or function. "I cannot identify the thing as a tool if I do not know what it is for. . . . [If] I come across a tool of which I do not know the use, it will merely strike me [*sic*!] as a peculiarly shaped object."[5] Thus, intrinsic to the description of an object as a *tool* is an under-standing of its usefulness. We might be mistaken in our understand-ing of its function; for example, we might confuse a screwdriver with an ice pick. But in the absence of *any* understanding of function or use, we can perceive it solely as an object and never as a tool.

This will help us to focus our discussion of the Christian concept of revelation. In the absence of a prior agreement regarding the function or purpose of revelation, all definitions are equally mystifying or, as I said earlier, equally arbitrary. Unless we first identify why the term even arises within the Christian vocabulary, and thus identify its use within Christian theology, we will not know how to distinguish between better and worse discussions of it. This awareness reflects the basic approach I follow in this book: to begin with the known (human beings) and with what is known about the known (the existence and hence the possibility of a relationship with God), and then to proceed to become clearer about what revelation must be in order for it to do what the Christian tradition has insisted that it does (say more precisely how that relationship is grounded in and hence revelatory of God.).

This basic approach, which I take to be essential to fruitful critical inquiry in all sorts of fields, will inform this book as follows. Chapters 1 and 2 will critically evaluate theories of revelation that proceed from what I have already described as an "arbitrary" foundation, meaning that these theories variously presume the meanings of God and human beings rather than deliberately considering them. Precisely what is presumed in each case will become clearer as I consider each proposal. My own theory will be proposed in Chapters 3 and 4. There I shall claim that an adequate understanding of human beings will observe that humans are moral beings, meaning that we are material beings who can know, love, and hope. Each of these constituent features is *moral* precisely in that it is grounded in goodness, and ultimately in that Goodness whom Christians call God. Furthermore, each is necessarily communitarian; one does not know, love, or hope in autonomous isolation from other beings. In sum, then, to be human is inescapably to-be-related and thence to-be-grounded ultimately in God.

This uncovers a second methodological presupposition of this book, namely that the concept of Christian revelation ultimately concerns finding out about persons (including, in this case, God) rather than discovering useful bits of information about objects (the history of Jesus, the origins of the universe, etc.). Granted, we often use the word in this latter sense, but even outside the specifically Christian context, that is not what we take its most important meaning to be. It surely does not seem to be the most significant meaning within the Christian tradition. Instead of *revelation* referring to advances in our understanding of things rather than persons, I shall assume that Christians use the word best when it refers to our being enabled to advance in our understanding of God's concrete offer of salvation, which is ultimately grounded in God's own self.

If I am correct in this assumption, then from this perspective, too, revelation may be seen as a relational concept. It refers to the dynamic growth in relationship of at least two discrete persons, one of whom is disclosing his or her self and the other of whom is receiving such disclosures or, as I shall argue in the last chapter, receiving that other's self. Revelation per se does not specify the limits either of knowability or of disclosures, although Christian revelation does by directing our attention to the saving aspects of such knowledge. *The purpose of the doctrine of divine revelation is to uncover the nature of the relationship between God and human beings so that we can participate in it more fully and deliberately.* Thus, the purpose of divine revelation may also be said to be *salvation*, meant here not solely in its narrower sense of justification from sin but in its wider (and older) sense of *health*.

I shall often assume this critical perspective when I argue against those theories that assume that the function of Christian revelation is to tell us things about the world that we would not otherwise be able to find out—for example, about the physical and organic beginnings of the universe. For my part, I shall assume that the function of revelation is not to compete with what the natural and humane sciences might tell us about historical facts but instead to disclose how we, as persons and as inhabitants of the natural universe, may see ourselves as related to the personal God whose good and gracious and steadfast character is not threatened by the caprice and banality of our experience of that universe.

One final methodological point remains to be considered as a guide to the organization of this book. It has been traditional in discussions of Christian revelation to distinguish between *general* and *special* revelation. Broadly put, the first type refers to the knowledge we gain about God from observing the nature and character of the natural universe. The second refers to the knowledge we gain about God from the Bible, which, according to this view, is divinely inspired and thus constitutes a sufficient summary of what we need to know about God.[6] In particular, it refers to God's saving interventions in the world, centering "in the redemptive acts of Hebrew history from the exodus to the resurrection of

Jesus of Nazareth, and in the communication of the meaning of these saving acts in both the prophetic and the apostolic word."[7] For Christians, what is critically central in special revelation is the interpretation of the life of Jesus, since without that interpretation it is assumed that sin would prevent us from correctly evaluating Jesus' life and we would thus lack precisely what the Christian tradition has insisted about Him, namely that He is God's ultimate act of salvation in and for the world.[8]

Regardless of the merits of this distinction or how it has historically been used by theologians, it indicates that in principle there are two different ways to come to know God. By definition, both ways are initiated by God, but each utilizes a different means by which God is made known to human beings. The way of general revelation assumes that there is an overall continuity between the ways human beings come to know about the world and the ways we come to know about God, and thus that there is an overall continuity between what we learn about the world and what thereby we learn about God. According to this view, coming to learn about the world is an indirect way of coming to learn about God. (In the nature of the case, of course, it should be stressed that faith insists that this be seen the other way around; that is, learning about the world is a *response* to the ways by which God allows us to learn about God since the initiative always rests with God.) I shall refer to this as the way of convergence or continuity, since it presupposes a drawing together of the ways we come to know the material world with the ways we come to know God.

The other way of coming to know about God is suggested by special revelation. The very notion of special revelation presupposes that there are acts of knowing that *cannot* result in increases in our saving knowledge of God (e.g., acts of knowing about the material universe). Unlike the way of convergence, this one presumes that human cognitive activity may take place independently of God and that when it does, such knowledge cannot contribute to a healthy or saved relationship with God. Thus, God must entirely take the initiative in communicating to us, since we need such knowledge for salvation but cannot acquire it apart from God's special interventions into our fields of knowledge. There are various specific candidates for this type of intervention, such as the Exodus, miracles, the incarnation-death resurrection of Jesus, the Bible itself, and so on. What all of these candidates share, though, is the assumption that they possess no soteriological or saving significance apart from the interpretation given them by God. That interpretation is the *special* revelation which distinguishes them from other sorts of things we might discover or come to know about the world and is thus the reason why they, and nothing else, are able to function as saving revelation. I shall refer to this way of knowing as the way of divergence or discontinuity, since it assumes that human knowledge unaided by special intervening divine interpretations cannot come to know what (or Who) is needed for salvation. What is specifically *dis*continuous here is the (at best) spiritually neutral knowledge our minds possess when they operate "naturally" and the spiritually saving knowledge our minds possess when they operate "faithfully."

This distinction will be reflected in the structure of this book. Chapter 1 considers various types of divergence theories of revelation, and Chapter 2 considers various types of convergence theories. Within each type I will survey what I take to be representative approaches and illustrations. I shall bring the following questions to each approach: What does it presuppose about the natures of God and human beings? How does it resolve or overcome the gap between them?[9] Thus, what follows is not a comprehensive survey of theories of revelation[10] but rather is simply intended as an analysis of certain signal or influential theories of revelation.

Following this evaluative work, my own understanding of trinitarian (or relational) revelation will then be presented in Chapters 3 and 4. Let me here say why I think that one is needed. The *Oxford Dictionary of the Christian Church* summarizes what I take to be the mainstream way of construing revelation: "In Christian theology the word is used both of the *corpus* of truth about Himself which God discloses to us and of the process by which His communication of it takes place."[11] According to this summary, the purpose of divine revelation is to inform us—or, worse yet, perhaps to instruct us—about God, following which we will allegedly learn or discover more about ourselves.[12] Not surprisingly, many treatises then end up so bedazzled by the vehicles of such disclosures (such as omniscience and omnipotence, in addition to miracles, "prophecies," etc.) that they never get around to the latter.

I think that this approach to revelation is religiously useless, as though the notion of omnipotence by itself, for example, considered apart from the need for salvation which we both have and cannot meet, were religiously interesting. I also think that it is backward. It is more in line with the notion of any revelation, I believe, but crucially of *divine* revelation as experienced within the Christian tradition, to say that its purpose is first to disclose ourselves to us and *thence* to tell us about the God who is our ground and our savior.[13] If the Christian notion of creation is correct and God *is* the "maker of all things visible and invisible," then self-discoveries are always and also discoveries about the God who created those selves and wishes to relate intimately with them. And furthermore, if the Christian notion of the threefoldness of God is correct, then the notion itself will necessarily reflect this threefoldness, since to say otherwise would imply that one of the three Persons of God were more involved in divine self-disclosures than either of the other two. Spelling this out is the task that awaits us.

It will help a good number of readers, although not all, if I acknowledge from the outset my dependence on the transcendental theology of Karl Rahner. He will not show up as a direct object of theological scrutiny within this study, because the form and content of his thought is so much my own. This is now the second book in which I have utilized Rahner's transcendentalist perspective to inquire into a topic that is of special interest to my own tradition, American evangelicalism. The first, *Evangelical Theories of Biblical Inspiration: A Review and Proposal* (Oxford University Press, 1987), critically evaluated what is arguably the most concrete instance of interaction between God and human beings. That book ended by briefly addressing the question of how faith could be certain that it was *God's* word, and not simply a human one, that is heard in the Bible.

This book expands upon the answer I gave there in order to account both for the question itself and for its presupposition, namely that some form of interaction or relationship between God and human beings is possible in the first place. In all of these reflections I have been immeasurably helped by Rahner. I hope that an increasing number of evangelicals will find him of use as well.

1

Divergence Theories
of Divine Revelation

Several times during the past year, I have been asked what project I am working on. When I have responded with "a book on divine revelation," most inquirers have blinked, nodded, and said something noncommittal, such as "My, that must be interesting." A few, however, have fumbled around in the apparent attempt to make a more contentious kind of statement without putting our friendship at risk. Eventually, encouraged by all sorts of reassurances, their statements took shape, and, interestingly enough, all took the same shape: "How can you have the kind of ego to presume to have something important, much less new, to say about a subject that is so close to the heart of the Christian vision of reality?" As a doctoral student, one becomes confident that everything one thinks or says about any given topic is important. Later on, of course, one discovers just how ungrounded that confidence is, usually as a result of an undergraduate's innocent but stunningly insightful interrogation. Thus, the more blunt the question, the more I have appreciated the questioner.

Several thousand years ago, at the intellectual dawn of what we now call the Western World, Socrates showed that questions, and not answers, are the greater dynamic by which our minds acquire knowledge and thus transcend earlier limitations. I think that this is because questions indicate a person's self-awareness of present limited knowledge and the intention to transcend that limitation in order to move to greater understanding of the world.[1] Questions, that is, are our way of showing our dissatisfaction with the present even before we know how to improve it.

That is probably the best place to begin to respond to the nervous question posed to me during the writing of this book. In reflecting on several accounts of divine revelation, it became increasingly obvious that most were flawed by avoidable errors. This chapter will serve not only as my attempt to represent and summarize the great bulk of Christian theories of divine revelation but, in addition, to point out these flaws. It can hardly be expected to include references to all such theories. In fact, I do not even claim to present a comprehensive representation of them. I only claim to have selected those that, when considered together, constitute a spectrum most interested readers will recognize as significant.

William Abraham presents probably the most widely used of these theories, namely that divine revelation is God speaking or acting in the world in saving ways. Carl Henry next reviews the claim that God's revelation is *the* truth about reality which is presupposed by our dependence on truth in rational discourse. Karl Barth then suggests, or rather insists, that revelation annihilates our common ways of determining truth, since by definition those ways and that truth are common to sinners. And since sinners are the very persons standing in need of what they cannot supply, revelation therefore must supply it if God is to be able to be believed in. Finally, James Packer defends another widely accepted theory, the stipulation of the Bible as God's revelation. Taken together, these constitute a useful taxonomy of discontinuist revelational theories.

As I implied earlier, questions are intellectually dynamic precisely in that they not only point out self-recognized boundaries but in addition strain to leap beyond those boundaries into new and fertile fields of reality. Thus, my intention in reviewing the theologians in this chapter is not merely negative. It is heuristic as well, in that I wish to gain from the past even if I discard various parts of it. My guess is that the nervousness of the questioners referred to above was grounded in their assumption that I was going to reject everything the tradition ever said about revelation in order to say something new about it. That would be silly, to say the least, especially for one who considers himself an evangelical. It is instead my intention to enrich, and perhaps to renew, what the Christian tradition has handed on to us so that we can be more aware and more appreciative of the many and varied ways in which God has been made known to us. The uncomfortable fact is that some of what previous generations of Christian believers accepted as true of divine revelation was both proposed and accepted rather uncritically. If we hope to do better ourselves, we must begin by asking blunt questions.

William J. Abraham

William J. Abraham is a Methodist pastor and professor from Northern Ireland. He has been lecturer in Philosophy of Religion and Christian Ethics at Queen's University in Belfast and currently teaches at Perkins School of Theology of the Southern Methodist University. He has published works in several areas of theology that bear upon our topic, including both revelation and its perpetual partner, inspiration.[2] His training in analytic philosophy is apparent in his defense of many traditional Christian interests, including the two just mentioned and several adjacent to them. With respect to revelation, his thesis is that its nature and purpose are most coherently conveyed by means of the events of divine speaking and divine acting.

Although the notion of divine *speaking* is perhaps what first comes to mind as the way in which God is revealed to the world, Abraham implicitly suggests that it may be less important than the images and possibilities available within the category of divine *acting*. He does this not so much by what he says but instead by the relative amounts of time he spends considering each, and even more noticeably by the essentially negative way in which he presents and inspects divine speaking.

Be that as it may, the notion of God speaking, surely an intrinsic part of both Jewish and Christian traditions, has come under intense fire within the past two or three centuries. Such fire has come both from theologians because of how the conclusions of historical criticism were alleged to bear upon the relevant biblical texts, and from philosophers who, if they believed in God at all, did not accept the coherence of the notion of God speaking in any mode that would justify its use within revelational contexts. Thus, the notion has been reinterpreted in many ways, but in general "as either a culturally conditioned or a dramatic way of expressing the results of intense spiritual reflection on history and experience."[3] This "reinterpretation" is significant, since it not only effectively does away with God's ability to talk but also reverses the agents of initiation and reception in the act of revelation: whereas previously God was said to initiate divine disclosures to humans in the world, now humans are said to discover, and in some senses create, insights about God. The obvious religious difficulty with this move, regardless of how warranted it might appear on other grounds, is how the rest of us can be certain that the insights thus discovered are the insights we need for salvation. Abraham discusses several objections to this view before moving on to consider the various ways of understanding the parallel notion of divine activity.

The first objection is that regardless of the cogency of contemporary arguments against divine speaking, "we cannot avoid positing some form of direct communication if we are to make sense of the [biblical] data as a whole."[4] This would appear to be a mere repetition of the traditional view and thus no real advance over it, but Abraham wishes to invest it with more significance than that. He employs it to substantiate his claim that "speaking has a privileged position when it comes to determining the intentions and purpose of an agent."[5] That is, while it is true that many avenues are open to us as ways to help us to understand another person, surely we should not ignore the fact that speaking is the initial, the widest, and usually the most fruitful one. It is only when we are barred from speaking with another (or, although this would not be the case with God, when we discover that the other person is a habitual liar) that we normally take recourse to the alternatives. Similarly, it is only if we knew antecedently that God could not talk that we should turn our attention to other ways by which God might be revealed to us. But this, says Abraham, is precisely what cannot be done in the case of divine revelation; to presuppose that God cannot be revealed by speech is gratuitous, and so to use that presupposition as warrant for restricting ourselves to the nonspeech alternatives is question begging at the very least.

Second, Abraham makes a stronger but still negative claim about a Christian theology that does not allow for divine speaking. Such a possibility, he says, would amount to a "radical agnosticism. . . .

[A] theology without the concept of divine speaking has of necessity a God who cannot forgive, command, or make promises." This rather stark claim is defended by noting that "forgiving, command-ing and promising are performative utterances."[6] A performative utterance is a linguistic form whose distinguishing characteristic is the immediate achievement of some behaviorally measurable inten-tion, even if only an internal one. So, for example, "John married Sue" is, if true, a historical report, whereas John's saying "I marry you" to Sue is a performative utterance. Similarly, "God forgave Mary's sin" is, if true, a historical report, whereas "Mary, I forgive your sin" is, if said by God, a performative utterance. Strictly speaking, performative utterances are neither true nor false but are only effective or ineffective with respect to accomplishing their intended behaviors. It is for this reason that Abraham claims that any restriction upon God's ability to speak, especially a radical one, would have devastating effects on the central Christian notions of forgiveness and salvation.

The final defense that Abraham makes of the appropriateness of divine speaking is more positive but also more terse and puzzling regarding the actual mode of such discourse. One of the principal reasons many began to be skeptical of the notion of God speaking in the first place was the straightforward and quite traditional insistence that God does not have a body. Because God does not have a body, neither does God have any of those somatic elements necessary for speech as we understand it—lungs, throat, larynx, tongue, palate, teeth, and so on. Thus, the tradition that claimed that God could speak could only explain this claim by saying that God spoke in ways analogous, but not identical, to the ways in which we do. The means of such analogous speech were never adequately spelled out, and for good reason: anything that would count as an adequate spelling out of it necessarily would have brought it into line with what we know about speech, especially with respect to its somatic components, and thus divine speech would have ceased to be different from ours. In general, therefore, the focused-upon feature of the analogous mode of divine speech was always its effect and not its performance as is the case with our more usual way of discussing the mode of speech. The effect on the listener was *as though* God had spoken normally, and even though all recognized that God had not, such recognition was suppressed in order to maintain the advantages of being able to think that God had.[7]

Abraham, though, does not take refuge in the analogous "as though." Instead, he seeks a univocal or identical way that God and humans might share in communicating verbal thoughts to others. He finds such a way in telepathy: "it is logically possible to conceive of someone communicating information without the use of vocal cords, and this is enshrined in dictionary definitions of telepathy."[8] Telepathy, he suggests, may serve as the preferred mode of discourse to keep in mind as we think of the ways in which God is revealed to human beings for the sake of their salvation.

There are two problems with this suggestion. The first is brought out by Abraham himself when he concludes his discussion by saying that "Much divine speaking could be construed as analogous to [telepathy]." Here he claims that the phenomenon of telepathy does in fact function as an analogy by which we can better understand what it means for God to speak and thus to reveal. However, I earlier referred to his intention to identify not an analogous but rather a univocal mode of divine (and human) speaking, and thus I take issue with him here. That is, although Abraham asserts that he will use telepathy as though it were only an analogous way of speaking about the actual means of divine speaking, in fact his discussion and use of it are better understood if we take it as the actual or univocal means itself.

The reason for this is clear: telepathy itself is an analogy, that is, a syntactic device which we press into service to give a name to a process that we clearly do not understand on its own terms. Because we believe it happens from time to time, though, we relate this kind of communication to something we do understand (actual speech), with the intention both of signaling our belief that it occurs and also of pointing out its present ambiguities. The dictionary definition accordingly refers to telepathy as though it were a type of speech with some specifically physiological features stripped away: "The communication of impressions of any kind from one mind to another, independently of the recognized channels of sense."[9] But recourse to one problematic analogy as a way of clarifying an even more problematic one does not strike me as a very constructive contribution to understanding what divine speaking actually is, especially for one who insists that the central truths of Christianity

cannot be known in the absence of it. It would thus seem that the
way Abraham uses the telepathy argument strongly implies that he
sees the divine and human uses of telepathy as univocal or identical.

   The second major problem with telepathy as the preferred mode
of illustrating divine discourse is also brought to light by Abraham
when he criticizes those who reject the propriety of divine speaking.
The claim has been advanced by some that revelation is simply but
strictly what a certain class of people (usually prophets and apostles) say it is. Abraham objects to this by asking rhetorically who
authorized them to function in this crucial way.[10] The same question can be asked of the receivers of divine telepathy, but in a more
straightforward manner. If we grant the actuality of telepathy as a
characteristic mode of divine revelation, we discover that it is a
quite private affair; that is the very nature of telepathy. Not everyone thinks that telepathy occurs, but even those who do never claim
that it is addressed to masses or communities of persons. Instead, it
occurs purely intersubjectively. But if this is so, then how are
subsequent generations of believers supposed to encounter this
divine telepathy in such a way that it becomes a saving revelation
for them? We appear to have here another version of the "private
insight" account of revelation which Abraham himself explicitly
rejects in this chapter and which, I think, he does well to reject. If it
really is true that God must "directly speak to particular people"[11]
in order for us to be assured of God's intentions concerning salvation, forgiveness, commands, and promises, then it cannot be true
that such certainty finds adequate grounding in telepathy unless,
and only unless, such telepathic revelation is instantaneously directed to all Christian believers everywhere. And nobody, I take it,
wishes to make that claim, both because it is counterintuitive and
because it renders the Bible useless to Christian theology.

   From this not terribly satisfactory discussion of revelation as
divine (telepathic) speech, Abraham moves to a much longer consideration of it as divine action. In particular, he inspects two
categories of divine activity by means of which revelation could be
said to be conveyed to human beings: miracles and incarnation.

   The point raised by Abraham in his chapter on miracles that is
most relevant for our purposes has to do not so much with whether
but rather with how a given unusual event may be said to be
revelatory for those who come to know more about God as a result

of reflecting upon it. Traditionally it was assumed that miraculous events, defined as contraventions of the laws of nature, were self-authenticating because nothing or nobody other than God could account for their occurrence, and thus for their interpretation as well. Abraham selects John Locke to represent this tradition:

> The number, variety and greatness of the miracles [of Jesus], wrought for the confirmation of the doctrine delivered by Jesus Christ, carry with them such strong marks of an extraordinary divine power, that the truth of his mission will stand firm and unquestionable, till any one rising up in opposition to him shall do greater miracles than he and his apostles did. Such care has God taken that no pretended revelation should stand in competition with what is truly divine, that we need only open our eyes to see and be sure which came from him.[12]

For Locke, the "real" revelation resides in the doctrines which Jesus "delivered," which are so clear that some are able to come to faith without aid from any other quarter. However, God so constructed the world as to create a congruence between those doctrines and certain kinds of empirical events such that any interested person not completely convinced by the doctrines themselves could find substantiation for them in those other events, especially the miraculous ones. In the nature of the case, the testimony of miraculous events alone is not sufficient to create Christian faith, since their place and purpose in the world is instrumental with respect to the more foundational "doctrines." Nor, interestingly enough, is it even enough to confirm such faith, since conceivably it might be overridden at any time by yet "greater" miracles and whatever religious system they attach to. No doubt Locke meant this rhetorically, and we should probably read him charitably rather than cynically here.

The weakness of this interpretation of revelatory miracles is not difficult to discover, and Abraham points it out. The only way any event, but especially a miraculous one, could be said to function in the confirming way Locke claims is if God and humans antecedently agreed upon exactly how events warrant doctrines. Such a step is necessary in order for humans to know precisely which miracle is confirming which doctrine and, in addition, how it does so. But of course this prior agreement would itself necessarily constitute a revelation, most likely a speech-type one and by definition *not* one confirmed by a miracle, and thus we are back at the point of wondering how events authorize doctrines in the first place.

Abraham concludes his consideration of the relationship between divine revelation and miracles by proposing and defending the relatively weak claim that miracles "can have some weight in a complex cumulative argument" concerning the exact nature of revelation.[13] His defense is essentially that miracles may function to warrant existing revelatory experiences "because they exhibit a design or purposiveness which will remain enigmatic or unexplained unless they are taken as direct acts of God." That is, certain events may serve to confirm previously accepted instances of divine revelation provided that they be construed as divine miracles rather than simply as odd and unrepeatable natural events. They may be construed in this latter sense, of course, but if so, then they will not have any relation at all to alleged instances of revelation or, by definition, to any more regular type of event. As an illustration of the propriety of believers' being able to take miracles in this weaker sense, Abraham notes the "cluster [of miracles] said to accompany certain key phases of special revelation in the past, [namely] Moses, Elijah and Jesus in the biblical traditions."

So far as I can determine, this display of the relationship between miracles and divine revelation is not only weak but fatally so.[14] To claim that unusual and unrepeatable events such as miracles serve to confirm the validity of the essential truths of Christianity but do not constitute revelatory experiences themselves is to increase rather than to reduce the effect that actions are said to have upon revelation. In so doing, this also seems to limit the arena through which God might be revealed to the world; for example, why only scientifically anomalous events and not more regular ones.

Worse yet, though, the mechanism by which this confirmation is alleged to take place fails to make any sense upon closer inspection. Abraham says, for example, that "such unparalleled events as miracles are of value in assessing a claim to revelation because they can be accounted for, given that the revelation is true." This repeats his earlier claim that the exclusive function of miracles with respect to revelation is to warrant or certify revelation claims. But this makes no sense, especially given Abraham's own description of a miracle here as an "unparalleled event." If an unparalleled event is one that literally has no parallel in history, then it could equally be said to confirm any claim to revelation as no such claim at all. In fact, it may be said equally to confirm everything, anything, or nothing at all. Thus, such an event would seem analogous to a logical self-contradiction from which, as philosophers love to remind us, anything at all may be deduced. It is only if we antecedently specify that the miracle is to apply to "this" divine utterance as opposed to all of "those" that it could function either to confirm or to disconfirm that utterance. But then, once again, the *prior* utterance would be the actual revelatory event, along with its antecedently agreed-upon specifications, and not the anomalous event, functioning as its confirmation.

An example will clarify this point. Suppose a graduate student is nearing the end of her doctoral studies in a field for which there are increasingly few professional openings. Suppose further that she is a Christian believer who takes it as true that miraculous events serve to confirm prior divine revelations, in this particular case those "natural" hints and proddings, those open and shut doors, through which she has always received God's direction for her life's path. Within these conditions we can all empathize with her as she prays that God would help her to decide whether or not to remain in her graduate field, since, among other things, she believes that God had approved her entering it in the first place. Furthermore, as time goes by and as the bleak employment stories of her predecessors filter back to her, she begins to suspect quite seriously that she should be looking for jobs outside of teaching altogether.

Now suppose that on a certain day "an unparalleled event" occurs in her life, one that so clearly violates the laws of nature with which she is familiar that she calls it a miracle: when she turns the key to start her car one morning, it does not start but instead tells her in clear English that she should serve hamburgers rather than chicken at the party she and her husband are hosting later in the week. Repeated turns of the key result in the same advice until she is quite convinced that it is a miracle. She subsequently takes this miracle as confirming the goal of completing her dissertation and assiduously pursuing a job in the teaching profession rather than venturing outside it.

Surely this is an unparalleled event, and it is clear that it is unparalleled in at least two senses. First, it has never (one imagines) occurred anywhere else at any time in the whole history of the universe. Second, and more to the point here, it has no parallel with the major question of her life: her professional future. That is, there does not seem to be any obvious congruity between it and her prayers that God would help her decide about her future. So what should she deduce from it, aside perhaps from what to serve at the party? The only answer that seems to be theologically appropriate is nothing. She could just as easily have deduced from this event that she should immediately change all of her life's plans and become a professional golfer as her actual deduction that she should remain in graduate school, so it is impossible to say that God was revealing anything to her, or confirming any prior revelation, by means of this unusual occurrence. Once again, since anything may be deduced from an unparalleled event, it is tendentious to insist that one particular thing should be.[15]

Thus, it would seem as though even the weak claim Abraham puts forward for the confirmatory nature of miracles with respect to revelation should be abandoned. And the reason for this conclusion is not that such events can have no confirmatory effects whatsoever upon bits of information, even divinely revealed ones, but instead that they may have confirmatory effects on any and all bits of information and thus do not do us any good in this context. In no way do I intend to be skeptical or cynical about the possibility of miraculous events occurring. Rather, it simply is not inherently clear what we should do with them if and when they do. Apart from some prior agreed-upon regulation telling us generally (and, it is hoped, precisely) how to apply such events to our concrete lives, they cannot serve to confirm anything. But if such an agreement were to occur, then it is clear that *it* would be the revelation in that situation.

Abraham's next chapter explores the incarnation in order to determine its significance to the concept of revelation. As Christians understand and use the word, *incarnation* brings to mind at least three possible levels or degrees of revelation. The first two are usually referred to as general and special revelation—that is, the understanding of God acquired through reflection upon the universe in the first case and through reflection upon the specific message of prophets and apostles in the second. Incarnation adds a third way in which God's character may be made known to humans in the world, a way that in the nature of the case is intended to be the most clear of all. The explanation for this has to do with the greater directness or immediacy by which we are able to know God if we are able to meet and deal with God face to face as opposed to being limited to the indirect reports, records, or impressions of others.

Of special interest to us here are the two ways by which Abraham defends the centrality of incarnation to revelation. The first is the way of religion or devotion, and the second is the way of epistemology or certainty of knowledge. I shall summarily review these two strategies and conclude that while Abraham seems to include all the right elements in these discussions, he presents them backward when viewed from the perspective of those in the first century who initially made the claim that Jesus was the incarnate self-revelation of God. If I am correct in noticing this, then to the degree that we intend for our faith to echo theirs, we, too, should reverse the order of priority that Abraham presents. My own suggestions concerning revelation in the final chapters will follow this reversed approach.

Abraham identifies at least three devotional problems that would result from any attempt to eradicate the incarnation from Christian theology.[16] The first is that such a loss would immediately precipitate a decrease "in the inspirational value of the story of Jesus" precisely because the doctrine of the incarnation is the doctrine that makes the story of Jesus a major part of the story of God rather than merely the story of an ancient Jew. Without it, therefore, one would only be able to think of Jesus as a human and not, as the church has always attempted, as both God and human. This would result in further problems: second, that Jesus would be stripped of His normative role within the tradition of Christian narratives (perhaps the life of a saint closer to our own historical context would better serve the need for an identifiable hero in the stories the church uses to shape its ethics and piety), and third, that any such story, including that of Jesus, would then formally be a story of our search for God rather than God's search for us. There is nothing inherently wrong with the former type of story; after all, at the very least that is the function of the stories of saints. But to see Jesus' story in exactly and only the same light as those of the saints would

constitute a significant alteration from how it has been seen traditionally, and I would agree with Abraham that it is both unneces-
sary and wrong to recast His story in this way.

The epistemological loss generated by the attempt to rid Christianity of the incarnation centers essentially around the claim that it
"provides a warrant for exercising trust and for believing God to be
a God of love. If God has acted as the incarnation specified, then it
is warranted to believe that God does love us."[17] So, for Christians
who wish to have a reason for their belief that God is primarily
loving rather than anything else, such a belief finds clearest substantiation in the doctrine that Jesus is God really loving concrete
human beings in history. This conclusion might be sustained on
other grounds, but there is no doubt that the incarnation, if true,
provides the best possible grounds for holding it. Abraham then
concludes the epistemological way of underlining the significance of
incarnation to revelation by noting that the incarnation is not a
"logically necessary" belief, since, among other things, it does not
reflect back upon a logically or even historically necessary event.
Instead, this doctrine functions more as a meeting ground or matrix
for all sorts of other beliefs, among which are the theological
doctrines of human sinfulness, divine love, and human redemption;
the philosophical doctrines of person, nature and essence, primary
and secondary causation; and so on. Christians are thus warranted
in accepting the incarnation to the degree that they find it an
illuminating way both of referring to and advancing their understandings of all of these beliefs, provided always that the criteria of
"advance" be the notions of God as Person and as love.

There are two problems with Abraham's treatment of incarnation
and revelation in this chapter. The first problem itself is twofold: (1)
Abraham only formally addresses the notion of incarnation itself,
and (2) he does not materially relate incarnation to revelation which
the reader had been led to expect in a book on revelation. That is,
Abraham contributes what might be more appropriate as a first
chapter in a book on the apologetic significance of incarnation,
setting out as he does the probable consequences of significant
alterations in that doctrine as it has come down to us in church
tradition. Had that been his intent, I would surely agree with much
of what he said. As it stands, though, he only succeeds in telling us
why we should insist on holding on to a notion of incarnation. He

does not do what we expected him to do in this context, namely say precisely how the incarnation functions as God's self-revelation either in the first century or in the twentieth. That is, he establishes only the much weaker claim that abandoning the notion of incarnation would lead to greater difficulty in holding to the belief that God loves us. True enough, I believe, but that in itself does not tell us why we should hold to incarnation ourselves; after all, our non-incarnation-holding Jewish cousins do not find it impossible to think of God in that way. And Abraham only obliquely hints at how the incarnation itself stands as the instance par excellence of divine revelation: by claiming an identity between a historical figure and God, with the result that that person's words thereafter present the character of God anew to those whose faith sprang from the initial claim.

The second problem with Abraham's presentation is much more significant and has to do with those first-century Jewish believers who initially professed faith in Jesus as God's in-the-flesh self-revelation. Here I refer to what I said earlier about Abraham having things backward. For example, at one point he says that "it is only because [Jesus] is accepted as God incarnate that the allegiance given to God can legitimately be given to Christ. Without the incarnation, worship of Christ would have to be seen as idolatry."[18] I would claim that this is historically anachronistic; that is, it might be true that *we* cannot believe in Jesus apart from a doctrine of incarnation, but it is textually unwarranted to think that of the persons we see coming to faith in Jesus in the New Testament. To claim, for example, that the faith of the Samaritan woman at the well in John 4 included some specific form of incarnational thinking strains credibility. And yet it is clear that John wants us to know that this woman did come to saving faith in Jesus, and furthermore that her testimony about Him served as proximate cause of the saving faith of many more persons in her city.[19]

What is backward in Abraham's account of faith for first-century believers is that he assumes they had available to them the entire conceptual framework of doctrines that the church subsequently and gradually constructed precisely in order to understand and structure how they lived and wrote about their faith. But clearly those believers did not. The Samaritans came to faith in Jesus, I would instead claim, because He was the one they would have expected God to be like had God become a person, in this case, "the savior of the world" (42).

This last claim deserves comment on two levels. On the more immediate but ultimately less significant level, it denies that holding to a given notion of incarnation is essential to genuine Christian faith. This point is well recognized among theologians[20] and will not occupy much time here, but it can quite quickly be demonstrated by reflecting upon the starting points of each of the four gospels. The earliest gospel, Mark, entirely omits any consideration of the birth or life of Jesus until His baptism, from which we must conclude that if Mark understood the notion of incarnation at all, he was able to do so without explicitly relating it to the life of Jesus. The next two gospels, however, begin their narratives at Jesus' conception and birth. Matthew and Luke both spend extensive amounts of time in theologically evaluating the historical and historic events surrounding the birth of Jesus. For them, in other words, the significance of Jesus did not "begin" at a certain point in His life, which is the most natural reading of Mark's baptismal beginning. Instead, their view was that the historical Jesus was never *not* religiously significant. From the very moment of conception, his life could only be understood if it were seen as *messianically* revealing the nature or character of God, His Father. John's Gospel, though, the latest to be written, clearly announces and affirms God's incarnation to Jesus: "In the beginning . . . the Word was God." By deliberately echoing the language of Genesis 1:1, John finally articulates what we today take as incarnation. If Mark's Jesus was the man whom God "adopted" at the baptism, and if Matthew's and Luke's Jesus was the historical man who always and perfectly revealed the character of His Father, then John's Jesus is God who became a human being. The point for us to notice is that each of these three ways, which do not exhaust the number of ways in the New Testament, is different but also (by definition) within the range of Christianly legitimate interpretations of Jesus. Only the latest, though, is "incarnation."

Thus, Abraham's claim about the intrinsic nature of incarnation to Christianity is justified, but not in the way he seems to have intended. His use of "incarnation" at no time reflects the diversity of ways specific incarnational events are presented in the New Testament. By implication, at least, he thus tempts his readers to think that there is only one such way which, were it to be excised from Christian theology, would fatally affect the shape of our belief.

I would agree that the incarnation is not an optional part of Christian theology but would argue that the New Testament forces us to recall that it developed historically and thus was not always present as a constitutive element in primitive Christian faith. The early church struggled to develop its understanding of incarnation, but even though today we accept only John's as canonically legitimate, we do not thereby throw out the more nascent expressions in the New Testament. What is common to all of them, and is thus that which each intends to reflect regardless of how adequately it is accomplished, is that Jesus was worthy of the worship the Jews had previously directed to Yahweh. We may safely conclude, then, that it was only after these early believers found themselves experientially worshipping Jesus *as* God that they began to reflect theologically upon His relationship *with* God. Incarnation arose as a way of conceptualizing something that was already happening: the worship of Jesus as God. And it is precisely because the experience of worshipping Jesus preceded the theological reflection upon it that there exists a gradually developing theology of incarnation in the New Testament. But this way of putting it is opposite to Abraham's, since it rejects the idea that they deliberately selected a specific incarnational theology *prior* to their encounter with Jesus in order to avoid an "idolatrous" worship of Him.

This leads to the second and theologically more significant comment on "the logic of faith" evidenced by the Samaritan believers. As we read the story in John 4, it is clear that both the woman and the townspeople had some understanding of God prior to their encounter with Jesus which by definition was not incarnational. In other words, they had what might be called dynamic expectations concerning God; they were not religiously inert. Thus, when they met Jesus, they were not persons in whom faith needed to be created ex nihilo so much as in whom it needed to be affirmed, challenged, refined, altered, and perhaps deepened. Of course, their prior faith was not Christian faith, but it was sufficient to ground their expectation that a person who "told me all that I ever did" must be the Messiah (John 4:29) and the savior of the world (42).

Abraham's account of faith is precisely opposite to this one. He insists that "the early Christians were only able to experience liberation through Jesus and thereby relate divine action to such experiences because they already believed him to be in some form or another a vehicle of God from whom liberation is to be hoped."[21] With specific reference to the incarnation, then, Abraham also says that it "explains why we respond to Jesus as Saviour and Lord. This explanation is epistemic rather than psychological; it gives rational grounds as to why we ought to respond to Jesus, rather than offering a psychological account as to why people have responded positively to Jesus."[22] By definition, this is true of Christians today, of course, since a Christian today is defined as (among other things) one who accepts certain specific beliefs about the propriety of worshiping Jesus as God. But we are not the relevantly interesting persons in this discussion precisely because we possess the more fully developed belief structure about Jesus which those believers then did not. Those who are theologically interesting in this context are those who came to faith when they historically encountered Jesus, for it is the account of their coming to faith that will uncover for us the relationship of faith (as effect), revelation (as proximate or secondary cause of the effect), and God (as remote or primary cause of the effect).

I shall consider this matrix more carefully in the last two chapters of this book, so here I shall only provide a brief criticism of Abraham's account of faith. The weakness in it that I can see resembles a problem already noted in this chapter. If it really is true that someone "already believed [Jesus] to be in some form or another a vehicle of God" prior to her actual encounter with Jesus, for example, then it is also true that (1) she was a Christian before she encountered Jesus, which is unusual to say the least, and (2) her actual encounter was soteriologically redundant since she already possessed an incarnational assessment of Him prior to meeting Him, which is even more unusual. Abraham's insistence that the cognitive aspects of belief always precede the experiential aspects of belief means that whatever accounted for those cognitive aspects is itself the saving revelation at issue, since it must be present in order to be able to have an "appropriate" understanding of the subsequent encounters. And since by definition it precedes the experiential encounter with Jesus, then it is impossible to say that the historical incarnation makes any difference at all to human salvation, since clearly one had to be saved (i.e., have a cognitively correct understanding of Jesus as God incarnate) before meeting

Him. The best alternative to holding this conclusion, it seems, is to give up the predisposition that assumes that cognition always and inevitably precedes experience.

Although I have only considered a small portion of Abraham's book, what we have seen is sufficient to warrant the suspicion that its subject matter might better have been described as incarnation (or, more broadly, divine intervention) than as revelation. And that is precisely how he concludes it: "The purpose of this study has been modest. It has attempted to show that belief in divine intervention is a permissible option for the modern theologian. . . . [Intervention] is at the foundation of claims about God's purposes and God's love that are unlikely to retain either their credibility or their inspiration if they are abandoned."[23] Perhaps so, but are we thereby given a clue to the nature of revelation? I believe we are, and that they fit nicely into the classical distinctions of form and material.

The formal clue is the one reflected in the methodology of this book, namely that theories of revelation may be distinguished as belonging in the two categories of continuity and discontinuity. Clearly a person who announces revelation as the purpose of his book and then spends the lion's share of that book considering divine intervention has said something significant (revealing?) about his concept of revelation. In following this procedure, Abraham presupposes that the notion of human cognitive activity unaided by God is itself a coherent notion (those discussed in the second part of this book will take issue here) and that it is entirely unable to arrive at knowledge that is savingly significant to the human knower. In view of this presupposition, then, it comes as little surprise that revelation, if understood as knowledge sufficient for salvation, must be delivered by the vehicle of divine intervention. The thorny question is then not primarily in what revelation consists but rather whether or not the notion of divine intervention may be held by thinking believers, for in the absence of a delivery vehicle it is useless to speculate about the contents of the package. That is also, I think, why Abraham spends relatively little time on the actual modes of revelation-intervention (i.e., speaking and activity) and more on defending the abstract notion of divine intervention in the scientific and philosophical context that seems to have erected so many barriers against it. Given his initial presupposition, this to be expected, but we shall soon see that the presupposition itself is susceptible to criticism.

The second and "material" clue that we may take from Abraham is seen in his statement that revelation has to do with God's purposes and love. (We encountered this thought earlier in considering performative utterances.) Although we would have wished for a more extensive treatment here, Abraham seems to agree that that which materially constitutes revelation fits within the parameters of ultimacy, prescription or normativity, and personality. To make the same point negatively, if a purported instance of revelation only concerns natural objects and not persons, or is of less than ultimate importance to how we live our lives, or is ethically tentative and variegated, then it is not revelation. It is not thereby useless but is simply not divine revelation. And here I would agree with Abraham.

Abraham's overall approach in this book presumes both that revelation occurs primarily as a cognitive action in the mind and that it is best construed as an intervention on God's part which occurs not only within history but more importantly within the minds of believers who need to have rational grounds for believing in Jesus as the incarnation of God. This approach is unsuccessful, though, when we attempt to use it to account for the effects of revelation on those who were the first to come to faith in Jesus, as we saw in the case of both the evangelists and the Samaritan believers. It is also conceptually problematic when taken with full seriousness, because in focusing as it does on the element of "the rational grounding of belief," the need to establish a rational ground for this element as *the* moment of revelation is completely overlooked. As already noted, Abraham reverses cart and horse by requiring persons to hold certain fundamental beliefs about God and Jesus in order to warrant the confession that Jesus is the word or self-revelation of God. We should seriously question the validity of any theology that insists that explicit faith be present before revelation can occur.

Carl F. H. Henry

Carl F. H. Henry is probably the most prominent evangelical theologian of the past thirty years, especially if measured by the scholarly criteria of productivity and degree of influence on that cross-section of the American church. He has taught at several campuses in the United States and lectured at numerous more internationally. He was the founding editor of the popular evangelical journal *Christianity Today* and served for many years as its editor-at-large. He is the author of some twenty books on philosophical theology and apologetics, christology, ethics, and (especially recently) revelation. Our interests focus on his latest work, a magnum opus of six volumes to date entitled *God, Revelation and Authority*. In these volumes we discover an understanding of revelation that is quite characteristic of evangelicalism.

Henry's latest work is his attempt not to establish but rather to demonstrate the rational credibility of traditional Christian theology in a world that often looks upon it as "an outmoded superstition, like alchemy or astrology, that has unfortunately survived from the ancient past or from the Dark Ages."[24] This suspicion is displayed in two opposite but equally deleterious attitudes: (1) that such theology is irrational and thus unable to be "integrated with any unified system of truth," and (2) that the only possible coherence of theology is based on "conclusions . . . laid down before the argument begins." Thus, his work is offered to a world that, far from being positively inclined or even neutral toward a theology that attempts deliberately to root itself in traditional thought forms, language, and experience, views all attempts instead as otiose and scarcely worthy even of denial.

In view of this, we may expect that Henry's antidote concentrates on the "truthfulness" of Christian theology, with truth being a measure not so much of the correspondence between experience and thought as of the systemic coherence of the whole of the theological enterprise. The person who sets himself or herself to the task of demonstrating such coherence must therefore be prepared to account for the "data of theology, . . . rational methods of inquiry, ways of argument, and criteria for verification,"[25] for in the absence of these there is no way to show Christianity's credibility either as a way of thinking about God alone or as a way of thinking about the God-human relationship.

Revelation is the area within systematic theology in which the truthfulness of rational coherence of Christianity is most easily tested, because it is defined as the area where the self-disclosure of God is made evident to humans and thus to human cognitive categories. "[God] is a very particular and specific divinity, known from the beginning solely on the basis of his works and self-declaration as the one living God. . . . God heralds his unchanging truth to man once for all and ongoingly; man meanwhile asserts a multiplicity of contrary things about God and his Word."[26]

Henry's first volume is devoted to "prolegomena," or notional categories that we must get straight if we are to be able to understand everything that follows. His second and third volumes discuss fifteen theses that constitute the framework of "what can be said for divine revelation in terms of the living God who shows himself and speaks for himself."[27] My specific interest leads me to review some of these initial notional categories and attempt thereby to uncover the essence and the structure of Henry's perception of divine revelation. In order to be most clear about his overall scheme of things, though, and in view of the fact that I will not consider most of his theses in detail, I shall here list all of them:

1. Revelation is a divinely initiated activity, God's free communication by which he alone turns his personal privacy into a deliberate disclosure of his reality.
2. Divine revelation is given for human benefit, offering us privileged communion with our Creator in the kingdom of God.
3. Divine revelation does not completely erase God's transcendent mystery, inasmuch as God the Revealer transcends his own revelation.
4. The very fact of disclosure by the one living God assures the comprehensive unity of divine revelation.
5. Not only the occurrence of divine revelation, but also its very nature, content, and variety are exclusively God's determination.
6. God's revelation is uniquely personal both in content and form.
7. God reveals himself not only universally in the history of the cosmos and of the nations, but also redemptively within this external history in unique saving acts.[28]
8. The climax of God's special revelation is Jesus of Nazareth, the personal incarnation of God in the flesh; in Jesus Christ the source and content of revelation converge and coincide.

9. The mediating agent in all divine revelation is the Eternal Logos—preexistent, incarnate, and now glorified.

10. God's revelation is rational communication conveyed in intelligible ideas and meaningful words, that is, in conceptual-verbal form.

11. The Bible is the reservoir and conduit of divine truth.

12. The Holy Spirit superintends the communication of divine revelation, first, by inspiring the prophetic-apostolic writings, and second, by illuminating and interpreting the scripturally given Word of God.

13. As bestower of spiritual life, the Holy Spirit enables individuals to appropriate God's revelation savingly, and thereby attests the redemptive power of the revealed truth of God in the personal experience of reborn sinners.

14. The church approximates the kingdom of God in miniature; as such, she is to mirror to each successive generation the power and joy of the appropriated realities of divine revelation.

15. The self-manifesting God will unveil his glory in a crowning revelation of power and judgment; in this disclosure at the consummation of the ages, God will vindicate righteousness and justice, finally subdue and subordinate evil, and bring into being a new heaven and earth.[29]

Here we see that theses 1 through 6 treat the nature of God as the initiator of revelation, thesis 7 treats the topic of special revelation, theses 8 and 9 treat christology or the significance of Jesus as both the historical and critical center of special revelation, theses 10 and 11 treat the form and location of what the church has recognized as canonical or authoritative revelation, theses 12 and 13 treat pneumatology or the doctrine of the divine confirmation of revelation by the Holy Spirit, thesis 14 treats ecclesiology or the relationship between church and revelation, and thesis 15 treats eschatology or the impact revelation will have upon the created universe when God's patience is eclipsed by the desire to be known unambiguously *as* God by all people.

The first question that must be addressed to Henry's program has to do with the methodological placement of his discussion of God. To begin a definitive defense of the rationality of Christian theology with several hundred pages discussing the nature of God is either very odd or very risky. It is odd in that it seems so clearly to be an instance of "basing theology on conclusions laid down before the argument begins." In this case, those conclusions have to do with the nature of God since that nature is scarcely unambiguous either with respect to its particular form or the method of uncovering it. That is, if it is true that God's nature is not objectively or universally known, which Henry certainly believes, and it is consequently and also true that no one way of attempting to come to discover God's nature is able to be canonized in advance as the only legitimate way, then to begin a discussion of how it is that God is revealed with an assertion of who God is constitutes a massive begging of the question.

The question begged here (i.e., the conclusion which is inserted as a premise) is, of course, how one knows the character of God apart from the revelation Henry has not yet begun to clarify. The only way one might chart a path through the various ambiguities noted above is if one already knew the revealed and therefore divinely authorized nature of God. But that is precisely what one cannot assume in a discussion of the nature of divine revelation, since that which makes a given revelation *divine* is its origin in God. Thus, one cannot antecedently specify a given body of knowledge as divine revelation if what makes something count as divine may only be known as a result of such revelation. Henry appears to be caught in this cul-de-sac, and some way out it is needed not just as a way of evaluating his proposal but more importantly as a way of overcoming the theological and religious difficulty here pointed out.

I will suggest both a critical and theological solution for this dilemma later on, but first I shall also discuss what I just referred to as the riskiness of Henry's approach. There is another way of reading him here which rescues him from the cul-de-sac, although perhaps at a price he would be unwilling to pay. I take my clue here from some contemporary forms of analytic philosophy that encourage us to explore certain kinds of discourse not so much for what they say as for how they function as logical units within discursive wholes.[30] This type of interpretation sees such units functioning within the larger whole in much the same way that grammar functions within a larger family of language.

Grammar specifies how language is to operate and thus is indispensable for a proper functioning of both written and spoken communication. At the same time, of course, grammar itself is language which, if it is to be a useful road map, must follow its own rules; an attentive primary-school student should properly be puzzled if his teacher were to say, "Don't ever use contractions." We can see two levels on which discourse operates in this example. The first is referential (we should never use contractions in written or oral communication), and the second is reflexive or grammatical (what form of language is used to tell us that we should not?). If information is conveyed to us referentially in ways that appear to violate the grammar or logical structure by which language conveys the reality of the world to us, and further if we believe that the speaker or writer is not simply being sloppy, then we are in principle licensed to look for other types of messages conveyed to us through the ungrammatical sentences.

So in this instance, if we choose to interpret Henry's opening discourse as "referential information about the nature of God," we would enter the cul-de-sac just noted. Alternatively we might attempt to interpret it as a "grammatical" suggestion concerning any and all discourse about divine revelation. Seen in this light, his first six theses could be interpreted as words about God *language* rather than words about *God*. They would thus serve as boundaries or parameters within which talk about revelation must remain if it hopes to be true to what we know about God from whatever other sources we have come to know about God.

Here is an example. Henry's fifth thesis says that "not only the occurrence of divine revelation, but also its very nature, content, and variety are exclusively God's determination." If interpreted in what we called the referential or informational mode, our attention is here focused on God's will as the ultimate origin of any and all forms of divine revelation. This interpretation brings to mind what has traditionally been called the double predestinarian view of salvation, the crudest form[31] of which is that God looks out over a vast sea of morally neutral people (i.e., people whose moral characters are irrelevant to God's decision concerning their salvation) and arbitrarily selects those to whom revelation will occur and salvation will come. All others therefore fall outside of salvation because God's equally arbitrary rejection of them strips them of their neutrality just as the previous acceptance had stripped the saved of theirs. "God determines not only the *if* and *why* of divine disclosure, but also the *when, where, what, how* and *who*. If there is to be a general revelation, . . . then that is God's decision. If there is to be a special or particular revelation, that, too, is God's decision and his alone."[32]

The alternative interpretation of this thesis does not call double predestination so readily to mind. It begins rather from the perspective of the reception of a disclosure of God's will and character and suggests the reverse of the prior interpretation: when one experiences the world in such a way as to learn something (more) about the character of God as well as something about the world, it is only because God initiates such self-disclosures through the media of the world. The world always serves as the means of those self-disclosures because it is God's creation. Seen in this light, thesis 5 functions as a grammatical reminder of how we are to use and interpret language about God, a grammatical rule that in this case we might phrase roughly as "One cannot learn about God except by learning from God, regardless of the means of such learning." Quite deliberately, nothing is here said about the number and nature of those persons in whom revelation will ultimately accomplish salvation. It simply states that reflections on divine revelation are off target if they concentrate on God's will as the sole determinant of those to whom revelation occurs and thus those who may ultimately come to salvation.[33]

We now turn to Henry's understanding of the place and nature of revelation. In my opinion this is most clearly seen not in his extended treatment of the fifteen theses in Volumes 2 and 3 but rather in his prolegomenal or preliminary treatments of Volume 1. It is here that he deliberately presents the skeletal structure of his thought which he rounds out in the subsequent volumes, and thus it is here that the whys of his later thought are most apparent. I will pay particular attention to what Henry calls "the theological transcendent a priori,"[34] asking first what that is and second how his treatment of it leads me to consider him as one of those affirming a discontinuity between the media of the world and God's self-revelation.

The latter half of Volume 1 is devoted to analyzing various conceptual approaches to theology, centering especially on the question of whether reason on the one hand or experience on the other is prior in our knowledge of God. Henry's answer is that reason has first priority here. He defends this response with recourse to the theological transcendent a priori, that innate or native presupposition that the possibility of rational activity by the mind reflects a rational order within the natural universe. Genuine knowledge of the universe would be impossible in the absence of such a presupposition, but because such knowledge is not only possible but also actual, the presence of this innate presupposition is warranted. Its truthfulness in turn depends on a previous one, namely that the universe is a divine creation and is thus reflective of God's ultimate unified rationality. Apart from these "biblical-theistic" assumptions, genuine knowledge of the universe could not exist in the ordered ways we presume every time we start to think about it. "[T]ruth is only God's revelation within the mind. Superhuman reason is the presupposition of the intelligibility of things, and man penetrates that intelligibility in virtue of rational relationships with the divine mind."[35] Experience is therefore secondary to reason because *its* intelligibility presumes the rational order of the universe of experiences.

Henry's understanding of this transcendental a priori finds anchor in three figures in the Christian tradition: Augustine, Luther, and Calvin. I shall pay special attention to the last because of the systematic deliberateness of his treatise. We shall see that Henry's treatment and evaluation of Calvin seem to present him as a continuist in this matter of how human knowledge relates with revelation. However, Henry's own treatment of the relationship between a priori divine revelation and the image of God in the second volume show him rather as a discontinuist, thus warranting my placement of him in this part of the present work.

Henry's major thesis in his treatment of Calvin here[36] is that the implied structure of Calvin's *Institutes* shows "a continuing divine-human relationship on the basis of creation" according to which "knowledge of God is no mere inference from the created world, but is immediately given along with self-consciousness, and becomes in turn a crucial factor in any knowledge whatever." Granted, he says, that the explicit interest of the *Institutes* has to do with salvation understood in Christian terms. Nonetheless, this interest is but an instance of the deeper function of God existing as (among other things) the presupposition of the possibility of genuine knowledge: "the divine accommodation in revelation exists for the sake of genuine knowledge."

A second feature of Calvin's understanding of the operation of human knowledge is that this a priori element is not ethically neutral or abstract. Instead, it has the actual aim or intention "of enabling man to glorify the Creator [through] worship and obedience and to own him as the source of all blessing. . . . The knowledge of God is . . . for the sake of the good life." Here it may be seen that worship and obedience, and not metaphysical speculation for its own sake, constitute the ethical dynamic that motivates, guides, and thus reveals the operation of the inbuilt a priori knowledge of God. Such speculation itself is an improper use of the divine a priori, but an improper use that nonetheless discloses the presence of that a priori; something cannot be used wrongly which cannot be used at all. Additionally, worship and obedience are not restricted to religious activities. They are not ends in themselves but rather the attitudes of the heart that underlie and motivate all of our daily affairs. The lack of such attitudes is attributable not to the absence but to the misuse of the a priori knowledge of God and thus of the good.

The third and final feature of Calvin's treatment of the divine a priori in human knowledge that Henry calls to our attention is that it adequately accounts for the unity of knowledge. It is only theories of knowledge, not acts of knowledge in themselves, that posit (artificial) distinctions among the conceptual, volitional, and affective realms of life. Knowledge itself ranges indiscriminately through each of these realms without transiting from one to another as through a barrier. This is not to minimize the significance of cognitive or conceptual forms of knowledge with respect to matters of religion but rather to include them as properly elemental, an emphasis Henry finds especially lacking in contemporary surveys of Christian theories of knowledge. Once again, this unity of knowledge presupposes and is sensible only in the light of the prior knowledge of the one God. The *Institutes* variously describe it as innate, naturally engraved on men's hearts, part of their very constitution, instinctive, universal, and indelible.

The question now arises about the effectiveness of this a priori knowledge of God with respect to present-day actualities. Clearly all individuals do not operate consciously with the existentially appropriated knowledge of God that is "innately" theirs. We need to ask why this is so. Having achieved an answer, we shall also need to inquire about the effects this answer has on the prior claim that such knowledge of God is *innate*.

It is the third feature noted above, dealing with the ultimate unity of knowledge, that is the key to Calvin's answer here. Because the distinction among the cognitive, volitional, and affective realms of life is more heuristic than real (that is, it is a distinction imposed by us upon the structure of knowledge to help us in reflecting upon and understanding reality, rather than a distinction residing in external reality itself), Calvin is able to claim that the knowledge of God available to us from transcendental reflection upon the conditions of the natural world is sufficient to ground an appropriate relationship with God. At least it would be, were we not so natively and intentionally committed to suppressing it because of our moral perversity or sin. It is because of sin, then, that the effects of our a priori knowledge of God are prevented from full actualization, and thus it is also because of sin that a second or "redemptive" type of knowledge is needed. That this second type of knowledge must be cognitive as well (in addition to being volitional and affective) is a given because of the ultimate unity of knowledge and our knowing faculties.

Our knowing faculties themselves are the seat, as it were, of our knowledge of God, whether of the initial and a priori type available from reflection upon nature or of the special redemptive type available from Scripture alone. In both cases, through, Henry notes an "interior" and an "exterior" side to revelation, to the origin of knowledge in God. The interior side is the knowing faculty itself which is presupposed by and revealed in any and all acts of knowledge.[37] One cannot know unless one is able to know, and thus the interior side of revelation is that God has created us with that which enables us to receive knowledge. The exterior or outer side of revelation then is that which God reveals about God's own self, whether through general (natural) means or special (scriptural) means. We are justified in presupposing that it is God who reveals this because such knowledge is about God; that is, unless God were the ultimate initiator of knowledge about God, we could never be certain that it was God, and not merely speculative ideas *about* God, with whom we were in contact. "Man is constantly related to God through inner revelation and through outer revelation, and these are correlative aspects of God's universal disclosure."[38]

Calvin finds two effects of the a priori knowledge of God present within human existence, although in the nature of the case they are both torpedoed by sin. The first effect is the innate knowledge of God's divinity, an effect manifest in the universal experience of religious worship. Sin causes such worship to be idolatrous, to be sure, but as we noted earlier in another context, there could be no possibility of false worship were there no prior possibility of true, and it is this prior possibility that itself signals the presence of the innate knowledge of God. The second effect is the human conscience, and this effect is manifest in the universal recognition of right and wrong. Regardless of how different societies structure their various systems of ethics or morality, the fact that none does *not* signals the second aspect of God's universal and a priori self-revelation. Reflection upon these two effects reminds us that the a priori knowledge of God is always and irreducibly both cognitive and moral. It is moral because both of its manifestations, worship and conscience, are irreducibly moral phenomena. It is cognitive as well because both worship and conscience are activities that engage our knowing or rational faculties. This is etymologically shown in the word *conscience*, which literally means the moral judgments that come along "with *scientia*" or knowledge.

Henry concludes his survey of Calvin's doctrine of the innate knowledge of God with an extended reminder of how it is real knowledge and not simply a faculty or port for the reception of other kinds of knowledge. He demonstrates this in both positive and negative ways. Positively he shows it by referring once again to the transcendental nature of knowledge in Calvin: knowledge cannot be actual if it is not possible, and it is not possible apart from the presupposition of the ultimate unity and rationality of the universe.[39] The correlativity of the rationality of the mind and of the physical/moral universe which the mind seeks to understand presupposes an ultimate unity between what *we* distinguish as the physical and moral spheres, and Calvin claims that God is the one who accounts for this ultimate unity. But if God ultimately accounts for the unity of knower with known, then God is thereby implicitly but really experienced as indirectly known in every direct act of knowing. Divine revelation is thus universally available as an indirect constituent of every act of knowing. To say the same thing the other way around, no act of knowledge can fail to terminate in and thus reveal God as the ultimate source and initiator of knowledge, and it does in fact terminate here if the knower wishes to extend the process this far.

Negatively Calvin shows how the innate or a priori knowledge of God is real by reflecting on the responsibility that humans have, and know that they have, to hold to the truth and to reject falsehood and error. The universal recognition of such responsibility is inexplicable apart from "the holy will of God." That is, it is impossible to account for this universal moral datum if one ignores God and attempts to explain it strictly from the empirical facts of the universe themselves. Empirical facts by themselves are unable to ground the universal moral imperative to hold to the truth and reject error, but that moral imperative is nonetheless recognized and accepted as universally operative. Thus, the twin senses of the appropriateness of holding to truth and the inappropriateness of holding to error, what we might call natural righteousness and natural guilt, point ultimately to the presence and activity of God in all acts of knowing. And as before, because these two senses are real, so too is the knowledge of God in which they are grounded.

Henry's summary of Calvin's doctrine of a priori divine revelation thus shows what we have called a clear continuity between such revelation and normally operating human knowing faculties. Revelation is available to all, even if only indirectly or transcendentally. Sin does not eradicate the actuality of such revelation, but instead only redirects its usage in ways that obscure but do not disrupt its origin in God and thus the uncovering of God.

> The Calvinistic view . . . is that man knows only in and through divine revelation; apart from God's revealing activity, man has no knowledge whatever. The various strata of general revelation are given together, but the knowledge of God has a logical priority, even if easily obscured by a concentration upon the other interests. There is no knowledge of the self without God-knowledge, no knowledge of nature without God-knowledge.[40]

My remaining treatment of Henry will consider his discussion of the image of God with respect to the doctrine of a priori revelation and whether he himself endorses the relationship between divine revelation and human knowledge as continuously as does Calvin.

Henry discusses the topic of the *imago Dei* in the tenth chapter of Volume 2.[41] This chapter is itself a subsection within his discussion of the fifth thesis concerning divine revelation, that involving the variety but also the ultimate unity of revelation. It reflects two sets of interests, the first of which essentially reproduces what we have just examined except on grounds taken more from biblical texts than from Calvin, and the second of which argues against biblical exegetes who Henry believes have distorted the traditional "Hebrew-Christian" meaning of the image of God. Our interests accordingly lead us to focus attention on the latter discussion.[42]

The major point at issue here is how one ought to treat the literary origins of the Old Testament passages that form the seat of the doctrine of the image of God, especially Genesis 1. Henry briefly cites several Old Testament critics who attempt to show the affinities between the Genesis passages and those from religious systems surrounding ancient Israel (Akkadian, Egyptian, Canaanite) and who argue that the biblical *imago Dei* is best interpreted as a recension and thus an elaboration of its meaning in those other systems. Henry vigorously rejects the validity of such an approach. We shall examine this interchange, noting from the outset that it is a difference not so much about the actual interpretation of *imago Dei* as about the theological legitimacy of source criticism. As Henry states, the "critically important question is whether Genesis 1:26 ['Let us make *adam* in our image, after our likeness . . .'] belongs to the genre of religious literary myth or whether it reflects divine truth." If the former, then "All that is said about the moral qualities of divinely delegated dominion loses its universal validity and ethical compunction." What we shall specifically look for in this interchange is whether divine revelation might be conveyed to and through humans who do not themselves stand within the biblical traditions of Judaism and Christianity. This in turn will help us to evaluate Henry's earlier noted claims concerning the actuality of the content of divine revelation in sinful persons.

As an example of the kind of interpretation Henry rejects, we may take Bernhard Anderson's analysis of the sources of the image of God passages in Genesis 1.[43] Anderson attempts to locate the cultural origins of certain distinctive phrases within Genesis 1, especially "*adam*-mankind," "chaos," and "image of God." He says that the use of these phrases would seem to indicate a sapiential or wisdom context located temporally around the time of David and culturally within Egyptian discussions of the relationship between Pharaoh and God as that of image bearer to image maker. These phrases imply that royalty or kingship is the prevailing political structure, a state of affairs that Old Testament Israel did not accept before the time of Saul and afterward only quite grudgingly. Anderson concludes that Genesis 1 was most probably written around the time of David because it reflects a cultural context that Israel began to face only as the Davidic kingdom began to expand southwest into Egyptian-held lands. Henry comments that "Anderson contends that the Genesis writer reinterprets the Egyptian myth of Pharaoh as God's image to stress the Creator's transcendent majesty, and universalizes the image to depict man generally."[44]

Henry rejects both this method of interpretation in general and Anderson's particular use of it here. He provides two reasons for this rejection. The first is that Anderson has elevated "myth" over "transcendent divine revelation," a move that "disallows any special truth-claim for the biblical representations." The relevant distinction here is between myth and truth-bearing ability; Henry assumes that the two are mutually exclusive. That is, myth cannot serve as the vehicle for God's self-revelation, and thus the contemporary and purely literary-scholarly designation of a biblical story as myth fully and retroactively disqualifies it from bearing the truth that God intends as the outer side of God's revelation.

I do not take issue with the popular meaning of myth used (and rejected) by Henry here, according to which a deliberately fictional story is used to tell us about transcendent matters and persons. This is the sense in which we all discuss the myths of Thor, of Zeus and Hera, and so on. It is to be hoped that no one today believes that such stories refer to actual historical events, and it is probably to be doubted whether many Norsemen or Greeks did either. My quarrel with Henry is not with the fact that he reflects (and rejects) the popular meaning and usage of myth. Rather it is that he does not reflect the more distinctive usage of it by Christian theologians, a usage that has arisen so far as I can tell because of conclusions with which Henry himself would agree and thus should have discussed here.

The New Testament: An Introduction by Norman Perrin and Dennis Duling can illustrate the meanings of myth and history as used within theology.[45] As some Christian theologians use these words (and it must be conceded that not all do), they reflect two emphases that I believe are quite proper. The first is that God is not like any human being; thus, whenever we speak of God we are using words beyond their intended fashion, and we must be careful to recognize that fact. Our language is inescapably designed to work in contexts that reflect the material universe and human kinds of participations within it. God, though, is not in the universe in the sense that everything else is, and thus any language about God will have to reflect our awareness of that fact. For simplicity's sake we may not always make that awareness explicit, but we should not confuse that *pragmatic* tactic with the belief that God-language works the same way as language about anything else.

The second emphasis is that I do not wish to cease speaking of God regardless of how difficult it is to do so "correctly," that is, regardless of how difficult it may be to use human language about a Being as far beyond human categories and limitations as Christians have traditionally insisted God is. For example, on the surface the sentences "God told me something" and "Susan told me something" appear to be identical with respect to how God and Susan are said to convey information. Of course, they cannot be identical since God does not possess the requisite physiological apparati we all presume (and thus rarely stop to think about) in the case of Susan. But neither do we want to bar the sentence "God told me something" from religious discourse, regardless of how difficult it is to know what we mean when we use it. At the very least, believers would want to say that it makes sense, even if we conclude that it can make sense only at the cost of distancing it from similar-looking sentences such as the one about Susan. This suggests that any sentence with "God" as the subject of its verb operates differently from any identical sentence in which some other word is the subject. "God spoke to the Israelites saying . . ." operates on a different level from "Moses spoke to the Israelites saying . . ." In the latter case we know pretty well how that sentence tells us about Moses and about the message conveyed to the Israelites. In the former case, though, we do not know how the sentence tells us about God or the Israelites. We know how it does *not* tell us about them, of course: we know that it does *not* say that God spoke using mouth, larynx, and other material phenomena in the ways Moses did. Thus, we cannot know with certainty about its mode of reception by the Israelites either. At the very most, I think, we can know positively about the message conveyed.

The point here is that theologians have come up with a way to characterize th?se two levels of discourse. Regardless of the variety of ways we have at our disposal to refer to various kinds of human discourse, it seems fair to place them all within the same category and distinguish that category from divine discourse. It is the latter category that, I believe, may properly be called myth. Granted, this is a loaded term, and quite frankly I would be happier with another word to perform the same function in this very restricted sense. (In fact, almost *any* word would be b?tter given the hue and cry that has attended the use of this one.) However, we seem to be stuck with it, and all we can do is define it as precise? as we can and then hold to that definition when others wish to attribute the wider and less appropriate definitions to our language about God. To sum up, then, and to put it somewhat crudely, any sentence in which "God" is the subject of a transitive verb is mythological according to this deliberately refined definition.

If we understand the meaning of myth in this sense, then it can be seen that there are relatively few sentences in the Bible that tell us about God that are *not* mythological. Let me hasten to add that I do not intend to decrease the truth-bearing function of the Bible when I say this; such an accusation overlooks what was just said about myth and more importantly the very traditional reasons adduced for why it was said. But if this way of talking about God is valid, then it would seem that to identify a particular story as a myth is not at all to preclude it from conveying genuine truth about, and therefore from, God. Any sentence in which God is said to do something, including those sentences saying that God has revealed something about God's own self, is mythological. Regardless of how odd this may sound, the only alternative is to say something odder still, particularly to the ears of faith, namely that God is a material being like any other in the universe. And that form of idolatry will not do at all. Paradoxically, it is only when theological discourse rejects "myth" in this sense that it is precluded from bearing theological truth.

This presents adequate if terse grounds for holding to the possible legitimacy of *myth* in theological discussions. I say "possible" legitimacy, of course, because there will surely exist theologians who use the word differently from my use here and with whom I would probably disagree. Such a disagreement would be about the meaning of the word, though, and not the bare use of it. Our understanding of things always outstrips our ability to talk about them, and thus some of our words will have to do double duty as we use them to represent our understanding. I believe that it is appropriate to say that many stories in the Bible utilize myth precisely as the ancients' way of holding to both the transcendence and the immanental activity of God. For that reason, then, and quite in contrast to Henry, I would say that myth *is* able to convey truth about God because it is those very sentences in the Bible in which "God" is the subject of transitive verbs that are most often taken to be revelatory of God's nature and character.

The second reason Henry gives for rejecting the propriety of Anderson's method of interpretation has to do with the fact that it locates the literary origins of foundational biblical concepts outside the Hebrew-Christian tradition, in this case within the Egyptian religious world. In Henry's view, such a move would additionally preclude the revelatory stature of the Bible because its origin in the speaking of God has been tampered with and perhaps jettisoned altogether. "Anderson's insistence that all man's religious views are cast in mythical form disallows any special truth-claim for the biblical representations. One is left with the impression that the Genesis writer was inspired by Egyptian sources, and that the passage more assuredly reflects a redaction of an Egyptian motif than that Adam . . . reflects the divine image." Here we get both barrels, as it were, and thus my task is to compare what Henry says here with what we earlier read from him concerning the universality of divine revelation not only as a possibility but also as a reality.

The summary of Calvin's "theological transcendentalism" above noted his insistence that the knowledge of God is both real and universal, a conclusion he warranted in both positive and negative ways. That is, all persons in history are actually in possession of God's self-revelation whether they know it or not and whether they respond to it as such or not. Positively this was shown by a transcendental analysis of the act of knowing, and negatively it was shown by a transcendental analysis of the universal moral sense of right and wrong. The fact that Calvin uses these two data as prelude to the discussion of God's wrath does not vitiate them; in fact, it only serves to underscore their applicability since Calvin uses them not merely to assert, but to justify, the divine wrath. Although I was not then interested to see the context of this discussion (i.e., the justifiability of God's wrath) because I was more interested in the outlines of Calvin's doctrine of revelation, the point still holds that no one is *not* in possession of the actual knowledge of God; such knowledge may be held down or suppressed by sin, but it cannot be eradicated altogether.

If this is the case, and clearly Henry agrees with Calvin that it is, then it seems odd for him to assert in the present context that the outer side of divine revelation cannot be mediated through non-Hebrew literary sources into the Old Testament tradition. One could more easily imagine that sort of restriction operating on certain New Testament notions; it is probably less to be expected that Paul would look to Egypt in order to clarify or explicate his notion of Jesus as Messiah or as second Adam. But in the Old Testament, especially with respect to the doctrine of image of God, what is to prevent the authors or literary communities from reaching beyond their own religious/political boundaries to acquire symbols by which to clarify their proclamation of humankind as "image of Yahweh" as a covenantally recast echo of Pharaoh as image of God? This question is put to Henry less as a historical one than as a systematic one: if God's knowledge is really present to all persons as actual constituents within all that they know, then whence arises our right to preclude that knowledge from showing up in the way Henry does here? He wants to deny the possibility of this sort of literary sharing, he says, in order to protect the "distinctive revelation of truth in . . . the Genesis *imago*-passage."[46] But why should the means of such revelation matter to the ultimate reception by the Israelite authors of this particular way of relating humankind to God, particularly to one who insists that God's self-disclosure is available to *all* persons even before their acceptance of salvation? And systematically speaking, how can the sinfulness of the ancient Egyptians preclude them from mediating divine truth to the world whereas the sinfulness of the ancient Israelites does not? Henry's restriction here seems grounded in a doctrine of human knowledge that he had earlier rejected, namely that certain persons or cultures are beyond the possibility of really knowing God while other persons or cultures are beyond the possibility of being wrong about God even in spite of their own sinfulness. One can hold to one of these positions or the other, perhaps, but not both.

It is precisely because of this bifurcation of Henry's thinking that I have placed him in this chapter. Were I confident that his representation of Calvin's doctrine of divine revelation constituted a summary of his own position, I would have been justified in seeing him more as a continuist than as a discontinuist. For Calvin, it is surely the case that human knowledge of objects within the universe is possible only on the presupposition of the human subject's knowledge of God. Thus, whether one is considering physical-empirical objects on the one hand or moral objects on the other, one cannot in fact *know* those things without at the same time knowing the God whose existence and character are the presupposition of any act of knowing. God is co-known every time any other object is known. Although this is clearly a theological analysis, it is not one that applies only to believers in God. It is part of what I might instead call a theological epistemology which is true of everyone if it is true of anyone.

For Henry in particular, though, his actual treatment of instances of divinely revelatory material in the Bible indicates that huge blocks of persons and cultures exist that are not related to God in the ways Calvin insisted that all persons and cultures are. That is, for Henry there are groups of persons whom God is prevented from employing as vehicles through whom to reveal God's character. Almost without exception those persons exist outside the Hebrew-Christian tradition. The presupposition of this exclusion can only be that genuine knowledge of God is available solely to those existing within that tradition. This is a very common presupposition within Christian theology, to be sure, but one wonders why Henry holds to it while simultaneously endorsing Calvin's universalisms. This perplexity is only heightened when one recalls Calvin's negative employment of the doctrine of universal revelation. The negative function of this doctrine is to relate all persons to God through sin (that is, through the use of knowing faculties in ways that negatively presuppose God) *so that* God could not fail to be seen as the savior of all persons. In placing great numbers of persons and cultures outside the possibility of knowing God's outer self-revelation, Henry has also placed them outside the possibility of being saved by God: if they do not natively know God, they cannot sinfully suppress the knowledge of God; and if they do not suppress the knowledge of God, then they cannot be saved by God.

It seems warranted to estimate Henry finally as a discontinuist— that is, as one whose understanding and use of the doctrine of divine revelation assume that such revelation interrupts and categorically redirects human knowing processes. My evaluation of him has discovered two weaknesses in this approach. The first and less important weakness is what we might call the rhetorical one, having to do with his puzzling use of Calvin. The second and more important weakness is the religious one according to which, by implication at least, Henry places most of the world's population outside the possibility and, worse yet, the need of salvation. My suspicion is that all Christian discontinuist theories of divine revelation do the same thing precisely because they presume that divine truth is not available to persons outside the Christian traditions. This presumption is, of course, part and parcel of my definition of discontinuist theories of revelation. What makes such theories religiously problematic, however, is not that they may all be grouped together but rather that the criterion that allows them to be grouped together is suspicious at best and worthy of rejection at worst. Christians should be quite skeptical, I think, about any theory of revelation that implies that only Christians can be saved.

Karl Barth

No assessment of recent theories of divine revelation could be complete without considering the contribution of Karl Barth.[47] For that very reason, it is nearly impossible to arrive at anything approaching a new interpretation of him. His celebrated break with his Protestant liberal background and orientation constitutes at once a massive critique of theological subjectivism and a creative reformation whose intent was to return to the traditional bases of theology, but now from within the categories of modern thought and theology wherever possible. This "reformation" reflected his own dynamic growth: away from the overt anthropocentrism of nineteenth-century liberal Protestantism, to an initial theological position in which he granted no possibility of continuity between

God and humans, and finally to a more mature position in which he conceded an analogy between God and humans. This later doctrine of analogy seemed, however grudgingly, to allow for a partial symmetry between the ways of God and the ways of humans and thus for at least the possibility of a method for talking about God. As we shall see, though, the analogy was more one of method than of content, for Barth never relinquished his postliberal insistence that all theology begin by considering the sovereign God rather than by considering the human act of faith which this God initiates and creates.

I will first summarize Barth's earlier position which he articulates immediately after rejecting liberalism. I shall take this position primarily from various emphases in the second edition of his commentary on Romans, *The Epistle to the Romans*, and from his own bird's-eye view of nineteenth-century theology found in the address "Evangelical Theology in the 19th Century." I shall then turn to consider his later position, as represented in the address "The Humanity of God."[48] Here I shall be especially interested to see whether this newer position justifies its reputation as a categorical advance over the former one or whether, on the other hand, it too suffers from the deficiency of being unable to say exactly how theology (literally, God-talk) tells us about God.

Barth's overall intention in the years immediately following his conversion from liberalism was to safeguard the objectivity or givenness of God's self-revelation at whatever cost, especially if that cost could be exacted from those features of liberal theology that were most clearly anthropocentric. Liberal theology was anything but faithful to its name, he believed, because beginning theology from the perspective of humanity rather than God unavoidably stripped it of its grounding in God. But this in turn precluded it from being able to say how it is that God's self-revelation could be a saving and thus liberating event. Divine revelation would at best be redundant, confirming what humans already discovered by themselves on natural grounds, and would at worst be damning, licensing a theology that reversed the positions of God and humans and thus precluding any exercise of divine saving activity.

If this was his general intention, the specific tactic used to apply it to divine revelation was to separate revelation from its reception by humans so widely that faith (i.e., the believing acceptance of revelation) itself could no longer even be spoken of as a genuinely human act. In place of the traditional twin poles of revelation (initiation) and faith (response), then, Barth substituted only one: faith-cum-revelation. Any attempt to make the initiative of God dependent for its completion upon a correlative response by humans would strip the former of all meaning and thus render the latter moot as well.

Instead, Barth argued, revelation created faith as its own object. Faith was not an inward capacity of created humanity that vibrated when struck with the hammer of God's revelation. Even less was it an internal predisposition toward God whose presence was signaled by the universality of the "religious" sphere of life within all of history. Rather, faith was a part of the revelation itself. The distinction between the two was thus merely one of logical priority, much as heads might be said to be logically prior to tails on a penny, and not one of a distinctly divine location on the one hand and a distinctly human location on the other. To speak of one apart from the other was to speak of something that did not exist.

The difficulties of this position are not hard to spot. The primary difficulty, of course, is that it simply avoids addressing the theological question it purports to answer, namely just how it is that God's revelation meets humans and transforms them from unbelievers into believers. Barth's early answer is unsatisfactory because it removes the category of "human" from the question altogether. Thus, one might even grant the appropriateness of his analysis here (although not many did) while still recognizing that it was ultimately an evasion rather than an address of the God-human question posed by the notion of revelation. If one wishes to say how revelation occurs within human history and does so by removing humans from the stage altogether, few will be found to applaud the suggestion.

Another and related problem with this approach is that it is fundamentally a way of saying that revelation works by way of miracle—that is, by ways that are inexplicable to human knowing faculties. It is fair enough to say that revelation is miraculous, but it is then puzzling to notice that Barth continues on to try to explain the miraculous event of revelation. If we define *miracle* among other things as that which we believe to occur beyond our (present) ability to explain or to account for it, then by extension all of our attempts to explain a miracle will only reveal our real disposition that the event in question is explicable and thus not miraculous. But what if we succeed? What happens if in our attempts to provide a reasonable account of an inexplicable event we should succeed in making it understandable or (worse yet) understood? What then of our original assessment of its miraculousness?[49]

Barth faced this question immediately after publishing the second and succeeding editions of *The Epistle to the Romans.* His resolution was to begin to redefine *miracle* in such a way as to make it more closely reflect the traditional understanding of revelation and faith, or of divine initiation and human response, without abandoning the overall critique of liberal anthropocentrism. His method here was to see the relationship of revelation and faith not as (chrono)logical priority but rather as dialectical. In any dialectical relationship, two elements are related precisely by virtue of their being diversely implied by each other; without much loss to anything except style, we might say that they are inversely and asymmetrically related to each other. The inverse shape of the relationship is entailed by the nature of dialectical relationships in general and thus is a given here. The asymmetric shape, though, is insisted upon by Barth here precisely to maintain his earlier reticence to grant any sort of correlativity between revelation and faith. That is, revelation and faith are not related as key to keyhole, where neither is identical to any part of the other but yet each implies the existence of the other. Barth rejects the possibility that faith implies the presence of revelation because that would grant the logical possibility of faith being considered apart from revelation, just as keys and keyholes may be. Instead, he says, we know from the presence of faith in ourselves that revelation exists not as the correlative to faith (or, as I shall later put it, as the condition of the possibility of faith), but rather as that which creates faith in a completely free and objective manner. Faith, then, is as much God's work as the revelation that precedes and creates it. And yet it is not analytically included within revelation, first because revelation is sovereign and thus need not create faith, and second because faith is, after all is said and done, a human act.[50]

Here we are in the presence of a genuine dialectic if there ever was one. On the one hand, faith must be a real creation of God alone because to say anything else is to grant to the creature that which properly belongs only to the creator and thus make salvation a work of humans even if only to a tiny degree. On the other hand, faith is a real act of humans in that it reflects the free and unforced spontaneity that is fundamental to human nature, in this case free and unforced faithfulness to God. To say anything else here would simply be to repeat, rather than resolve, the problems inherent in his earlier analysis. Thus, faith is a contradiction. It is both passive (because it is created by God) and active (because it is active obedience); both knowledge (because knowledge is requisite for certainty and trust) and not knowledge (because knowledge is always bounded by creaturely limits); both an affirmation (of divine sufficiency) and a denial (of human sufficiency even when it is granted that humans are creatures of the divine). As contradiction, therefore, faith always points dialectically away from itself to the sufficiency of revelation. Considered methodologically, therefore, and not materially or intentionally, the overall purpose of faith is to bring one into the presence of revelation, because one who is in the presence of revelation is in the presence of God.[51]

Before proceeding to discuss the later Barth of "The Humanity of God," we need to pause for a criticism of the middle one. I take it as a given that theology is the systematic and reasoned effort to come to terms with, and to express, the church's experience with God.[52] Thus, theology is a reflective activity in that it looks back upon such experiences as the data it seeks to interpret in understandable ways. So, as with all reflective activities, two sorts of phenomena are present and need to be accounted for. The first are the data themselves, those experiences of God that Christian believers throughout the centuries have had and that constitute the vast bulk of the tradition present-day believers accept as "handed on" (*traditio*) to them by those former generations. The second is the conceptual method or structure into which those data are fit as the grid that organizes raw and chaotic experiences into understandable pieces of knowledge and thus into critical tradition.

Optimally it should be the case that the method or structure of theology reflect as closely as possible the actual shape of the experiences themselves, and this for two reasons. First, as Christians we believe that God is not capricious; that is, God does not savingly approach some persons in ways that are incompatible with how God approaches others. Thus, even though there may be differences among the patterns of experiences that various individual believers

and communities of believers have (had) with God, theology posits
that the differences are not as fundamental as the unifying similarities we implicitly presume every time we recognize another individual's or community's pattern as a *Christian* pattern. Second,
method should reflect content as closely as possible because the
overall intention of theology is to be both reflective and constructive. Theology does not simply "look back upon," but it also "looks
forward to" in the sense of making the past understandable to
present-day believers who may thereby grow in their Christian love
of God and service toward others. Clearly the constructive intention
will be imperiled to the degree that the structure or logic of theology beclouds the actual ways in which God is savingly revealed. If
we believe that God only works in certain ways because that is what
our church's theology tells us, then we will most likely miss it if God
decides to work in some other way. This is precisely why theologians pay so much attention to methodological matters, and thus why
until the relatively recent past so little attention was addressed to
the actual experiences Christian believers have (had) with God. To
notice this is not to condemn interest in methodology. It is rather to
recognize it for what it is: an interpretive tool and not an end in
itself.

This is important in a treatment of Barth because he quite deliberately distinguishes content (the believer's experiences with God)
from method (the systematic categorization of such experiences).
As noted above, Barth begins all theology at the point of the
meeting between God and humans in Christian faith. Since this is
not an empty or purely heuristic category (in fact, it is precisely *not*
that for him), it must be the case that human beings are concretely
able to experience God. However systematic thinking subsequently
recasts such experiences into understandable conceptual form, the
point is that Barth grounds all theology in the personal experience
of God.

But this is what makes his methodology so peculiar at this stage,
for it simultaneously refuses to concede any point of continuity
between God and humans. Feelings such as piety (Schleiermacher)
and ultimate dependence (Tillich) cannot function as such a point,
first because they result from faith in Christian believers, and
second because they are observably present in non-Christians too,
and thus are as much a witness to the kind of "godliness" Paul

condemns as idolatry in the first chapter of Romans as to genuine Christian faith.[53] Knowledge cannot succeed for the same reasons. And finally faith itself cannot constitute such a point because when considered from the divine perspective it is a miracle wrought by God, and when considered from the human perspective it is a dialectical pointer to the reality of revelation and to itself only as a negative sign of that reality. Faith, then, is a contradiction of what is not-present signaling the actuality of the incomprehensibly present. The believer's ultimate experience is of that which is present, but since it is incomprehensibly present, theology can go only as far as to say that it is incomprehensible, and no farther.

It is over this latter point that Barth's position itself changed later in his life. The reason is straightforward: method constitutes a boundary or fence inside of which understanding can take place. To ignore or reject the methodological implications of one's content thus risks a very troublesome understanding of that content. "[I]gnoring the question of thought-form or method might actually make some thought-form so dominate content and objective intention, that the net effect would still be the production of something remarkably like [liberal] theology."[54] In this particular instance, his deliberate failure to provide a methodological description of faith resulted not in a troublesome understanding of it but something far worse: none at all. To make God everything and human beings nothing was hardly a satisfactory response to the liberalism that (in his opinion) had done the opposite.

And so Barth changed. By the time of his 1956 address "The Humanity of God," his appreciation of his former opponents is almost startling: "We are called upon today to accord to that earlier theology, and the entire development culminating in it, greater historical justice than appeared to us possible and feasible in the violence of the first break-off and clash. This is an easier task today than it would have been earlier."[55] The methodological key here is his use of "historical," for what the nineteenth-century liberals had drawn upon, and thus what he had earlier skirted, was christology, the doctrinal location of greatest significance to the Christian understanding of how God acts in history. It is not surprising that the evolution of the center of Barth's theology from the sovereignty of God to the humanity of God should find its dynamic and critical axis in christology.

"The Humanity of God" proposes five theses as consequences from his methodological realignment around christology, of which the fourth will be of greatest interest to us. They are:

1. The distinctiveness of man as such.
2. The distinctiveness of theological culture in particular.
3. The dialogical attitude and alignment of Christian theological thinking and speaking.
4. The necessity of a fundamentally positive sense and sound of Christian proclamation, including the possibility of a distinct notion of universalism.
5. A thankful and serious affirmation of the church.[56]

In each of these, Barth vigorously redresses the weaknesses of his earlier theology in light of his newer appreciation of humanity as the vehicle of the self-expression of God.

The fourth thesis departs so radically from the theologian who broke with liberalism that one is tempted to call it un-Barthian. In fact, it seems to be virtually identical in form if not in content to what Karl Rahner has termed "the anonymous Christian," a concept that has scandalized many in the church but nonetheless may be found in this conservative Calvinist.[57] Here Barth says that the "No" of the cross of Christ is in reality a "No" addressed by God to the sinfulness of humanity, a double negative that turns out to be an affirmation of humanity:

> God does not turn towards [man] without uttering in inexorable sharpness a "No" to his transgression. Thus theology has no choice but to put this "No" into words within the framework of its theme. However, it must be the "No" which Jesus Christ has taken upon Himself for us men, in order that it may no longer affect us and that we may no longer place ourselves under it. What takes place in God's humanity is, since it includes that "No" in itself, the *affirmation* of man.[58]

What humans are is precisely what God loves, and became, in Jesus Christ. *This* is now the most radical statement of the sovereignty of God, not that God rejects humanity but rather that God assumes it into God's very Being.

> [Man] is the being whom God has loved, loves, and will love, because He has substituted Himself in Jesus Christ and has made

Himself the guarantee. . . . And with this explanation the statement that the human spirit is naturally Christian may also be valid as an obstinately joyful proclamation. That is what we have to testify to men in view of the humanism *of God*, irrespective of the more or less dense godlessness of *their* humanism—everything else must be said only in the framework of this statement and promise.[59]

Barth rightly notes that this is nothing other than universalism, and he coyly introduces three rhetorical "observations" with the denial that he is affirming universalism.

1. One should not surrender himself . . . to the panic which this word seems to spread abroad, before informing himself exactly concerning its possible sense or non-sense.

2. One should at least be stimulated by the passage, Colossians 1:19,[60] which admittedly states that God has determined through His Son as His image and as the first-born of the whole Creation to "reconcile all things (*ta panta*) to himself," to consider whether the concept could not perhaps have a good meaning. The same can be said of parallel passages.

3. One question should for a moment be asked, in view of the "danger" with which one may see this concept gradually surrounded. What of the "danger" of the eternally skeptical-critical theologian who is ever and again suspiciously questioning, because fundamentally always legalistic and therefore in the main morosely gloomy? Is not his presence among us currently more threatening than that of the unbecomingly cheerful indifferentism or even antinomianism, to which one with a certain understanding of universalism could in fact deliver himself? This much is certain, that we have no theological right to set any sort of limits to the loving-kindness of God which has appeared in Jesus Christ. Our theological duty is to see and understand it as being still greater than we had seen before.[61]

One cannot even conceive of the earlier Barth saying that the human spirit is naturally Christian, or that theology can set no limits to the mercy of God. Had that Barth died and become the keeper of the heavenly gates, the later one would never gain entrance.

In a yet later address, Barth clarifies why this evolution became imperative. The greater the emphasis one puts upon the sovereign and autonomous God, the greater the reflexive validity given to the autonomous human being. But when this is done, it becomes a matter of mere accidental coincidence, or ancestry, or self-interest, whether or not that human being is grasped by the saving God. Barth insists that authentic theology cannot simply be content to assert the human need for God but that it must go far beyond this and demonstrate that it is actually constitutive of the definition of human being to stand in need of God and thus to be loved by God. "It cannot be simply supposed that man naturally stands in need of, and is subject to, the authority that encounters him in the Word. Before human thought and speech can respond to God's word, they have to be summoned into existence and given reality by the creative act of God's word."[62]

What that word of God creates is precisely the realization that God is "man's father, brother, friend [and] primary partner of the covenant—himself as *man's* God."[63] Here, in a simplicity that belies both the profundity of the message itself and the surprise in discovering it to be a Barthian message, is the core of his understanding of revelation. Revelation is the word and thus the act of God that places humankind in its fundamental theological context. Human beings are partners with the saving God whether they know it and confess it or not. They may be faithful or unfaithful partners, but they cannot fail to be partners. And conversely, God is the loving partner of humankind. The threefold God is inescapably self-bound to humanity. Revelation is the act of God that discloses this, and discloses it precisely as good news.

Barth moved nearly from one end of the spectrum to the other. But there is an important sense in which he did not move at all. I will expand upon it in my own proposal concerning revelation later on, so here I shall note it rather simply. In insisting that humanity constitutes the actuality of the possibility of God being able to love and to become that which God is not, namely human, Barth retains his early focus on two traditional notions: that God always initiates the revelation or disclosure about God's own self-becoming, and that this revelation concerns the person or character of God and not simply new information about the world. The only notion of divine revelation that is religiously interesting is that which holds to this insight: revelation is the personal God freely disclosed and thereby delivered to the world for the sake of human salvation.

James I. Packer

There are probably few theologians who have influenced thoughtful evangelicalism as much, and as long, as J. I. Packer.[64] He is a writer whose simplicity conceals sophistication and for whom faith, church, doctrine, and ethics are all of a piece. Two things may be said of his beliefs concerning the ground and shape of revelation which will help us in interpreting them. First, Packer is very representative of mainline (or what he often calls "orthodox") evangelicals in English-speaking countries.[65] His cautious criticism of traditional theological doctrines discloses very little desire to reformulate them in significant ways, particularly in ways that would align with nonevangelical assumptions about the nature and structure of experience and knowledge. This is especially true of his understanding of revelation. Second, his treatment of revelation exhibits some very representative evangelical mistakes, ones not yet seen in this chapter but which nonetheless reside in a great many contemporary conservative theories of revelation. My own attempt at a credible notion of revelation will thus be strengthened to the degree that these mistakes can be identified and avoided.

Two such difficulties in Packer's discussions of revelation will be of use to us. First, there is a contrast between method and execution in his revelational writings. His hints about how one ought to construct a theology of revelation differ from his actual construction of one. Second, he commits what might be called the classic double standard of traditional expositions of revelation, namely the ambivalence in specifying the criteria for defining something as divine revelation. The double standard in his case is that he views the Bible as identical with divine self-revelation until pressed for the critical authorization for this view. Then the authorization is always something much more fundamental but also much more arbitrary; for Packer it is the Bible's own self-description, while for others it might be ecclesiastical definition, miracles, or the like.[66] My treatment of Packer will attempt to clarify both of these weaknesses, suggesting resolutions where possible, with a view to my own construction in later chapters.

Method and Execution

The first chapter of Packer's *Knowing God* proposes "five basic truths, five foundation-principles of the knowledge about God which Christians have" (or should have) as their lodestones in the study of God.[67] The expressed intention of this chapter is to guide the interested student of God in his or her path toward the goal of knowing God. This seems appropriate enough. However, there appears to be a contrast between his reason for suggesting these five basic truths and the actual shape of them, a contrast that will inevitably have a bearing on what can count as knowledge of God. In brief, the contrast is between Packer's rationale for these basic truths, which is experiential in nature and thus in principle invites the personal contribution of the experiencing subject, and the actual five basic truths themselves, which are abstract or universal in nature and thus constitute a priori rules that are impervious to subjective contribution.

Packer is on good evangelical ground in hinting at a subjective intention for the study of God. The end of such study is not knowledge per se but rather the saving knowledge of God by persons needing salvation. Thus, this kind of knowledge has the potential (at least) of leading us to God and having fellowship with God; it is neither static nor objective. It is instead an historical relationship that will allow us more wholly to enjoy God, love and be loved by God, enlarge our acquaintance with God, and communicate with God.[68] That is, the end of any study of God is the enrichment of a person's knowledge of God,[69] and by definition this end is determined more subjectively than objectively, more concretely than abstractly. This is because the rules for the enrichment of concrete interpersonal relationships cannot be exhaustively specified in advance. A relationship is always a relationship *with* and *for* and by definition is never unilaterally or objectively imposed. I suspect that we are more likely to value and appreciate those relationships whose partners "fell" into each other's lives, where partner A discovered that partner B met her expectations joyfully and deliberately rather than as an agenda item within a contractual or obligatory context.[70] To the degree that this occurs, though (assuming the perspective of partner A), it is A's subjective reality and situation that determine what B will do and how B will go about doing it. "Recognising, then, that the study of God is worth while, we prepare to start. But where shall we start from? Clearly, we can only start from where we are."[71]

But Packer then proceeds to start entirely elsewhere. His five foundation principles are a priori regulations abstracted from Christian tradition. They are clearly intended to provide limitations upon subjectivity—that is, upon "where we are"—rather than to move from that subjective location to where God's person becomes more intimately known to us. And although traditional within evangelicalism, they are rather narrow limitations at that:

> 1. God has spoken to man, and the Bible is His Word, given to us to make us wise unto salvation.
>
> 2. God is Lord and King over His world; He rules all things for His own glory, displaying His perfections in all that He does, in order that men and angels may worship and adore Him.
>
> 3. God is Saviour, active in sovereign love through the Lord Jesus Christ to rescue believers from the guilt and power of sin, to adopt them as His sons, and to bless them accordingly.
>
> 4. God is Triune; there are within the Godhead three persons, the Father, the Son and the Holy Ghost; and the work of salvation is one in which all three act together, the Father purposing redemption, the Son securing it, and the Spirit applying it.
>
> 5. Godliness means responding to God's revelation in trust and obedience, faith and worship, prayer and praise, submission and service. Life must be seen and lived in the light of God's Word. This, and nothing else, is true religion.[72]

It is a rare person indeed who can say that these principles describe "where we are" and thus where we as receivers of divine revelation begin the journey of being disclosed-to by God. In fact, we should all hope that this is the case, for as we saw above in the consideration of William Abraham, we should be nervous about any theory of revelation that insists upon explicit faith as the precondition for receiving revelation in the first place. Regardless of how many marital veterans share their experiences with us before our own walk down the aisle, our spousal histories must be written one day at a time. We cannot be expected to begin marriage with our own completed experiences in hand as marital road map. But Packer's rules require just that.

The Double Standard

Chapter 4 of Packer's *Knowing God* is entitled "The Only True God." In it he attempts to distinguish between true and false concepts of God (or, perhaps, between concepts of true and false gods) by critically employing the second commandment.[73] His interpretation of this commandment emphatically describes two religious (and thus critical) consequences of the toleration of images: they "dishonour God, for they obscure His glory," and they "mislead men [in that] they convey false ideas about God."[74] The net effect of the commandment is negatively to warn us "against ways of worship and religious practice that lead us to dishonour God and to falsify His truth," and positively to summon us "to recognise that God the Creator is transcendent, mysterious, and inscrutable, beyond the range of any imagining or philosophical guesswork of which we are capable; and hence a summons to us to humble ourselves."[75]

Packer aims this injunction against his own evangelical tradition as well as others. He rejects the legitimacy of *any* image making, whether aesthetic-symbolic or verbal-symbolic. "To make an image of God is to take one's thoughts of Him from a human source, rather than from God Himself; and this is precisely what is wrong with image-making."[76] However judicious this may be in principle, though, it is impossible in fact; if one were to subtract every thought about God derived from an identifiably human source from one's entire set of beliefs about God, which I take it would amount to what he commends here, nothing would remain. Surely it is easy to think about removing statues of Jesus from our churches; what remains might be dull, but at least it is conceivable. But how in principle could one go about removing *verbal* symbols from the life of faith? Words and thoughts would then have to go, because they, too, are created for the purpose of imaging God. And in particular, Packer's words about God would have to go unless he were ready to admit that he has captured the totality of God with utter and radical faithfulness in his own theology, an admission that is both counterintuitive and impossible on his own grounds given what he said about God in the last paragraph. If one believes that God is transcendent mystery, then everything *not* God is not. This is nothing else than the reverse of the doctrine of creation, which insists that God may in principle be revealed through all parts of the creation precisely because they are parts of creation and neither God on the one hand nor independent of God on the other. I shall return to this thought time and again in my consideration of convergence theories of revelation later on, including my own.

Packer provides a delightful though presumably unintentional illustration of this critical inconsistency in this same chapter on "the only true God," where he uses the two examples of Aaron's golden calf and a crucifix to show how images blur rather than focus theological truths. The golden calf was perhaps passable as a bovine symbol but scarcely as an indication of God's "moral character, His righteousness, goodness, patience . . . and glory." Likewise the crucifix "displays [Christ's] human weakness, but it conceals His divine strength [and] the reality of His joy and His power. . . . [It] is a matter of historical fact that the use of the crucifix as an aid to prayer has encouraged people to equate devotion with brooding over Christ's bodily sufferings; it has made them morbid about the spiritual value of physical pain, and it has kept them from knowledge of the risen Saviour."[77] That is, since images are in principle limited, at best they omit necessary features of the realities they symbolize, and at worst they obscure or obliterate those realities altogether.

All of this would be acceptable were it possible for Packer to avoid his own symbolic imaging of God. In what one hopes is a mere oversight, he repeatedly uses *Jehovah* as the transliteration of the tetragrammaton (*YHWH*). *Jehovah*, though, "is an artificial form that arose from the erroneous combination of the consonants YHWH with the vowels of 'Adonai' by a Christian during the late thirteenth century A.D."[78] Thus, the name of God that Packer himself uses is a symbol, and an historically inaccurate one at that. But clearly he anticipates that his readers will know the reality to which *Jehovah* points, and thus that they will overlook its unsatisfactory historical and theological features, gazing instead on the features he wants them to consider. This latter set of assumptions is quite legitimate given the wide range of ways in which symbols relate knower with known, but in this particular context one would hardly expect *Packer* to ask his readers to make them.

My intention here is not simply to point out inconsistencies in Packer's thought, as though throwing rocks through someone else's glass house served any purpose in building one's own. It is instead to repeat the theological truth that I assume is central to the Christian understanding of creation, and yet which is interpreted inversely, in one form or another, by all of the discontinuist theologians we have considered. If God alone is creator, then everything in the universe is a creation of God and thus "usable" by God as a vehicle through which God's self may be disclosed to us. But if this is the case, then by definition everything in the universe may be a symbolic representation of God to those who view it with the eyes and the intention of faith. Obviously some symbols are going to be clearer than others in imaging God, but none may be conceptually precluded from doing so. Such a prohibition would amount to a declaration of autonomy between that thing and God, which is nothing other than a denial that it is a creation of God, and that is *ex hypothesi* unacceptable to faith.

The concepts of revelation that we have seen in this chapter invert this insight, claiming instead that a relatively tiny percentage of objects and ideas in the world may carry the possibility of divine self-disclosure even in principle. (The four most common candidates are the Bible, the life-death-resurrection of Jesus, the church and its sacraments, and miracles.) As I have repeatedly noted, though, the theological mistake committed by such a restriction is that it ultimately boils down to there being a single real instance of divine revelation, that by which the others are authorized *as* revelational. Apart from this one, none of the others could be certified as revelational, and discontinuists do not like uncertainties at such fundamental locations. But by definition, this "ultimate" authorization could not be Bible, Jesus, church and sacraments, or miracles, and so its status as authorizer is also beclouded by uncertainties. This appears to be a trap with no escape so long as one precludes any one part of God's creation from being able to function as a vehicle for God's self-disclosure in preference to other parts. An exclusion requires criteria; these criteria function as ultimate revelation but are shrouded in mystery; revelation then becomes in practice whatever those in authority say it is.

Clearly, I think, Packer's belief that "Scripture has complete and final authority over the Church as a self-contained, self-interpreting revelation from God"[79] needs modification. But just as clearly, some way out of the impasse noted above is needed since the question of whether the Bible (or Jesus, or the church and sacraments, or miracles) is the primal revelation of God turns out rather quickly to be a cat chasing its own tail. That is, traditional responses to this question are all formally identical, regardless of their material differences, in that they cannot break through this critical impasse. Something else is needed, and in the nature of the case it cannot merely be fifth variant on the same order as "Bible, Jesus, church and sacraments, or miracles." Rather, as I will try to show in the next chapter and especially in my own understanding of revelation afterward, I believe it is more consistent with what Christians have long meant (if not said) about revelation to think about it initially in terms of its reception by human subjects, and only then move to a consideration of the God whose person and character accounts for that reception. As we shall see, this approach clearly locates divine revelation in a religious context, and more precisely in a soteriological or saving one, which I would insist is the point of Christian reflections on God's relationship with the world.

We shall leave off our consideration of discontinuist theories of divine revelation with Packer. It is not at all cynicism or sarcasm to say that he has been helpful in the two ways implicit in my critique of him. First, we have seen afresh that proper theology must align method with experience. This is not because of arcane or arbitrary rules of procedure but instead because theology is faith seeking understanding—a certain kind of thing (an experience of God) undergoing transformation into another kind of thing (a notion about an experience of God) with the ultimate intention of understanding the original experience both practically (on the level of the experience itself) and systematically (on the level of its interrelationship with all other similar notions). This is not a straightforward task. And because it is *salvation* theology that we are ultimately interested in, we must always and in principle align our cognitive and theoretical constructions with our experiences of the saving God. To proceed in the opposite direction risks far more than mere cognitive confusion.

Second, we have seen that Packer's careful doctrinal structure rests upon a foundation that is ultimately unable to decide whether a given datum is revelational because it is in the Bible, or whether it is in the Bible because it is revelational. His explicit theology claims the former whereas his rationale for it is forced to claim the latter. I say "is forced to" quite deliberately, for it is clear that Packer does not want to deal with any type of revelation outside of the Bible. This is because he is comfortable with the norms of revelation that he believes the Bible contains self-referentially, and also because of what I earlier called the inverted interpretation of the doctrine of creation with which he and a great many others operate. Thus, my own suggestion concerning revelation will have to avoid *this* bifurcation while resting within the foundation of the human experience of salvation, providing criteria for how the subject of that experience may be certain that it is God, and nothing less, who is ultimately encountered.

Conclusion

We have seen various ways in which divine revelation is said to cut across our usual ways of thinking and acting in order to establish itself as *divine* revelation. There are other ways of explaining discontinuous revelation, but those discussed here will give us a measure of familiarity with the entire family so that we can think of it as a whole. I believe that the instinct on which this family of theories rests is commendable in itself but is typically misconstrued in practice. Its legitimacy lies in what it seeks to protect, namely the belief that God intends for revelation to be a message of salvation rather than of confirmation. Regardless of how many nuances the notion of divine salvation brings to mind, all of them incorporate some understanding of change. The notions of salvation and of business as usual are not the same, for reasons I discussed in the Introduction when I talked about the gap between divine intentions and human actualities. So the discontinuity theories we have examined and others aligned with them are on good grounds in seeking to reflect this change throughout the scope of the notion of revelation.

Exactly where such theories falter is difficult to say because of the particular diversities among them, of course, but of necessity almost all encounter the problem we saw in William Abraham's discussion of revelation and miracles. That is, because revelation is here seen to cut across and in some sense to negate, or at least override, our normal thought processes and behavior patterns, and because we need some measure of certainty to ensure that it is *divine* revelation doing the cutting and negating, some form of prior agreement to this effect must be secured. The individual believer or receiver of revelation must know how to discriminate between the unusual that comes from God and the unusual that comes from elsewhere. The Christian tradition has characteristically located this prior agreement in the doctrine of biblical inspiration: the divine authority (i.e., author-ness) of the Bible grounds its use as the primal as well as critical self-revelation of God.[80] This is prefectly acceptable so long as the discussion is confined to the self-disclosure of God to the Christian community in today's world.[81] It is less acceptable, though, if one wishes to think of how God is disclosed to the larger non-Christian world, and I am convinced that the most important distinction between biblical inspiration and divine revelation is that the latter enables us to do just that. The problem with Abraham's suggestion concerning miracles, as noted above, is that it is precisely the content of whatever is defined as this prior agreement that becomes the functional content of divine revelation; all else flows from this.

This does not appear to be a significant or important discovery, and by itself it may not deserve mention. What is criticizable about it, though, is that the great majority of revelation theories that have been suggested throughout the history of Christianity have been blind to it; they have been far more interested to say how a particular verse (or notion or event or datum of knowledge) was revelational than to recognize that to say that anything was revelational implied a criterion of revelation. What we need to do is pay careful attention to *how* we are going to frame this prior agreement ourselves so that we do not fill it with hidden content that is critically operative but beyond our reach because we keep it both prior and hidden. I shall try in Chapters 3 and 4 to define and defend a formal notion of what would and would not count as disclosure from God. We shall be helped in that task, though, if we first consider the other general approach to the notion of divine revelation, what I have called the way of continuity or convergence.

2

Convergence Theories
of Divine Revelation

Divergence theories of revelation generally suffer from begging, in various ways and with various consequences, the question of how the believer can know that he or she is in the presence of God's self-disclosure. For the person who is neither scornful of nor satisfied with the traditional answers to this question ("because the Bible says so," "because the Church says so," etc.), more is needed. Something must occur in his or her life to point to the divine origin of whatever it is that is called revelational, and thereby point out as well that other events, pieces of information, and the like are not revelational. In the very nature of the case, this thing cannot be, or even be like, the first premise in a syllogistic argument. Rather, it must function more as the presumption or presupposition in which all syllogistic arguments are grounded, and thus which serves collectively to warrant them.[1] It is these presuppositions that generate the possibility of successful argumentation in the first place, and thus which a person who constructs one is in the presence of, whether consciously or not.

It would not be unfair to characterize divergence theories of revelation as reflecting an outmoded and inadequate view of subject and object. In them, as we have seen, the initial assumption is that God and humans are opposed to each other to such a degree that the relationship between them can only be negative until and unless God dynamically compels some kind of saving improvement. Because of sin, humans are taken to be morally inert (at best) except insofar as they can receive revelation. For the same reason, there is little or no attention paid to the means or media of revelation, since those that are identifiable are all part of the structure of the sinful world and not of God. By definition, then, revelation reflects the form only of the divine and not at all of the human. As subject, God is fully responsible for launching and sustaining saving revelation in the world; and as object, human beings are called to be passively obedient to it. As a partial preparation for my own theory of revelation, the critical question to raise against this option focuses on the conditions of this negative relationship: negative relationships may be actual only if relationships themselves are possible. If no relationship at all is possible, then it is obviously moot to discuss how negative one might be. In this chapter and especially the later ones, I shall ask where the possibility of a relationship between God and human beings is seen, and then the more fundamental question of what the grounds of its possibility are.

Another rather general way to characterize and criticize divergence theories of divine revelation is that they divorce the Christian doctrines of creation and christology and then interpret all notions of divine creation in view of the latter. We saw this in Henry and especially in the early Barth, for whom all acts of God's revelatory self-disclosure are interpreted as events that overcome sin. If these doctrines are not separated and ordered, though, but are instead seen as distinct yet equivalent moments of the same self-revealing act of God, then the "discontinuity" that characterized the above theories is healed. God no longer needs to do different things in different ways to different groups of human beings. Instead, God's self-disclosure may always be seen and interpreted as actualizing a single divine intention: drawing persons into closer conformity to authentic moral expression, into closer relationship with God.

In the following chapters I will be more interested in presenting what I take to lie behind traditional notions of revelation, offering an outline of how we know that we are in the presence of persons and, by careful extension, the personal God. Here, however, I will try to show how some other theologians have wrestled with the notion of revelation itself. Those I consider do not accept the validity of the dynamic we saw in the previous chapter, namely that God's self-disclosure cuts across natural human faculties, subverting or at best ignoring them in favor of its own purposes and agenda. Instead, we shall see that they identify God's revelation *in* the natural and the mundane without identifying it *as* the natural and the mundane. Thus, the revelation of God cooperates with the natural, especially the humanly natural, neither impugning it nor canonizing it in advance.[2] This type of theology does not require new ways of thinking about God that are uninformed (at best) by usual ways of thinking about things, as divergence ways do by definition. Instead, it invites us to pay more careful attention to what we already do as believing persons, not only in the explicitly religious spheres of our lives but additionally and perhaps more revealingly so in the others.[3] If God is co-present to all of reality, not accidentally but intrinsically so in view of reality's being the expression of God's creativity, then in principle no part of it may be rejected a priori as vehicle for God's self-disclosure.

Avery Dulles

"Theology, in conformity with St. Augustine's famous dictum, seeks in order that it may understand; but it understands in order that it may seek still more. If we so understood that we no longer had to seek, it would not be the God of revelation that we had found."[4] Few contemporary theologians have been so deliberate in constructing means by which to aid this function of theology as Avery Dulles. Although he is probably best known (especially outside the Catholic church) for his ecclesiological classic *Models of the Church*, that work turned out to be an extensive albeit important interruption within his longer interest in the history and nature of revelation.[5] Here I shall discuss and evaluate what he says about that topic which, he says, is at the heart of the greatest questions human beings can ask about themselves:

> The great Western religions—Judaism, Christianity, and Islam—are based on the conviction that the existence of the world and the final meaning and value of all that it contains ultimately depend on a personal God who, while distinct from the world and everything in it, is absolute in terms of reality, goodness, and power. These religions profess to derive their fundamental vision not from mere human speculation, which would be tentative and uncertain, but from God's own testimony—that is to say, from a historically given divine revelation.[6]

Reality, within which historical goodness and power are preeminent, is grounded in and dependent upon the personal God. Evidence testifying to that contingency is contained within the world itself (indeed, where else could it be?) and especially within human inquiries concerning ultimate meaning and values. That which endures from such inquiries is neither invention nor conjecture on our part but is instead the "received" or historical pole of the self-disclosure of God.

It is precisely because the divine self-disclosures are most clearly located within these ultimate and perennial human questions that the notions of method and criteria are crucial. My first task accordingly will be to summarize the conceptual grids, those structures of critical thought by which our minds are nurtured in the advance of understanding, which Dulles offers as relevant to the topic of revelation. I shall then turn to material matters and examine his suggestion that *symbol* is the operative manner in which God's revelation comes to us. Finally, I shall assess his project in order to determine how it both does and does not help us in specifying the actual nature of divine revelation.

In the three works that address the question of divine revelation most directly,[7] Dulles offers the following criteria as the structures within which revelation thoughts will be most insightfully located. It will be most helpful simply to list these grids rather than to discuss them, since my overall task is the material one of constructing a theory of divine revelation and not primarily the epistemological one of assessing Dulles's criteriology. I shall also distinguish (where possible) between those criteria that appear to be more formal in nature and those that appear to be more materially bound to the notion of revelation.

In *Revelation and the Quest for Unity* (1968):

Formal: None.
Material: Revelation is historical; doctrinal; mysterious.[8]

In *Revelation Theology* (1969):

Formal: None.
Material: (A) Revelation is a completely gratuitous disclosure of God's mind and purposes, salvific in intent; it is heralded through the apostles; it is to be proclaimed universally; it is

eschatological (i.e., both fulfilling and final); it is historical, conveyed in both word and deed.[9]

(B) Nine different epochs have understood it in slightly differing ways: in the *Old Testament*, Yahweh's word is a dynamic force demanding prompt obedience, empowering men to action, and promising prosperity to those who rely on it; in the *New Testament*, Jesus is the manifestation of the covenant between God and all persons, not only Israelites; in the *patristic* period, revelation inwardly enlightens the soul with an obscure but deeply satisfying anticipation of the eternal vision; in *medieval scholasticism*, revelation is a body of divine doctrine furnishing answers to important questions about God, man, and the universe, with which philosophy had grappled in vain; in the *Reformation* period, it is the response to man's anxious quest for a gracious God, the good news that God offers to sinners through the merits of Jesus; in the *Counter Reformation*, it is reaffirmed as the content of an objective body of doctrine, drawn from Scripture and Tradition and taught authoritatively by the Church; in *nineteenth-century idealism*, it is identified with the emergence of the Absolute Spirit in history; in *nineteenth-century moralism and sentimentalism*, it is seen as the religious experience of God as Father and all humans as brothers; and in the period *between the two World Wars*, revelation influenced by existentialist philosophy is seen as the source of meaning, value, and courage. Dulles brings this chronology to the present under two headings: Protestant and Catholic. Here these terms are not used in their denominational senses but instead to indicate different perspectives: the "Protestant" outlook wrestles with the historical and the eventful, while the "Catholic" wrestles with the divine and the transcendental.[10]

(C) Finally, Dulles isolates three basic mentalities which give rise to three distinct styles of revelational theology: the positive or factual mind, which concentrates on revelation as concrete event; the conceptual or abstractive mind, which fastens on the eternal truths in revelation; and the intuitive or mystical mind, which tends to depict revelation as an ineffable encounter with the divine.[11]

In *Models of Revelation* (1985):

Formal: The criteria for evaluating among theories of revelation are faithfulness to the Bible and Christian tradition; internal coherence; plausibility; adequacy to experience; practical fruitfulness; theoretical fruitfulness; and value for dialogue.[12]

Material: (A) The five models or types of revelation which this book considers are revelation as doctrine, as history, as inner experience, as dialectical presence, and as new awareness.[13]

(B) Theories of revelation must situate themselves between families of negative and positive conclusions:

Negative assertions	*Positive assertions*
1. Revelation does not initially occur in the form of propositions, still less that of prefabricated propositions miraculously inserted into the human mind.	1. Revelation has cognitive value that can be expressed, to some extent, in true propositions.
2. It is not a series of events in the remote past.	2. The chief symbols of biblical and Christian revelation are given in specific history, mediated to every generation through the canonical Scriptures, and read in the light of living and ongoing tradition.
3. It is not an ineffable mystical encounter between God and the individual soul.	3. By evoking participation, the revelatory symbols mediate a lived, personal, and thus immediate communion with God.
4. It is not an unintelligible word or an absurd message to be accepted in a blind leap of faith.	4. The words of Scripture and Christian proclamation are, under favorable circumstances, imbued with the power of God, who speaks and acts through them.
5. It is not a mere invitation to adapt one's attitudes and	5. Revelation is not merely speculative truth, but instead

behavior to the needs of a particular phase of the evolutionary process.

has implications for human existence and conduct, demands obedience, brings new horizons and a new consciousness.[14]

(C) Finally, Dulles notes the three functions of revelation: it grounds the faith of the Christian believer, it directs the mission of the church, and it undergirds theological argument.[15]

All of these criteria may be taken as formal because they are more interested in how the notion of revelation is to be properly bounded for the sake of proper comprehension than in the actual phenomenon of revelation. This is scarcely a criticism. In fact, as Robert McAfee Brown repeatedly mentions in his Foreword to *Revelation and the Quest for Unity*, Dulles is one of the earliest theologians to pass beyond thinking about ecumenism and to begin to think ecumenically. These criteria represent the central theological ideas of Western or Catholic theology.[16] The reason I discuss them first in my consideration of Dulles, and more basically yet the reason I discuss Dulles first in my consideration of convergence-type theories of revelation, is precisely that they are both adequate and comprehensive for their critical purposes. We shall surely be benefited to the degree that we keep them in mind as I move to the construction of a theory of revelation in Chapters 3 and 4.

The closest Dulles approaches the actual phenomenon of divine revelation is his discussion of symbol and symbolic mediation. Even here, though, the focus is as much upon the mode of transmission as upon the divine reality disclosed. Drawing upon the works of Paul Tillich, Paul Ricoeur, Michael Polanyi, Ian Ramsey, and others,[17] he makes two fundamental and apt claims about the relationship of symbol and revelation. First, in contrast both to positivist philosophers and other sorts of skeptics earlier in this century and also to religious fundamentalists and biblical literalists closer to our own day, symbol is a perfectly appropriate way to convey meaning. In different but related ways, both positivists and fundamentalists attempt to restrict the mode of language to what Polanyi calls the "indicator" mode and what linguists often call the "referential" mode. According to this understanding, the sole function of language is to point out or to indicate meaning to the human knower. Words and sentences "have an exact identity of reference thanks to their abstract quality."[18] That is, they neither point to nor evoke anything beyond the exact and precise lexical meaning assigned to them. Furthermore, they themselves are referentially transparent; "without being attended to they direct our attention to other objects which are focally known. When, for example, we read a letter, we hardly notice the print or even the language, since our attention is directed to the meaning."[19] Certainly, though, this is an unwarranted restriction upon the ways that language, much less other kinds of vehicles such as art and environment, brings us into contact with meaning and truth. That language does function in the strict indicative or referential mode is clear; that it functions in broader ways is even clearer.[20]

The category of symbol accounts for the residue of meaning beyond the strictly lexical which resides within ourselves as we experience the full meaning of the word.

> A symbol is a sign pregnant with a plenitude of meaning which is evoked rather than explicitly stated. . . . In symbolic communication, the clues draw attention to themselves. We attend to them, and if we surrender to their power they carry us away, enabling us to integrate a wider range of impressions, memories, and affections than merely indicative signs could enable us to integrate. Thanks to symbols, we can bring an indefinite number of diffuse memories and experiences into a kind of focus.[21]

As both near and remote literary instances of the category of symbol, Dulles discusses analogy, myth, metaphor, parable, allegory, and ritual.[22]

Dulles identifies four similarities between symbolic communication and revelation which he says buttress but do not conclusively prove the idea that revelation functions symbolically. First, both convey meaning and truth by participation rather than by objective observation. In symbol as well as in (the reception of) revelation, truth is appropriated more by inhabiting an environment than by simple memorization. "A symbol is never a sheer object. It speaks to us only insofar as it lures us to situate ourselves mentally within the universe of meaning and value which it opens up to us."[23] Second (and third; I do not think that these can be distinguished in practice), symbol both "transforms the person" and "has a powerful influence on commitments and behavior."[24] Symbol equips the person for change and also constitutes the goal of change. Finally, and most importantly for our particular purposes, symbol awakens and uncovers realms of reality not accessible to referential or indicative discourse.[25] That is, it puts us into contact with what is beyond us, beckoning and luring us to itself and thus to self-transcendence. By definition, "what is beyond us" is mysterious, at least for the present, although it is not radically inscrutable (which would render it permanently inaccessible and thus doomed as either the ground or the goal of self-revelation and self-transcendence). Dulles concludes this critical comparison by showing how revelation, too, is participatory, transformative, ethically influential, and disclosive.

This is the heart of Dulles's proposal concerning the nature or essence of divine revelation. I hope that it is a forgivable oversimplification on my part to note that it is of greater critical help than religious help. Dulles has constructed enormously useful fences within which any notion of divine self-disclosure must reside if it intends to reflect and thus be of use to the Western (or catholic) Christian tradition. The scope, brevity, and clarity of his writing make these three works central to any contemporary treatment of the topic, an assessment that would only have been reinforced had our purposes included the historical treatment found in *Revelation Theology: A History*. He seems equally comfortable in the disciplines of history, systematics, and philosophy, and almost any reader will feel the same.

Nevertheless, Dulles has not completed the task that I believe that this topic deserves. He makes two assumptions that invite further explication in any work on divine revelation than he gives to them. The first assumption has to do with symbolic mediation, and the second has to do with God. In particular, he has not said *how* symbol mediates truth and meaning to us, but only *that* it does. Dulles is surely correct in insisting that the "route" of divine revelation is most often through symbolic mediation, but more explicit cartography is needed in order to feel more comfortable with it. Second, and also in line with the great majority of the catholic tradition, he assumes that God reveals and that human beings can receive what God reveals. But he does not say how this is intrinsic either to what it means to be human or to what it means to be God.

Thus, both the initiation and the reception of divine revelation might appear to be extraneous or arbitrary to human existence, which is contrary to the centrist catholic tradition that he and I wish to occupy.[26] Accepting both of these at face value from the tradition allows him to focus his energies elsewhere, and so here I shall attempt to supply what Dulles has not.

The overall intention of Dulles's works on revelation seems to be to provide the theological community with a critical taxonomy by which to understand the history, lived as well as theoretical, of this doctrine. What it does not do, I think, is say what human beings are in the presence of when they are, or are not, experiencing the self-revealing God. My objective in the last two chapters of this book will be to propose an answer to this question.

John Macquarrie

Anglican theologian John Macquarrie is the first theologian we shall look at who deliberately peruses divine revelation from a conceptual or perhaps global perspective rather than simply a Christian one. He brings two worthwhile emphases. First, more clearly than Dulles and especially the discontinuists of Chapter 1, he inquires into revelation as a statement about God and not merely about Christianity. In so doing, though, he retains his particularity as a Christian theologian and does not attempt the (ultimately useless) enterprise of trying to explain revelation from an allegedly neutral base.[27] Second, he will show us how revelation is both at home in and elicited from the world in which we live as receiving human beings. This, too, will contrast sharply with the assumptions of Chapter 1.

This second accent is noticed as soon as one opens Macquarrie's book. Of its three major divisions, the first is entirely devoted to what he calls philosophical theology, described as the discipline of laying "bare the fundamental concepts of theology and [investigating] the conditions that make any theology possible."[28] That is, the discipline of philosophical theology attempts as much as possible to prescind from the historical and doctrinal particularities of a given religious tradition, and from thence to show how those specifics are precisely grounded in the universal, the knowable, and the believable. In this first division, then, he lays the groundwork for being able to hold to that which he will later discuss as specifically Christian.

Because he is here working in a field vastly larger than Christian but with the ultimate intention of returning to it in order to ground and defend the explicitly Christian, the need to select a careful and effective method is crucial. The one he chooses is phenomenology, an investigatory and explanatory approach that has three advantages over alternative methods: its beginning point (phenomena or things in themselves, uninterpreted as much as possible); its fundamental dynamic (the relationship between words and the phenomena they bring to our attention); and its overall intention (a descriptive account of reality, rather than a normative or deductive evaluation). Accordingly, Macquarrie's section on philosophical theology moves methodologically from the observation that human beings have revelatory experiences, then backward to the presupposition of such experiences which (or who) is God, then forward again to the meaning of "God," then to how theological language serves to link the human experience with its divine origin, and finally to how such revelatory experiences may be understood even in the face of the enormous variety of religions present today and throughout history. My own interests in this book impel me to pay special attention to the first three of these.

All religions, Macquarrie insists, operate from the presumption of some form of revelation, whether it is as explicit as the classic prophetic formula in the Old Testament ("Thus says the Lord") or as inchoate as animism and other primitive religions.[29] For both extremes and everything that stretches between them, religion or faith is seen as a response to God. This is not simply a gratuitous or optional response, because it is one that reflects the dynamic of humankind's ineluctable search for resolutions to problems or dilemmas inherent in life itself. Thus, it is a religious search, even when undertaken by persons who are deliberately neutral or even hostile to explicit religious faith, because it reaches beyond the mundane to that which ultimately grounds the meaningfulness of the mundane. Responses that succeed as effective groundings do so precisely in that they place one in some kind of contact with God (once again, regardless of whether or not this contact is consciously affirmed as contact with *God*).

Revelation is thus neither ancillary nor accidental to the essence of human being. Constitutively, humans are beings who both perceive and address existentially debilitating polarities: between possibility and facticity, between rationality and irrationality, between responsibility and impotence, between anxiety and hope, and between individuality and sociality.[30] Precisely because these are debilitating, the net result of serious reflection upon them is that both we and the world are best characterized by "nothingness."[31] And since resolution cannot arise from nothingness, resolutions are experienced precisely as gifts breaking in from outside of the condition of nothingness that necessitates them. Such resolutions might reside in either approval or accusation, but in any case as new, and *that* is revelation.

Revelation acts like all knowledge in that it is an unveiling. All knowing is a movement from the chaotic to the organized, with truth (or some functional equivalent) as both critical catalyst and ultimate intention.[32] Ever since Kant, it has been difficult to avoid the idea that the knowing mind itself holds the initiative in overcoming such chaos, particularly when *our* knowing mind is the one at issue. In revelation, though, we sense the opposite: it is because our minds themselves impress the kind of order that they do upon the data of reality, an order that paralyzes us within the above polarities, that revelation must come from beyond the universe of those minds and data themselves. This is why revelation is always *divine* revelation, or *God's* word: reality cannot dispose of the debris that reality itself hurls onto the beach.[33]

Further, revelation per se does not concern itself with new bits of "real" data. When revelation invites us into the presence of that which is new, whether in approval or its opposite, we are not merely in the presence of another feature of the universe that had previously escaped our attention. In fact, we are not even in the presence of a feature that had previously escaped everyone's attention. Instead, it is a new and different kind of perspective on our existing familiarity with reality that grasps us and revises us in that very familiarity. Macquarrie's language here is relational and ontological. Revelation does not simply introduce us to another being, but rather to being itself which grounds the individual being of all things that are. This being (or Being) is prior to all particular instances of being; it is the "lets-be" or "allows-to-be" or the "letting-be" of all existing beings. This being is God even though, as we shall see, *being* and *God* are not synonymous.[34]

As do all theologians who insist that God is not a something in the universe but is instead that in relation to which all things stand and thus receive their ex-ist-ence, or thingness, Macquarrie is forced to proceed more by way of negation than proposition in his attempt to say what, how, and who the God is who is the "lets-be" of all beings. My specific purpose in this book leads me to focus on his depiction of God as *holy* being, an adjective that draws attention to two existential or relational dynamics: God as ultimate source of morality and value, and God as one to whom persons are related in faith or unfaith rather than simply in observation and distance.

Although "God is the key word of all religion and of all theology," Macquarrie waits until he is halfway through his account of the nature and purpose of philosophical theology to introduce and describe what he means by the word.[35] He briefly recounts three stages through which humankind and thus theology have traveled in the attempt to understand God more clearly. The first is the mythological stage, in which God was imagined to be like us except bigger, more powerful, and (occasionally) less embodied. The second stage is traditional theism, from which the cruder mythological anthropomorphisms have been removed but other personal specifications have not, so that God is still treated as another being within the universe of beings. Finally, Macquarrie identifies the stage called existential-ontological theism, in which God's genuine ultimacies can be understood more precisely because all known inhibiting limitations have been removed. This signals an appropriate ontology of divinity: God is not a being but is instead being itself. Definite and indefinite articles have no place in the grammar of divine ontology. They serve only to discriminate between and among things of similar kind, and not between all of those things and that which grounds and thus constitutes the possibility of their thingness in the first place.

The movement from earlier to later stages here may be interpreted as theology's increasingly successful attempt to strip from the notion of God any feature that is not both transcendent and moral in essence. The reason for this is straightforward: what is not moral does not contribute to humankind's distinctive attribute, namely conscious and intentional self-transcendence.[36] Self-transcendence is a moral dynamic whose ground is God, and not a morally neutral or static given whose ground and possibility is fully immanent within the structures of the physical world. To speak of God, then, is to speak of holy being; "holiness" is the radical term of the moral spectrum, and God is the "allows-to-be" of all existing beings.

Now Macquarrie's assertion that human beings are essentially or constitutively related to God may be understood. Both poles of what humans constitutively are, namely existence or beingness on the one hand and moral self-transcendence on the other, are grounded in God, the Holy Being.[37] To be human is to be related to God; or, better, to be human is to be grounded in God. This is not optional, and neither is the need to account for it in understandable ways. In fact, it is even less optional than other human attributes that limit and condition our existence and experiences, such as being female or being intelligent or being healthy.[38] One can neither create nor eradicate this ultimate feature of human existence but instead can only affirm it or deny it. The affirmation of God as constitutive ground of all (and therefore human) existence is called faith, and the denial of that is called unfaith. Because God is not another being in the world but rather the condition of the existence of all beings, faith and unfaith are stances toward the world rather than discrete sets of knowledge and data about it.

We can now understand more clearly what Macquarrie means by revelation as well. Revelation is that initiative of God whereby we experience our particular existence in the world as grounded in God, which reflexively makes us more aware of who we are as persons in the world. Or to say the same thing more expansively, revelation is that initiative of God by which we experience both the ultimate ground of our own being in Being which allows all beings to exist (ontology), and by which we progress toward a deeper understanding of the possibilities and thus the responsibilities that are ours as beings capable of intentional self-transcendence precisely because we are grounded in the self-transcending God (existentialism). Accounting for this complex is the true task of an existential-ontological theism.

In Chapters 3 and 4 of this book I shall discuss the meaning of divine revelation as that self-disclosure of God whereby we are constituted as, and can account for ourselves as, free beings capable of knowing, loving, and hoping. I take these as the three essential and distinctive features of *human* being, and the "purpose" of divine revelation is taken precisely to account for how the self-transcending and self-disclosing Holy Being grounds, and thus precipitates, human beings who possess and exhibit these features. Although *objectively* the dynamic of divine revelation always moves in the ontological direction, from God to us, *theologically* and subjectively the dynamic always moves in the existential direction, from us to God.

The dyadic movements just referred to remind us that we need to pay particular attention to epistemology, to the checking procedures by which we verify as best we can the rightness and appropriateness of our thoughts about the self-disclosing God. It is here, I think, that Macquarrie's phenomenological orientation requires crutches. This is not very surprising, since phenomenology is intentionally descriptive rather than normative. Nevertheless, I think that greater conceptual resources can be harnessed by which to certify or evaluate the conclusions of our thoughts about revelation than what he grants.

Immediately after Macquarrie discusses the notion of revelation itself,[39] he draws critical attention to what some have called its self-authenticating nature. The claim has often been advanced that divine revelation is self-authenticating because that has seemed to be the only way out of the epistemological merry-go-round discussed in Chapter 1 and represented by the following questions: How do we know that a given statement or proposition is revelation? Because it comes from God. How do we know that it comes from God? Because it is revelation which, by definition, cannot deceive us. The formal precision of this argument is more than offset by its material emptiness, and some theologians who noticed this came up with the notion of the *self*-authentification of revelation. This stops the merry-go-round by asserting that the epistemological warrants for the identification of a given proposition as revelation reside simply in the proposition itself and are both present and obvious to any who do not bend over backward to deny them.

This is not much of an advance, if it is one at all. For one thing, it seems at least as empty (or purely formal) as what it tried to displace; anyone who could be satisfied by stipulating an abstractly self-authenticating revelation was probably not suffering from merry-go-round motion sickness in the first place. Even more problematically, especially for religious purposes, it innocently (?) locates the warrant for the identification of divine revelation *outside* the revelatory proposition or event itself, and *in* the decision to end all uncertainty by arbitrarily stipulating "these" propositions and events as revelatory rather than "those." This is not terribly helpful. Apart from some inclusion of the experience of revelation and, I would claim, of the difference that such experiences make in the life of the believer, the stipulation of given propositions and events as revelatory turns out all too easily to be entirely philosophical, gratuitous, and nonreligious.

Macquarrie would agree entirely with this analysis. Where he does not go far enough, in my estimation, is in emphasizing the positive critical role of human moralness identifying divine revelation. That is, Macquarrie is comfortable in affirming the idea that we can discriminate between genuine and deceptive instances of divine revelation by testing whether or not the revelation helps us to overcome the polarities mentioned above. And he further specifies how this discrimination is to occur by applying what looks to be a quite pragmatic test: Does the alleged revelation confirm our conscience by being creative of selfhood and community? If so, then it is genuinely, although never incontrovertibly, from God.[40] But throughout this discussion he seems to back away from an unambiguous declaration of the human moral capacity as the location of that which is uniquely human and thus that which is the target of divine revelatory activity.

I shall try to add to Macquarrie here in three ways. First, he seems to distinguish between "conscience" on the one hand and "that which is creative of selfhood and community" on the other. I will argue later that these are really the same thing. To put the matter more accurately, conscience (or human moral capacity) has two poles: the inner one or selfhood, and the outer one or community. The critical test which assesses and thus ultimately grounds the inner pole is knowledge (or truth), while that for the outer pole is love.[41] Both are essential to our natures as moral beings who are capable of self-transcendence, and thus both find their ultimate ground in God.

Second and closely consequent to what I have just said, Macquarrie does not spend much time saying *how* that which is creative of selfhood and community functions retroactively to assess alleged instances of revelation. I shall try to do so. As I have already said, the route of this attempt will be to relate that which is distinctive to human beings (our moral capacity) to God in such a way as to ground it adequately in God, *and* ground it in God in such a way that the two prime constructs of our moral capacity, namely self-hood and the community, are both accounted for.[42]

Third, Macquarrie's understanding of revelation functions pretty much independently of christology on the one hand and trinitarian theology on the other. (His initial discussions of both occur only subsequently in Part Two: Symbolic Theology.) It is the failure to try to relate these topics, or else the botched attempt actually to do so, that renders most discussions of divine revelation unhelpful.[43] If we really do intend to suggest a theory of divine revelation that is both intellectually coherent and distinctively Christian at the same time, then it does not do us much good to overlook this matrix.

As is obvious by now, the understanding of divine revelation that Macquarrie presents in his *Principles of Christian Theology* is one I find immensely useful. For the first time in those we have considered thus far, we see the attempt to ground all of reality within the self-disclosing activity of God. In more classical terms, Macquarrie attempts to ground creation within revelation in such a way as to remain faithful both to the universality of creation and to the particularity of revelation as Christians experience and understand it. And he does so by means of an approach that holds forth the promise of critical responsibility and of broad, if not universal, responsibility and awareness. If his conclusions limp here in the ways I have tried to indicate, they do so because he has not been sufficiently responsible to the centrality of the Christian notions of christology and trinity. Since these are the two primary avenues by which Christians categorize or reflect back upon their experiences of the self-disclosing God, any notion of divine revelation *not* including them will be unhelpfully truncated. Macquarrie's definition of revelation does not return fully to home in its movement from "Christian experience" to "philosophical theology" and thence back to "Christian theology."

Gerald O'Collins

Gerald O'Collins is a professor of fundamental theology at the Gregorian University in Rome. Just what "fundamental theology" is is a matter of no small debate,[44] especially in the Protestant theological world where the designation is rarely if ever used. In general, though, it may be said that fundamental theology is that discipline of thought which inquires into the linguistic and conceptual presuppositions made by theology itself (and thus theologians) since theology is thought, spoken, and written in culturally shaped patterns. Thinking and speaking in such patterns is inescapable, and this determines in large part the kinds of conclusions that may and may not be reached by given theologians employing given theological methods and patterns. Examining them is thus essential to the discipline of theology itself, since making a mistake at these hidden or presuppositional levels will have enormous and potentially deleterious effects at the more visible ones. As such, then, fundamental theology is functionally equivalent to what Macquarrie and many Protestants call philosophical theology.

Although the how of all of this is also a matter of debate, fundamental theologians must be attentive to philosophy, history, sociology, psychology, and other humane disciplines in order both to discern and to correct the patterns of thought operative in given theological constructs.[45] This results from the contemporary discoveries of these very disciplines that the influences that shape or determine our patterns of thinking, speaking, and acting are rooted in those realms of reality to which philosophy, history, sociology, and the rest draw our attention. Quite clearly, individual human beings are not the blank slates that many of our Enlightenment forebears believed. Just as clearly, though, neither are human beings the mere or simple expression of all of the external forces and influences that operate upon us. We are instead responsible employers of those factors and influences, called upon to use them both creatively and wisely. It is the task of fundamental theology to identify and evaluate the influences, especially the conceptual and critical ones, that operate within given theological systems and result in the particularities of one.

O'Collins's *Fundamental Theology* is a recent discussion of both the presuppositions and the content of the notion of divine revelation. It divides itself into four parts: theology and experience (i.e., what is properly "fundamental" to the notion of revelation), revelation, tradition, and inspiration. It will be of enormous use to us as we consider these things ourselves in the third and fourth chapters of this book. I will especially take much of value from his "transcendentalist" perspectives, those concerning the nature and critical value of human experience in general, and of religious experience in particular, in uncovering what is at stake in the Christian notion of divine self-revelation. I do not believe, though, that O'Collins goes far enough in his identification of the content of such revelation, especially with respect to Christian believers applying what we have learned about God from within our own community of belief to those who stand outside it. By the end of this book, I hope to have outlined what I take this content to be more clearly than he, not so much as a way of correcting him but rather as a proposal for how Christians today may see God's presence permeating all of reality, including crucially those aspects of reality that are not obviously Christian and are not in a conscious relationship with God as Christians understand God. It will perhaps be of even more use to that proposal, then, to consider O'Collins's shortcomings.

I shall try to do two things in my consideration of *Fundamental Theology*. First, I shall summarize the content and method of the features of revelation that surface in that work. Like Dulles, Macquarrie, and myself, O'Collins has gained much from his use of the transcendentalist methodology so often associated with Karl Rahner. Second, and much more briefly, I shall say where I believe that his treatment of revelation only barely glances at the most crucial aspect of God's character, and thus of God's presence in the world, and thus of the content of God's self-revelation in the world. The third and fourth chapters of this book will give me the opportunity to graze in these pastures with greater leisure and care. At the moment, therefore, my purpose is more to learn from O'Collins than to criticize him.

"[My] book will center on the human experience *of the* (*historical and transcendental*) *divine self-communication in Christ*. As a Christian theologian I would find it pointless to discuss the conditions and nature of human experience by itself, as it were."[46] This quite nicely encapsulates each of the major components of O'Collins's understanding of revelation: its origin in human experience,[47] the distinction between historical experiences themselves on the one hand and the transcendental conditions or parameters of human experience itself which govern or condition both the nature and the content of actual or historical experiences on the other, and the need to integrate "abstract" or universal estimates concerning human experience with what the Christian tradition confesses about human beings as creatures concretely and necessarily related to God. This serves not only as an overview of the content of O'Collins's theology of revelation but additionally as a methodological clue. Here we see that his treatment will proceed from the human experience of receiving God's self-revelation, to the nature and content of that revelation as experienced both inside and outside the Christian tradition. I shall follow him as he outlines his transcendentalist understanding of God's self-communication.

Human Experience by Itself, as Transcendental, and as Historical

O'Collins's discussion of the nature of human experience is both dense and succinct, and it would be tedious for me simply to summarize his summary.[48] Given the relationship between "experience" and "being human," though, a relationship whose terms are so intertwined that we can scarcely understand either apart from the other, we will not get very far in our consideration of how persons experience God if we do not first pay careful attention to what experience itself is. O'Collins begins by dividing this notion into three components: the subject, the experience itself, and its consequences.

Regardless of what the (human) subject experiences in particular, which we might call the content of experience, the experience itself or that which mediates the content retains certain stable features. These features include immediacy, personal involvement in the rational but more especially the encountering sphere of life,[49] disclosiveness, and breadth or holism.[50] From both the inside and the outside, then, or constitutively and expressively, the human realizes itself in and through experiences. I shall return to this thought repeatedly in my effort to show how the concept of human experience includes or presupposes the concept of moralness.

Experience itself[51] includes four features. It has intentionality or meaning (which is not to say that we immediately and clearly recognize that meaning; in principle, at least, we may never do so);[52] it is concrete (it is never the case that I fall in love abstractly, but instead I fall in love with Sally); it is properly both new and old (contrary to prevalent usage, which normally prefers the word for the novel and unexpected above the mundane and the foreseen); and finally it is morally evaluable. It is this last feature that I shall be most interested in as I attempt to specify more clearly than O'Collins just what divine revelation is in its reception by human beings and (thus) in its donation by God. For the moment it is useful simply to note that an essential part of what makes something a *human* experience is that it can be assessed by some mark on the moral yardstick that ranges between good and evil. I think that this is the ultimate distinction between events that occur to animals and events that occur to human beings; even if in all other respects the nature and shape of those events might be identical, they are not ultimately identical in that humans can, and animals cannot, perceive them as good, bad, or indifferent.[53] This is because, as far as we know, human beings are the most highly developed earthly beings in possession of the requisite conditions for being able to make moral evaluations. Those who cannot experience given things do not experience them, as any reflection on logic makes clear.

An analogy here would be living in the world of color. We take it for granted that the real world is colored, but we can do that only because we have the requisite physiological apparatus for being able to perceive colors. If we were like some forms of sentient life on earth that have retinas that are innocent of all the complex cones and rods that humans have, then our world would not be colored because it could not be colored. We can only experience the world in ways that reside within the bounds or conditions of experience that constitute us as the kinds of beings we are. Similarly, if we do possess the conditions of experiencing the world as moral, then "our world" is moral.[54] I think that this is what is essentially and distinctively *human* about human beings and that all of our notions of divine revelation need to seat themselves within this essential and distinctive human capacity.

Finally, O'Collins discusses the consequences of experience. He distills it into four components: discernment, interpretation, expression, and memory.[55] Interestingly enough, although he is much interested here in distinguishing between authentic and inauthentic experiences (especially religious ones), and in fact devotes a few paragraphs to determining the difference, he fails to address what would seem to be the relevant constituent or attribute of God that befits the distinction, namely God's goodness. His reader is left only with an implicit notion of God when an explicit one is available, and with a rather anecdotal connection between that God and the human critical task of discernment and evaluation.[56] Overall, though, O'Collins offers a rich and valuable discussion of the complex interplay among the various factors that comprise us as human beings: individual and social, contemporary and historical, interior and expressive, cognitive and experiential.

O'Collins's summary of the difference between transcendental and historical experiences arises in his first explicit treatment of religious experiences, and thus of God. Here he draws upon Karl Rahner's *Foundations of Christian Faith*, arguably the clearest locus of this contemporary distinction.[57] It is one of Rahner's most fundamental and dynamic insights that all knowledge and experience display our relationship with these two "horizons." The historical horizon is what we encounter in usual acts of knowing and experiencing: things, persons, colors, values, and memories. But if we do encounter things on the historical horizon, however, then we do not simply encounter *it* when we encounter them. Instead and more fundamentally (in fact, *so* fundamentally that we rarely pause long enough to think about it), whenever we encounter them we also encounter the horizon that makes them possible in the first place. This ultimate horizon is not experienced in the same way that the historical or proximate one is, though, because as source or condition of the closer horizon it cannot be surrounded, objectivized, and contextualized in the same way as things within that closer one.

> The ultimate horizon is not one determined object among others. Knowing it is not just one more instance of knowledge in general. It is there as an unthematized and unreflective element. Even when through subsequent reflection it becomes the object of explicit attention, it can never be totally and adequately thought through and objectivized.
>
> The human subject enjoys a "transcendental" experience of his horizon, in the sense that the experience goes beyond any particular acts of knowing and willing. This horizon not only transcends all specific acts as acts, but also does not depend upon this or that particular content. Hence the experience of [this] horizon can be called transcendental.[58]

This horizon, then, is inescapable. It is experienced along with our experiences of everything else as "the a priori condition for the possibility of any human experience. When, for instance, some specific act of knowledge occurs, that is because there already exists a knowing subject oriented toward this horizon."[59] It is thus the ultimate seat or source of those things that we take to be fundamental to our presence in the universe, and as "absolute fullness of being, meaning, truth and goodness, this ultimate horizon is to be identified with God."[60] A summary here would be that any concrete experience we have puts us into objective contact with the "this" or "that" of the experience, but in addition puts us into contact with the conditions that trigger and govern the possibility of the "this" or "that" in the first place, and thus of the possibility of having *that* experience. It is most recognizably the case, but only this and nothing more, that we accept the ultimate horizon of realities such as being, meaning, truth, and goodness to be God.

In principle and in fact, then, all experiences are religious insofar as they are all indirect experiences of the transcendent ground of the possibility of any experience whatsoever, namely God. Common usage invites us to specify this further and say more precisely that all experiences share a religious dimension, whether recognized or not, an invitation we do well to accept. Common usage invites us as well to divide between those experiences that are religious and those that are not. But this is an invitation I think we should decline, both because it ignores the distinction between transcendental and historical (some historical experiences are not explicitly religious, but if the above characterization is correct then no transcendental experiences are) and because it rejects the universality of God's creativeness (claimed in, among other places, the Nicene affirmation that "We believe in one God, the Father, the almighty, maker of all things visible and invisible").

In fact, not only should we decline this second invitation, we should go further and recognize that it is precisely around this reality that faith and unfaith revolve. Religious faith does not see what is not there to be seen, as has so often been claimed in the past. It sees precisely what is there, but "there" as the invisible ground of what is there and visible. It is unfaith that resists the opportunity to look beyond what is seen to that which makes the seen and known both seeable and knowable, and thus it is unfaith, and not faith, that ultimately distorts the reality of the world.

It is essential to the possibility of religious experiences both that God exists and that God exists as a self-disclosing God whose self-revelation constitutes the ground of the possibility of religious experiences being authentic experiences of God. This is a purely formal claim in that it says nothing about who God is *as* ultimate horizon within which reality is experienced by human beings, but instead says only that if experiences of God are possible, then what makes them possible is God making them possible.

On the other hand, this purely formal nature is not unhelpful, because it shows us (formally) what revelation is as well. Revelation is the gratuitous self-disclosure of God. It is self-disclosure in that God is the ultimate or transcendent horizon against which all human knowledge and experience become possible. And it is gratuitous or gracious in two ways. First, although it is necessarily true that if anything else exists then God exists as the transcendent condition of the possibility of that thing's existence, the opposite is not the case. God's existence does not transcendentally presuppose the existence of what is not-God in the way that what is not-God transcendentally presupposes the existence of God. God's creation of the universe was not forced upon God by any feature not already an intrinsic part of God's character.[61] Second, revelation is gratuitous in that humans may or may not accept it as divine self-disclosure. Indeed, humans may freely choose to reject the legitimacy even of the possibility of divine revelation as ground of knowledge and experience. In and of itself such a rejection does not dismiss the reality of divine revelation or of God's presence as transcendent ground of reality. But it does distinguish how it is that we know transcendent objects of knowledge from historical or categorical objects of knowledge.

Negatively put, this distinction can be seen in the consequences of rejecting conclusions of either kind of knowing. Rejecting the conclusions of historical or categorical knowledge usually involves us in some form of pragmatic difficulty because for most of us, we "know" when given bits of data expand or nurture the possibility of living coherently and comfortably in the real world.[62] Rejecting the conclusions of transcendental knowledge, though, does not implicate us as quickly in the same pragmatic predicament. Rejecting the existence or the graciousness of God presents us with a more subtle sort of difficulty than rejecting the validity of mathematics or of formulas depicting the surface tension of water. It is part of the graciousness of God and thus of the universe which functions as the means of God's gracious self-communication, I think, that this is so.

Before moving to O'Collins's discussion of the content of revelation and thence to my observations concerning its incompleteness, a couple of more formal matters need to be addressed. Before this century, most Christian treatises on divine revelation innocently (one hopes) identified revelation with certain truths or propositions that God directed toward the world that were both necessary for salvation and unavailable from other sources. O'Collins notes, though, that this naive identification has lately broken down both inside and outside of Catholic contexts. What has replaced it usually goes under the name of personal or dialogical revelation, including but not at all limited to the impartation of propositions; here the intrinsically religious essence of divine revelation is signaled by the question "Who is revealed?" rather than the previous "What is revealed?"[63] Because the "Who" question intends to inquire about God, though, and not simply about facts and data, one must have a fairly clear notion of who God is in order to be able to distinguish revelations that authentically disclose God from revelations that only putatively do so. O'Collins notes here that the consequential difference between these two questions was that theology became much more convinced of what it had professed all along, namely that the intention of divine revelation was the establishment of a personal relationship between human beings and God. And if this were true, then salvation itself was transformed from adeptness in conceptualizing all sorts of divinely released propositions to (simply) a healthy and positive relationship with God. "Almost inevitably the [former] terminology of revelation fails to cover the full human condition and the scope of what God does for us. It narrows things down to our quest for meaning and the answer to our mental bewilderment—in brief, salvation for our intellect and reason."[64]

Finally, then, O'Collins notes the historical (or nontranscendental) parameters of religious experiences that serve to distinguish between authentic and inauthentic religious experiences.[65] In brief, these parameters surround the following insights: authentic religious experiences are liminal or profound (they are beyond the mundane, but "beyond" in ways that have reflexive meaning back upon the mundane); they are optimistically intentional (they reorient our approach to the future in ways that give concrete expression to hope and to love); they are somehow christological (they are correlative to what the Christian tradition identifies as the difference made by Christ, especially "the creative, revealing and redeeming presence of Christ"); and finally they are vestigially trinitarian (not, surprisingly, in the transcendental sense but rather in the explicit historical-categorical sense; examples here are the "Hindu triad representing the three aspects of the Absolute Spirit [Brahma, Vishnu, and Siva], the Yin, Yang and Tao of Taoism, and other religious experiences that speak of an absolute origin of things, some principle of meaning and order, and the unity of love").[66]

Finally, O'Collins launches his explicit discussion of the content of divine self-communication. It, too, is surprising, with respect to both its placement and its brevity. It is launched within his initial discussion of faith, the human response to revelation, which seems to presuppose a developed notion of revelation itself.[67] Instead, though, the discussion is introduced as his answer to the question:

> What is that self-communication itself supposed to be like? The previous chapters have in fact often been in the business of offering replies to sub-aspects of that question. Here we need to summarize some dominant features of those replies, add a few details and, above all, focus matters for the key discussion on faith.[68]

The structure of his developed response follows along the lines of Kant's famous three questions: What can I know? What should I do? What may I hope for? Perhaps because he *is* summarizing, he answers these questions in the briefest of terms as the marrow of God's self-revelation.

First, we know that God's self-revelation is gracious, or giftlike, in that it springs from God's initiative. It is historical and communitarian in that it seeks the concrete salvation of living human beings, who are themselves irreducibly both. It is thus also a mediated gift as a reflection upon the how of God's presence; because God is real but not phenomenal, because God is Mystery but not mere conundrum, because God is transcendent but God's people are ephemeral, God's self-revelation is interwoven into the fabrics of those persons and cultures who inquire about God. Thus, it is woven into the fabric of history as well, especially and "classically exemplified by the history of Israel up to its climax in Jesus Christ."[69] Second, divine revelation is not a mere transferring of information. Rather, because it intends the wellness of the whole human being in the culture and context in which that precise person is located, it calls for personal involvement and response. "[It] makes drastic claims on us to live in new ways."[70] (This is where the present theological notion of divine self-revelation swerves most noticeably from the popular notion. "New revelations" about JFK's love life or about Napoleon's hidden wealth are not likely to challenge us to any new type of action or way of being in our world.) Finally, it is intentional, although in the classically bifurcated sense that Christian theology habitually names "the already and the not yet." Here we recognize both the completeness of God's self-disclosures and the historical incompleteness of them. Roughly put, we do not expect to discover anything qualitatively new about the Father of Jesus, but we do expect to augment our own appreciation for God's presence in the world as well as to perceive more and more persons historically doing the same. "If 'now is the day of salvation' (2 Cor 6:2), we must still hope for the day which will bring the future of this 'now' in Christ."[71]

This account is avoidably unsatisfactory. The less important reason for this assessment is that it is not only brief but painfully so. O'Collins spends the better part of half of this book outlining formal considerations that serve to ground and bound the notion of divine revelation, but then only about four pages saying what that revelation is in ways that reflect and illustrate those formal considerations. Because brevity is not a mortal sin, but is instead often a signal of unmet expectations, it is the second and more important reason that will be of greater usefulness to us as we think both about O'Collins and (later on) about divine revelation itself.

I hinted at this reason when I observed earlier that O'Collins paid more attention to the historical indicators of vestigial trinitarianness than to transcendental ones. It is not mere critical obscurantism that notices that transcendentalist (and Rahnerian) thinkers rarely do this. The reason, I think, is that it is of the essence of the transcendentalist method, and thus of the fundamental distinction between the transcendental and the categorical, to look beyond the historically specific and seek the comprehensive and the generic, not out of a prior and hidden disposition in favor of reductionism but instead out of a prior and explicit belief that God really is the "creator of all things visible and invisible." If this is so, then it is the essential function of Christian theology to see how it is so, especially in those anthropological and cultural expressions that are not explicitly Christian, and thus whose relation to God is real but only "vestigially" christological and trinitarian. O'Collins never identifies that universal constituent of human nature which is both the link through which God's revelation is mediated and the criterion that distinguishes between authentic and inauthentic expressions of that revelation.[72] He does not even do this in the chapter where it is most expected, "Christ and Non-Christians."[73] To be sure, his formal considerations in this chapter are crucial to a discussion of revelation both inside and outside the Christian tradition; we have already appreciated them under the names of the liminal, the intentional, the christological, and the trinitarian. Aside from these, though, his most explicit attempt at such identification is essentially a restatement of the distinction between the transcendental and the historical itself:

> [Inasmuch] as *the divine Word is present and active in the ultimate, transcendental horizon of all experience* and inasmuch as *all particular religious experiences remain conditioned by their transcendental horizon*, any specific divine self-communication in human history will in fact enact a saving dialogue with Christ— even if this is never consciously known. The divine Word actively influences the human history of religious experience at the transcendental *and* the categorical levels.[74]

With this we might all agree but still find the need to ask ourselves precisely how it is that the Christian notion of divine self-revelation is historically and concretely, even if obscurely, actuated in persons and cultures not consciously Christian.

What is divine revelation? O'Collins has told us the answer clearly in its explicitly Christian form, thereby hinting at its explicitly Christian content, too, at least as much as one could expect in a book on fundamental theology. But in focusing as he does on that which is categorically Christian, he runs an enormous risk of circularity, observing what Christians receive as revelation and then identifying that as revelation *because* Christians receive it as such. This obscures the usefulness of the distinction between the categorical and the transcendental precisely in that it seems to identify, at least by default, the categorically Christian and the transcendentally real. My own instincts go in the opposite direction. If the Christian view of reality is the closest human approximation to what history mediates to us from God (a claim that, to be sure, makes most sense to those within the Christian tradition), then at the very least there should be vestiges of this view of reality outside that tradition, embedded, in fact, within the very notion of human being itself. In chapters 3 and 4 of this book, I shall try to identify this constituent element of human nature and say why it constitutes the essence of divine revelation, both ontologically and critically, both formally and materially. Before doing so, though, we will find it useful to consider one more theory of revelation and add one more necessary ingredient to our final construction of such a theory.

Personalism:
Ian T. Ramsey and Michael Polanyi

My intention in this section is to discuss a final component within what I have called the continuist theories of divine revelation, namely the personal God as the other and the initiating pole of such revelation. Thus far, I have more or less assumed both God's existence and God's personal nature. Methodologically this assumption is justified by the nature of my task, which is theological and hence primarily critical and explanatory rather than apologetic. Specifically, this means that I have been able to agree with some revelational theologians and to disagree with others, but never the latter from the perspective of the outright dismay that is a permanent feature of (say) atheism. Now I shall address myself somewhat more carefully to the question of God's personal nature, still from the perspective of theology rather than philosophy. Thus, I shall not try to "prove the existence of God," but instead, presuming that existence, indicate what it means to say that God is personal.[75] Once we have made sufficient headway on that topic, I will be able to outline in a systematic fashion what I take to be the core structure and insights of a Christian doctrine of divine revelation.

Two persons are of great interest here: Ian T. Ramsey and Michael Polanyi. Ramsey (1915–1972) was a British cleric, theologian, and philosopher. With only the slightest intention to be facetious, it can be said that the title of his first-ever sermon at Oxford ("Why be religious—isn't it enough to be good?") constituted both methodologically and materially the agenda for his intellectual work during the remainder of his life.[76] As I progress into the final part of this book, it will become evident how significant these two questions are for me as well. Michael Polanyi (1891–1976), also British, was a chemist and social scientist whose ongoing pursuit was the integration of values and intentionality (i.e., decision-making capacity) within understanding. Both he and Ramsey took significant issue with an assumption that was common during the early decades of this century and thus to their own intellectual context, namely that knowledge was objective and value-free. Proceeding instead from the opposite perspective, that knowing involves the knower with the known and thus relates them in a manner that symbolizes their commonality, they will be of great help in our attempt to show what it means to receive God's self-disclosing revelation.

Ian T. Ramsey and the Experience of God

The early twentieth century abounded in philosophical criticisms of traditional Christian claims and doctrines. Most of these intended to go beyond previous post-Enlightenment attacks and demonstrate the incoherence or non-sense of Christian claims rather than their mere incorrectness. Not surprisingly, these criticisms spawned many intense reactions from within the Christian camp. Some of these rejected the entire conceptual agenda of the critics of religion altogether, while others attempted to respond from within the context of those criticisms and turn them on their heads. Ramsey tried the latter. He was especially interested to provide an empirical basis for theological claims and language that he hoped would demonstrate not the necessity but instead the meaningfulness of such language.

> [T]heological assertions must have a logical context which extends to, and is continuous with, those assertions of ordinary language

for which sense experience is directly relevant. From such straight-forward assertions, theological assertions must not be logically segregated: for that would mean that they were pointless and, in contrast to the only language which has an agreed meaning, meaningless.[77]

I do not intend to retrace the entire demonstration of this claim, but instead to pick out that feature of it which illustrates his understanding of God's personal nature, and show how that nature may be recognized on grounds that reflect how we recognize other beings as personal. In particular, I shall consider Ramsey's discussion of the disclosure theory of language with special interest in "cosmic disclosures," and then point to his discussion of discernment and commitment as his account of how we identify certain kinds of experiences as personal as well. If this is intelligible in accounting for our confidence in experiencing other subjects as personal, then it can also guide our thoughts when thinking about experiencing God.

Ramsey was a empiricist, a philosophical orientation which for our purposes can be summarized fairly tersely. Empiricism views language as the only dependable bridge between the knowing mind and the real or empirical world. Language, that is, is our best clue to the nature and shape of the world outside of ourselves in that it is precisely our primary (if not sole) means of cognitive and critical acquaintance with that world. But language itself is also an interior sort of thing, both a construct of our imagination and a reflection of it. Thus, careful attention paid to it will yield insight into both knower and known, insight which itself is shaped by the nuances of interiority and exteriority and is thus relatively less susceptible to criticisms addressed against either pole by itself.

Ramsey's overall intention[78] was to show that there is an empirical basis to religious language, a basis resident within human experience itself which thus satisfies the external or "real" pole of critical knowledge. This stance put him squarely between two worlds, a philosophical one that believed that any form of empiricism committed one to denying the validity of religious and metaphysical outlooks, and a religious one that believed that "empirical religion," like "airplane food," is oxymoronic. Not surprisingly, he begins his defense of this thesis by inspecting experience itself.

Careful and unprejudiced attention to experience yields certain conclusions that, although not observations in the strict sense, reside within experience and are thus discernible within it. For example, one's own *I* is more than merely the sum of those behaviors and sensory impressions collected and collated by oneself. Typically, in fact, it is this "more" that we have in mind when we say something like "I walked downtown this morning" or "I have a cramp in my leg." The behavior of walking downtown, or the pain of a cramp, are resident features within the entire thing we think of as our *I*. But so, too, are all of the other individual behaviors and sensory impressions in which we participate; that is, we are more than the complex set of all of them even when considered together. Reflection upon this leads to the suspicion that it is in fact our *I* that dynamically collects and relates all of these individual behaviors and impressions, resulting in the possibility of our self-identification over time. I am quite certain, for example, that I am the same person I was when I was in Mr. Adams's sixth-grade class at Parkmead Elementary School, even in spite of the fact that molecularly, behaviorally, psychologically, and intellectually very little resides in the adult that also resided in the boy. What provides the continuing possibility of my self-identification over time, then, beyond and thus presupposed by the changing molecular (and other) constituents of my identity, is my *I*.

If this is true, then we may safely presume the same of other persons. We do not typically restrict our beliefs about others to the concrete empirical experiences we have of them, as though "Sally" is nothing more than what my five senses encounter by themselves when in her physical presence. We do not restrict our beliefs about the existence of others to those times and events in which we participate with them in a first-person sense, as though they snapped into and out of existence strictly with respect to our empirical experience of them. Instead, we have a native and well-founded suspicion that they exist even in the interstices. It is in fact this very suspicion about the makeup of the real world that grounds the distinction between subject and object, hence nominative and predicative, in our language. "[The] subject-object distinction [itself] presupposes that there is at least one subject, and all language presupposes a subject using language."[79]

Karl Rahner observed this same suspicion about the correlativity between language and the shape of the external world in the writ-

ings of Thomas Aquinas. In any affirmative predication (for example, in the sentence "John is a man"), a particular "what" is always
reduced to a more universal "something." All identity predications
operate by means of this reduction of particularity to generic being
itself, and what remains left over, which Rahner calls the "excesus,"
is the intellectual dynamic that draws out attention to what is
beyond *and* incomprehensible (precisely because it is beyond). This
dynamic incomprehensibility, says Rahner, is a permanent feature
presupposed by the dynamic activity of human knowing itself and is
rooted in the incomprehensibility of God. Returning to the language encountered above in O'Collins, we might say that the cognitive incomprehensibility historically encountered in even the most
basic of affirmative identity statements is an echo of the transcendental incomprehensibility of God, not in the sense that they are
two distinct and unrelated incomprehensibilities, but precisely that
they are the same approached from different sides. The incomprehensibility of God is that which human knowing presupposes as the
condition of the possibility of its own movement and growth.[80]

Thus, there is a "more" to empirical experiences of other persons,
itself grounded within such experience but not empirically observable to it. It is a dynamic sort of a thing in that it accounts for the
process whereby we surround and identify a progressively growing
number of behaviors and sense impressions as belonging to an *I* or
to a *you*, that is, to a person.

> The unity of personality is to be found in an ongoing integrating
> activity. While it is always possible to describe scientifically the
> genetic, biochemical, endocrinal, electronic, neurological and
> psychological manifestations of personality's embodiment, the
> peculiarly human integrating activity which gives rise to personal
> existence is that "more" which escapes the net of the categories of
> natural science.[81]

If this is true, though, then the empirical reality of the nonobserv-
able and subjective *I* has been justified in two different ways. First,
in the way I discussed a little earlier, namely that the "more" of
objective experience points to something that is beyond but clearly
resident within the sum of all of the behaviors and sensory impressions themselves. But second, the subjective *I* has been justified in
that it may now be seen as the dynamic initiator or disclosing

ground of the external behaviors themselves, beyond them but in a way that actually presupposes them as necessary for the possibility of observing those behaviors in the first place.

> Let us argue by a *reductio ad absurdum*. Suppose nothing more were to be said about human beings. Then each human being would be a set—admittedly very complex—of discriminated observables, scientific objects, discerned behavior patterns, a set of these and no more. This may seem not at all implausible about everybody—except ourselves. As an account by ourselves of ourselves it would clearly be a logical blunder. For any of us to talk of a group of *objects* presupposes a correlative *subject*. Whatever is observed implies an observer who is a presupposition of the resultant discourse and cannot be netted within it.[82]

"Person" is that which resides as the "more" or the "beyond" of empirical observations, not passively but dynamically, accounting for the patterns and continuities we all presuppose as the possibility of personal identification and relationship. The dynamic process that calls us to burrow through the observations themselves and beyond to the subjective *I* or *you* is what Ramsey calls discernment. Correlatively, the evocative or initiating dynamic of the subjective self itself in this process is what he calls disclosure.[83]

The subjective or personal self, then, discloses itself through and by means of experiences that can be observed. If the observer wishes, nothing more need be done here; that is, it might be odd or lethargic but would not be illogical or antiempirical not to seek for "the more beyond the observations." Those who wish to seek, though, will find themselves in contact with that dynamic and subjective self. The way this is disclosed is signaled by our responses; typically we respond to personal selves in personal ways. For example, we disclose the difference between our spouse vacuuming the living room and our robot vacuuming it by exchanging personal tokens with the former but not the latter; I might well ask Sally to stop vacuuming for a while and discuss how her day went, whereas I would never do that with my robot. Even if in all other observable respects these two experiences were relevantly identical, I disclose my awareness of their difference by infusing personal and subjective possibilities into the one but never into the other. My awareness of the personalness of the one experience and the non-personalness of the other is disclosed by my commitment to act personally in the one and not in the other, at least in part because *persons have a "claim" upon us that nonpersons do not.* There is a mutual dynamic that is triggered by personal experiences which, although not empirical in the narrowest sense, is nonetheless quite real. When we are in the presence of this dynamic, we are in the presence of another person. It is in this complex of discernments and commitments, then, that Ramsey finds the greatest hope in saying what an empirical experience of the personal God is like.

When one experiences the world in certain ways, it is appropriate to say that a personal self resides beyond the experiences themselves, giving shape and identity to them while yet remaining beyond. Empirically speaking, the appropriateness of this response is grounded in our response to it (i.e., our commitment): doing certain kinds of things that we know are personal precisely as our response to what we have discerned as a personal experience breaking in upon us from the outside. There are times, though, when there is no identifiable human person who can stand as the axis of our commitments and discernments; certain kinds of objective experiences evoke personal responses from us in spite of our certainty that no identifiable human being did the evoking. What are we to think then? And what are we to think when the commitments elicited in such situations are our most ultimate—when we can imagine no greater or more intense? Ramsey's response brings us to cosmic disclosure situations, and thence to God.

Terrence Tilley reminds us that "talk of God parallels talk of who I am,"[84] and Ramsey himself summarizes the transition from person-talk to God-talk by saying that "'I' will never cease to be a useful guide for us when we are confronted with puzzles about 'God.'"[85] Guided by these methodological hints, we can inquire further into the questions raised in the last paragraph. Let me do so by reflecting on a personal experience that Ramsey would characterize as a cosmic disclosure situation.[86]

One summer when I was in college, I went backpacking in the Sierra Nevada mountains of California. One particular night I lay down on a large outcropping of granite to watch the galaxies and the shooting stars, so obscured by city lights but so brilliant in the high mountain air. My companions were back at our camp, asleep after a long day's hike. As I contemplated the sky and its display, I felt myself grasped by a sense of acceptance and love such as I had previously experienced only from my parents and family. Nothing else surrounded me for long moments of this event, not tiredness, aloneness, or fear. I was loved, or, more accurately, I was being loved. By what? I wondered? By granite rocks, or tired friends, or shooting stars, or galaxies—by the universe itself? In one sense, I supposed, by all of these.[87] But even altogether they could not account for the vitality of the love that held me in the cool quiet, because that love was at least as intense as that which I had previously experienced only from my family. However, none of those things then present to me were as familiar, and most were not even persons. All I could say for certain was that this event was just as "external" as prior experiences of being loved (we all know the difference between loving ourselves and being loved by others) without any known or identifiable "face" being present. (I recall a humorous thought occurring to me even then: "Evangelicals are not supposed to have experiences like this because, among other things, they tend to justify those who absent themselves from church on Sunday mornings and instead try to find God on the golf course." Ever since then, I have had much greater sympathy for those whose resistance to church attendance appears to be similarly grounded.) Several minutes later, without anything really changing, I noticed that the feeling of being-loved was gone; it had not been dismantled but had simply left. Several years later, then, I discovered Ramsey's work and his discussion of cosmic disclosure situations.

No doubt, if one were to construct a model or paradigmatic instance of a cosmic disclosure situation, this story would lack some useful features. But I believe that it is helpful in illustrating some of Ramsey's suggestions about how we are licensed to think of certain kinds of experiences as personal. For example, although it lacks some features of commitment,[88] both evocation and discernment are present—the awareness of being accepted and loved and thus of being in a *relationship* with the subject of those evocations. And the commitment features that are present are precisely those that I shall later explore as essential to the notion of divine revelation, namely the responses of comfortability and congeniality rather than of terror or estrangement.[89] As a "proof for God's existence," this fails.[90] But as a way of showing the reasonableness of Ramsey's notion of empirical experiences of God, it rather succeeds.

At the very least, Ramsey's notion reminds us that wḷ ᵔn we respond to experiences in ways that are undeniably and fundamentally personal, we have responded to something that is itself personal and thus initiates or evokes those responses in us. There is nothing especially necessary in this conclusion, but as I have said before, believers in God do not usually stand in need of this kind of necessity. For them, it is enough to make ever-greater sense of what is already experienced and participated in. Ramsey is useful in precisely this way.

Michael Polanyi and the Knowledge of God

Michael Polanyi might seem a fish out of water in a book on divine revelation, particularly one whose author is an evangelical. In addition to being a chemist, he was a philosopher of science and of language, and a social and political critic (especially) of the Marxist-Leninist socialism raging through European intellectual communities in the middle decades of this century.

My selection of him is not arbitrary, however. It reflects my appreciation of him as an empirical philosopher who, like Ramsey, attempted to bridge the gap between objectivity and subjectivity in a way that resulted in a fully believable theory of knowledge (and hence of living in the real world) while yet respecting the special characteristics of religious faith. Polanyi's work does that, not because he was a theologian but rather because he, again like Ramsey, noticed that both the act of knowing itself and the possibility of being convinced about the rightness of what one knows point to a source of knowing outside oneself as well as of the specific object of knowledge. But this "outside" is not objective in the depersonalized sense that the early logical positivists had insisted. Instead, it was outside in a way that required something analogous to an act of faith (or what Polanyi calls a "fiduciary commitment") as a foundational constituent of each and every act of knowing. Thus, we can bring to him the same question we brought to Ramsey: How are we reasonably able to infer God's personalness from reflection on our usual modes of thinking and knowing? I will allow his answer to this question to arise from his distinction between focal and subsidiary awareness, and then from what that distinction brings to mind, namely the difference between explicit and tacit knowledge, and finally from his insistence that all personal knowing and experiencing relies upon "fiduciary commitments," probably, for our purposes, his most compelling term.

All acts of knowing, says Polanyi, necessarily involve two levels of conscious awareness. He labels these the explicit and the tacit. The difference resides entirely within the knower and not at all within the objectively known. I may illustrate it by being more attentive to what I am presently doing. If I were asked what I am doing now, I would answer that I am writing a book on divine revelation. In fact, at this instant I am thinking about Michael Polanyi, typing on a keyboard, watching words march across a screen in front of me, pausing occasionally to look out the window, feeling the approach of numbness that gradually ovetakes one's middle regions when sitting for too long, letting my eyes range over the shelves of books in front of me, wondering what the temperature has become in the four hours since I was last outside, taking sips of coffee, answering the telephone when it rings, thinking about my family at home, and so on.

Of the ten activities just listed, I am aware of the first two focally and the latter eight only subsidiarially. That is, because it is my intention at present to write about Polanyi, my mind distills all of the experiences presented to it into two camps: those that directly contribute to this intention and those that only instrumentally do so. Shifting my focal awareness to one of these subsidiary experiences, as I had to do in order to write the last sentence of the previous paragraph, deflects the concentration that I was otherwise able to give to the project of thinking about Polanyi and revelation, and thus had an effect on me that was similar to stage fright: thinking about experiences that were real enough but were not centrally applicable to the limited context into which I placed myself this morning when I came to the office, thus interrupting them and causing delays in that intention. "The kind of clumsiness which is due to the fact that focal attention is directed to the subsidiary elements of an action is commonly known as self-consciousness. A serious and sometimes incurable form of it is 'stage-fright,' which . . . destroys one's sense of the context which alone can smoothly evoke the proper sequence of words, notes, or gestures." The reason for this is straightforward: "our attention can hold only one focus at a time and . . . hence it would be self-contradictory to be both subsidiarily and focally aware of the same particulars at the same time."[91]

Focal awareness, though, depends upon subsidiary awareness even though the two are mutually exclusive. This can be shown to be true both by commonsense reflection on our everyday experiences such as that discussed above, and also by logical reflection on the fact that a particular "this" always presupposes a larger number, and hence category, of "these." It is our intentions, then, upon which we depend implicitly and tacitly, which perform the discriminatory work necessary for us to be productive. To put this another way, as centers of experiencing we are unable to differentiate *in advance* those features of the external world that we will, and will not, allow to pass through our five senses and other experiential receptors.[92] But clearly we need such differentiation to occur since we could never be critically and appropriately attentive to each and every feature of experience if it did not. What we call upon for this critical funneling, then, is our intentions; once they have operated, then our experiential world is safely and pragmatically divided into focal and subsidiary pigeonholes.

If this is true of our awarenesses or experiences, then it is also true of our knowledge of such awarenesses and experiences. Knowledge, too, that is, will differentiate itself into two echoes of focal and subsidiary, which Polanyi calls explicit and tacit knowledge. Objects of which we are directly and focally aware are objects we explicitly know. But then these explicitly known objects depend for their knowability upon things that are only tacitly known, and thus upon things that may never become explicitly known because they exist in a region so fundamental to our ways of being in and experiencing the world that we rarely, if ever, get adequate access to them.

A couple of examples will suffice to illustrate this structure. First, Polanyi turns to the widely discussed mathematical theorem of Kurt Gödel, who showed in 1931 that it was impossible for any deductive system (such as mathematics) to be rationally warranted by means of hypotheses or axioms that are internal to it. That is, neither the pragmatic usefulness nor the theoretical consistency of mathematics can be defended on strictly mathematical grounds. Instead, such a defense arises from grounds that are tacit (and hence external) to mathematics per se and are paradoxically both mathematically useless and mathematically necessary.

The same is true of our ordinary use of language. Language depends for its meaningfulness on its bearing or relation to concrete experience. In this can be seen the justification of the common realization that some languages are "dead" while others, notably our own, are "alive." But language itself is neither dead nor alive; it is instead a formal and fairly stable system of grammatical rules that govern the order in which we may string together logical units called words. The logical units (nouns, verbs, pronouns, etc.) are themselves not the language, as becomes obvious whenever we try to converse with someone who is grammatically either sloppy or innocent. The grammatical rules themselves are not the language, either, of course, for they only tell us how and how not to string words together but do not tell us about what we really use language to find out about: the meaning of the world. Furthermore, these rules cannot tell us in advance of the ways words can be variously strung together to form meaningful sentences never before envisioned. *Language* is thus a complex of units and rules, but in addition and most fundamentally, also of the native and generally uninspected (i.e., tacit) belief that it will tell us about the world that we want to know more about. If we wished to be completely Cartesian about all of this and attempt to justify this latter belief, we would discover the truth of Gödel's theorem: we could never succeed with respect to the general belief upon which the possibility of language itself rests, but instead only the specific beliefs which ground "this" or "that" specific linguistic reference.

> Thus to speak a language is to commit ourselves to the double indeterminacy due to our reliance both on its formalism and on our own continued reconsideration of this formalism in its bearing on experience. For just as, owing to the ultimately tacit character of all our knowledge, we remain ever unable to say all that we know, so also, in view of the tacit character of meaning, we can never quite know what is implied in what we say.[93]

This double indeterminacy results from our inability to step sufficiently far away from our language to be able to distinguish with utter *and* prior finality whether new uses of language are going to be creatively and organically meaningful on the one hand, or just plain gibberish on the other. Polanyi suggests three criteria for coming to some degree of certainty here: "the *text* [itself], the *conception* suggested by it, and the *experience* on which this may bear."[94] Of these, the third, which he also calls "indwelling," is most directly applicable to our upcoming theory of divine revelation.

All knowledge is a search for truth, says Polanyi. Truth, however, is not what many have alleged it to be, namely either an objective and static quality of the external world on the one hand or a purely subjectivist and solipsistic feature of private interiority on the other. The reason each of these extremes must be denied is the validity of the other. We may be certain that the objectivist extreme is invalid[95] because of how we experience knowledge as self-involving; none of us ever says, "I know that *x* is true, but it doesn't matter that it is," or "I know that *x* is true, but it's OK if I act as though it is not." When we "know" something, that is, *we commit ourselves to it* in a way that supersedes and thus invalidates the allegation that its truthfulness is merely a formal and thus non-person-involving feature of it.

Similarly, we can see how the subjectivistic alternative is defective because of how we treat knowledge: we do not act toward it as though it were privately true merely for us, but instead we believe it to be universally applicable, exerting some kind of call not only upon ourselves but also upon larger and larger communities of persons.[96] This is the ultimate linguistic presupposition: that words make sense. Thus, it is the presupposition of every use of language as well, especially, for example, its use in teaching and learning. Of course, we might later on turn out to be wrong about a particular thing that we knew and thus about the universality of its particular call upon us and others, but that does not efface our responsibility to treat that datum of knowledge as objectively true prior to discovering whatever it was that prompted our change of mind. And not only does it not dislodge the reality of the general presupposition itself, but in fact it confirms it.

Personal knowledge, then, is a seeking after truth that is prompted and motivated by the two responsibilities we have just seen: the responsibility to ourselves to conform our lives and experience with whatever we have discovered to be true, and the correlative responsibility to share truth with others because of the "call" such truth has upon us all as members of the human community. The former responsibility is easily seen as personal, but the latter may not be because it might look nearly indistinguishable from other universal calls upon us, such as the "call" of gravity. This possible discrepancy may be overcome, however, if we accept

> the framework of commitment, in which the personal and the universal mutually require each other. Here the personal comes into existence by asserting universal intent, and the universal is constituted by being accepted as the impersonal term of this personal commitment. . . . [Thus,] the freedom of the subjective person to do as he pleases is overruled by the freedom of the responsible person to act as he must.[97]

Commitment, that is, relates the personal with the impersonal in acts of knowing made by personal agents. Such commitments reflect the ultimately ungroundable belief that the impersonal world may be personally known, and that it may be known truly and nonsubjectivistically.[98] Because this is a belief it may be wrong, but because it is unavoidable we cannot act as though it were; that is, we cannot be utter skeptics, postponing any gain of knowledge until we have determined with logical finality how the personal and the impersonal connect.[99]

Knowing, then presupposes two things that are relevant to this study: (1) that the dynamic of knowing includes the notion of responsibility (seen here as the obverse of "the call to universality"), and (2) that it always intends to approach truth as its goal, truth that is constantly hidden but also constantly presupposed and hence present. The actual or historical identification of truth, whose importance cannot be underestimated, is not at issue here since the actual identification of truth presupposes the prior intention to discover it. The universality of this intention, then, discloses the universality of the belief that it may be discovered, and it is *this* belief that is at issue here.

What has all of this to do with God and divine revelation? Two things, I think. First, if knowing is an action taken as a response to a universally felt responsibility, then it is not meaningless to ask the question: Responsibility to what or to whom? By its very nature, a responsibility does not arise ex nihilo but instead as antipode to a prior action or expectation that is (usually) located outside the responding person. And if the responsibility we are considering in this case is universal in both geographical and chronological extent, then that to which it is antipode is extrauniversal or transcendent for the same reason.

Second, if knowing is a distinctively personal affair,[100] then the transcendent antipode is personal as well, because the relationship of responsibility exists solely between and among personal agents; that is, it is "subjective" rather than "objective." We simply do not share responsibilities with the impersonal world; even the areas where it is most tempting to think that we do are in fact the areas where that impersonal world is the arena or environment in which other personal beings do or will exist.[101] But if we do observe a universal responsibility to know the truth and to express it, then the "transcendent antipode" that elicits such responsibility must be personal.

> So far as we know, the tiny fragments of the universe embodied in man are the only centres of thought and responsibility in the visible world. If that be so, the appearance of the human mind has been so far the ultimate stage in the awakening of the world; and all that has gone before, the strivings of a myriad centres that have taken the risks of living and believing, seem to have all been pursuing, along rival lines, the aim now achieved by us up to this point. They are all akin to us. For all these centres—those which led up to our own existence and the far more numerous others which produced different lines of which many are extinct—may be seen engaged in the same endeavour towards ultimate liberation. We may envisage then a cosmic field which called forth all these centres by offering them a short-lived, limited, hazardous opportunity for making some progress of their own towards an unthinkable consummation. And that is also, I believe, how a Christian is placed when worshipping God.[102]

Polanyi has deposited us at just the point where we are ready to begin an explicit construction of a theory of divine revelation. He and Ramsey have shown us how both experience and knowledge of the objective world may be integrated into one's thinking about God's self-disclosure. Although not modally necessary in the ways some philosophers would like us to believe it should be, it is surely reasonable to believe that experiencing and knowing the external world echoes the dynamic whereby God initiates the process of self-disclosure and thus relates with personal beings in that world. This is enormously useful, because it is another way of saying that God's self-disclosure is presupposed by each and every act whereby we express who we are and who we will become as human beings.

Conclusion

We have seen five ways in which divine revelation may be construed. All are modern in that they differ from traditional theories of revelation both in perspective and in methodological orientation. By now it is no surprise that the different perspective shared by Dulles, Macquarrie, O'Collins, Ramsey, and Polanyi is the one I have called, perhaps clumsily, the continuist perspective. That is, each author considered in this chapter has indicated his belief that God's self-disclosure employs our experiencing and thinking faculties, rather than ignoring, annihilating, or cutting across them. Thus, without claiming that this was explicitly intentional on the part of any one of them, it can also be seen that each also posited a greater correspondence between the Christian notions of creation and redemption than those we considered in the first chapter were able to do.

The theories just considered also differ in method from those in Chapter 1. The traditional approach to the notion of divine revelation, represented tersely but I think adequately by Abraham, Henry, Barth, and Packer, commonly assumes that the gap between human beings and God is so great that it can only be bridged by a special self-disclosing act of God. I criticized these theories not primarily for their content, with which my evangelical background is largely in sympathy, but instead for the hidden and yet utterly crucial assumption each one makes. In saying that divine revelation cuts across normal human experiencing and thinking faculties, and does so in saving ways, these theories leave unexamined the decision each human being must make about how to distinguish unusual events that do disclose God from those that do not. As we saw in Abraham, we cannot even say that miracles escape the necessity of this decision since a miracle is nothing but a statistically anomal-

ous physical event until and unless it is linked with some divine
intention and thereby rendered the earthly conduit for that intention. Since by definition this linkage is not a part of the anomalous
event itself, but is instead settled upon independent of the event in
question in an act usually called faith, it cannot be shown that any
self-disclosing act of God occurs outside of the need, and thus the
parameters, of human decisional and experiential faculties. Hence
"the shift to the subject" of each of the authors in this chapter.[103]

What this "turn to the subject" involves with respect to my
purposes in this book is the observation, expressed in the conclusion to the first chapter, that traditional theories of revelation have
typically focused on the *content* of given revelational events and
have thus got themselves into the difficulties I enumerated there.
Acting upon this observation, I then attempted to show how it is
not the *content* of given events, but instead the very possibility of
seeing certain events as revelational and then the concrete intention
to do so, which is revelation. To put the matter simply but accurately, if someone does not wish to see the world as the target of
God's self-disclosing and saving acts, then for that person the world
is not God's target. This is not, of course, to say that the world is
not God's target but only that it is part of the experiential and
decisional configuration of human beings to see the world in certain
ways and not in others. One's decision to see it "thus" and not "so"
is thus the crucial arena of interest to us. And this decision, in turn,
is grounded in the capacity to "see" it as anything at all.

We have now completed the survey of revelational theories. Chapter 1 considered various ways to construe the content of events (and
words) as revelational. Chapter 2 considered various ways to
construe experiential and decisional matrices as revelational. I wish
to go one step further in my analysis of divine revelation. What is
left to do now is to move through content, and through experiential
and decisional configurations, back to the human being as abstractly or generically considered. I shall attempt to show how
God's self-revelation is what makes human beings different from
every other created being of which we are aware.[104] This is not to
say that it is the content of such revelation, much less the way
humans respond to that content in either faith or unfaith, that

makes the difference in human beings; saying this would only point out my theory as another tired attempt to do what the tradition has unsuccessfully tried to do for millennia. Instead, it is to say that God's self-revelation is what makes certain created beings able to be *human* beings. Thus, it is the capacity to be human, and only thence the actuality of what we do with our humanness, that is at the core of the theory to which I now turn.

3

Human Beings as Receivers of Divine Revelation

I have spent most of my time considering what others have expressed as the formal boundaries of a theory of divine revelation. It is now time to attempt the same thing myself. Gaining from what we have learned thus far, both positive and negative, how should one approach the notion of God's self-disclosure?

Although we will encounter this thought later and more extensively, the place to begin a response is to say that I think that we are true to the best instincts of the Christian tradition if we insist that "divine revelation" refers primarily not to content but instead to constitution. That is, God's self-revealing word ought not be seen as formally identical to knowledge acquired about the cosmos from whatever other sources convey it to us, what we might call cultural knowledge. This is because such knowledge is always filtered through the cultural grids that both grasp us and condition how we know what we know. Nor is divine revelation analogous to those cultural grids themselves, since they, too, change from epoch to epoch and from culture to culture and yet remain exhaustive and exclusive throughout, regardless of their stage of evolution.[1]

Instead, I wish to begin considering divine revelation from the perspective of human beings as the image of God. I do not wish to treat this notion taxonomically, since that would take me too far afield. Rather, I will use the notion of *imago dei* as my methodological beginning point, noticing that it licenses us to begin thinking about the self-revealing God from the vantage point of the receiver of that revelation, namely us as human beings. I believe that divine revelation *is* what constitutes us as human beings and thus formally distinguishes us from all other known beings. As I have said already, this claim should not be misunderstood as a material one; to return to the distinction between transcendental and historical that we saw in O'Collins, it should not be treated as an historical claim. Interpreting it this way would imply that there was a rather loose connection, if any at all, between being human on the one hand and being able to receive God's revelation on the other. But if this were the case, then one could be human and *not* be in possession of God's revelation, a state of affairs that directly clashes with the biblical portrait of all of humanity included within the image of God and therefore responsible to that God in virtue of their possession of it.

Having said only this much, it should be fairly clear where I come down on the traditional and thorny question of how God's revelation resides in human beings, to put the matter spatially. Are there three categories of human relationships with God (those who respond in faith to God, those who respond in unfaith, and those who have never heard of God), or just two (those who respond in faith and those who respond in unfaith)? I do not believe that there is any legitimate justification for the first alternative here, in view of both the *imago dei* doctrine and its negative implication, namely that the third group of "nonhearers" is thereby divested of its transcendental relationship to God and of its consequent transcendental responsibilities to God as well as to other human beings.[2] And, to return to the thought of the last paragraph, it would also imply that it would be possible for a being to be human but not related to God, which in itself is nothing other than a suggestion that faith and unfaith in God are formally gratuitous,[3] more or less the spiritual equivalent of gastronomic and aesthetic tastes, all of which I think is wrongheaded. Most of the next two chapters will try to show how this is.

I ended my comments in the introduction to this book by saying that it would divide itself into three parts: theories I do not much care for, theories I care a great deal more for, and my own theory. Let me now suggest the plan of this third and final part. I will begin with the stipulation (and it can only be that, although I think that it

is an exceptionally well-grounded one) that human beings are constitutively moral. To be moral is to be able to be good, and this
means to be able to know, to love, and to hope. Because each of
these is dynamic, each necessarily implies a receiver as well. Thus,
human beings are also constitutively communitarian, an observation that is correlative to the one that says they are constitutively
moral.

I shall then discuss how God is the ultimate ground of the
possibility of this characterization of human beings. First I will
consider God's goodness per se and how God's knowledge is the
ground of our own, then God's love as the ultimate point of
christology, and finally the Holy Spirit as the ground of goodness,
in particular the goodness of the experiences of knowledge, love,
and hope. My intention is to reflect on how the trinitarian God is
the ground of the human (or moral) order. If my account is successful, then divine self-revelation is, formally considered, the condition
of the possibility of being moral and thus of being human.

Systematic reflections upon the relationship between God and
human beings are bound up within two sets of critical polarities
which are closely related but not, I think, identical. Thus, they must
proceed delicately lest sensitivities and commitments be needlessly
offended. The first set is common to all disciplines (especially
within the humanities): that between the descriptive and the normative, or between what is and what ought to be. No serious thinking
about our topic can ignore this polarity. Of its very nature, divine
revelation is intentional in the literal sense of the word; it intends an
accomplishment within human existence and thinking that reflects,
or better establishes, the relationship between God and humans. If
that is the case, then I must continually ask myself where this
intention has, and has not yet, been realized. More traditional
accounts of divine revelation had an easier time with this question,
for they were able simply to postulate a given thing *as* instantiated
revelation (for example, the Bible, or the death-resurrection-ascension of Jesus, or miracles, etc.) and proceed from there to assess the
religious adequacy of all other things against that one, thereby
generating both a critical theological and a critical historical dynamic which served to measure how near or far reality was from
God's intentions. The simplicity of this approach is attractive, but
unfortunately, as we have seen throughout this study, it suffers

from begging too many important questions. Another approach is needed.

The second polarity bounding discussions such as ours is that between faithfulness and unfaithfulness. Here we are in even more of a circular dilemma, because what counts as "faithfulness" is precisely dependent on what one has antecedently accepted as divinely revealed. (This is similar to what we saw in Dulles, namely that theories of revelation often presuppose what they intend to clarify.) My approach here will attempt to minimize this dilemma without, of course, being able to dispense with it altogether.[4] I shall presume only that God intended the material world to eventuate in the possibility of morality—that is, knowledge, love, and hope—as human beings now express that possibility.[5] Faithfulness is thus not so much the actuality of such morality, which *ex hypothesi* is present within all human beings as the condition of their being human in the first place, but is instead the willing grasping and acceptance that one's ability to be human is grounded in the goodness of the self-expressing God. And unfaithfulness is the unwillingness to recognize this grounding. So far as I can see, these are the ultimate or generic stances toward God and reality between which all persons must decide. Part of the reason for writing this book is my hope that more persons will opt for the alternative whose ground and goal is God.

Centuries ago, St. Augustine faced the issue of how to introduce the notion of the Trinity to an audience that had accepted it experientially in faith but was apparently unsure of much of what it had accepted. In many ways his method blazed the trail down which we shall now proceed ourselves. In framing his discussion, he insisted upon what most theologians today would accept as a thoroughly modern approach: "We are not yet concerned with things in heaven, not yet with God, Father, Son, and Holy Spirit; but with this image, inferior but still an image, which is man—so much more familiar and less difficult for the infirmity of our mind to study."[6] In this one simple sentence, he says *where* the discussion should begin (with human beings and not with God), *why* it should begin there (because we will understand things better if we move from the known to the unknown rather than the reverse), and *how* it forecasts meaningful progress toward the goal of understanding God (because human beings are images of the Trinitarian God). Many

subsequent theologians would have done well, I think, to have
heeded this plan.

With our eye ultimately on God, then, and not simply on anthropology or psychology, we begin the construction of a theory of
divine revelation by musing on those who receive it. I have just
indicated that I believe that the necessary starting point for this
discussion is that which distinguishes human beings from all other
known material beings, that we have the capacity for moralness. I
shall more regularly say that we are moral, not intending the
popular meaning of this phrase which is that we are emotionally or
behaviorally *good*, but instead the more fundamental meaning
which is that we are able to be good or evil. Only human beings can
be good or evil. A person who does evil is not doing something
good, rather obviously, but he or she is *not* doing something
amoral; neither common sense nor careful inspection of language
can defend the popular reduction of *moral* to *moral goodness*.[7]
There is a difference between being good and being moral: the
former differentiates us from evil persons, while the latter differentiates us from animals. Thus, in the sense in which I am here
interested in the word, both Adolf Hitler and Desmond Tutu are
equally *moral* beings.

To be human, then, is to be moral. It is more than that, to be
sure, but distinctively that. What does it mean to be moral? It
means to be able to know, to be able to love, and to be able to hope;
and these, as I said before, all constitute a community in history.

Moralness and the Capacity for Knowing

There are, I think, two broad arenas in which goodness may be seen
as fundamental to the notion of human being. They are the critical
or intellectual on the one hand, and the behavioral on the other.
Because my next section will consider the latter, focusing especially
on love, here I shall spend more time on goodness as the condition
of the possibility of human critical capacities.[8]

It is incontrovertible that human beings are able to know. In fact,
the only way one can begin to make sense out of the great welter of
hypotheses and theories about what it means to be able to do so is
to recognize that all of them presuppose this very capacity and

intend to make sense out of it. Here I am not concerned with defending any of these theories against all of the rest. Instead, I want to reflect somewhat on the focus of this presupposition itself: what does it mean to be able to know?

To know something is to believe strongly that there is a basic agreement between it and the region of the real or external world to which it draws attention. (I am not collapsing the difference between knowing and believing here, although of course there is an important difference between them. For my present purposes, though, the difference can be stated as a matter of the degree of confidence about one's state of mind with respect to the external world rather than two different kinds or types of states of mind.) When I say, for example, that I know that my filing cabinet contains folders of letters, manuscripts, and courses, I disclose my commitment that there is such an agreement between a bit of knowledge in my mind and the shape of the external world. All sorts of deliberations can serve to clarify both how I came to acquire that bit of knowledge and later on how I might confirm it, but these are ancillary to what it is that my mind does in holding to the datum of knowledge itself.

Clearly, however, it could well be the case that my filing cabinet does not hold all of the files that I know that it does.[9] I surely know that there was a time in the past when it did not, and I know as well that there will be a time in the future when it will not. There is nothing essential or necessary, therefore, about the knowledge I have about the contents of my filing cabinet at the present. Knowledge, that is, is not pressed in upon us exclusively from the outside, and especially not from the objects of knowledge *in* that outside, as we learned from Polanyi. What, then, accounts for the security or comfortability of my state of mind in its knowledge of those contents?

Fundamentally, I think, what accounts for the security that underlies the very notion or possibility of knowledge is the agreement that we perceive between it on the one hand and the pragmatic shape of our lives in the real world on the other. Our lives operate more smoothly and comfortably the greater the degree of agreement or correspondence we sense between what we know and how things are. Of course, there is no "how things are" that is independent of our "what we know," since such an alleged thing would either be radically unknown to us or else be a part of what we know. So we can only *presume* this agreement or correspondence, as Polanyi noted, and test it out by observations and experiments whose ultimate assessments move along the spectrum we might informally call the pragmatic spectrum of comfortability and security. And to return to the difference between knowing and believing, the more comfortability and security that we actually experience, the greater the degree of correspondence that is disclosed and that we can presume between our state of mind and the external world. Thus, the closer that datum of information is to being certain knowledge rather than more doubtable belief.

At this point, it looks as though I am seating my theory of knowledge ultimately on comfortability and security, which looks a great deal like what Polanyi called the subjectivist or solipsistic extreme. But I am not, because it is a constituent part of my observation of the world, and thus in principle a part of my knowledge of it, that all persons seek out this same goal of comfortability in the fit between their inner knowledge on the one hand and the real world on the other. Wherever we go, that is, human beings disclose their trust in this fit by displaying what we might call a relaxation of intentionality when they perceive it and a prolongation of intentionality when they do not. This is only another way of saying that pesons typically stop trying to acquire further knowledge about a given slice of reality when their comfort level with respect to it reaches a certain point, which we might dub Point S (for "satisfaction"). Once Point S has been attained, then, presuming no future perception of difficulty or uncomfortableness with it, the pursuit of knowledge about *that* particular slice of the external world relaxes or ceases altogether, and the person's attention is shifted to the intentional quest for other bits of knowledge.

Although I realize that this reduces an enormous array of complex theorizing down to simplicity, we can also say now what truth is. Truth is the attainment of Point S with respect to the relationship between any given or new bit of information on the one hand and what we have antecedently experienced as the unity among all the previous bits of information we have acquired on the other.[10] That is, we disclose that a given datum of information is the truth when we perceive such a degree of fit between the slice of reality to which it points, the rest of what we know, and the real world as we experience it, that no relevantly significant facets of that slice of reality remain unresolved and hence intellectually uncomfortable. In addition to many other things that need to be said of it, truth is a psychological phenomenon. Psychologically, its presence is disclosed by the resting or the relaxation of intentionality that follows upon the attainment of some bits of information about the world. Its absence is disclosed by the continuation of our intentional intellectual activity even in the face of a similar attainment of bits of information. The difference between these two attainments is that the former does, and the latter does not, put us into contact with what we perceive to be the truth, a comfortable even if tangled co-integration of all of our bits of information with one another and the consequent and hence presupposed "fit" between them and the external world.

Now the question that relates knowing and goodness may be tackled more directly. Why does the intentional pursuit of knowledge relax, or shift focus, when Point S has been reached? And why is this relaxation or shifting of intentionality a *universally* perceived phenomenon? I think that the ultimate answer here can only be that our minds instinctively and reflexively relax when they achieve Point S.[11] And why do they do that? Because that is the realization of their intention; there is no further perceived or known unresolvedness; the lack of unresolvedness is identical with and thus neutralizes the dynamic of intellectual intentionality itself; *and this is a good state of affairs.*

If this is so, then it is *good* in two very different senses of the word. More obviously, it is good in that a given unresolvedness has been overcome. Regardless of where critical intentionality might next shift its gaze, or how short the interval before it perceives some additional difficulty with this given datum of knowledge and thus fall short of a new Point S, for the time being (at least) the mind is able to place this datum into the category of subsidiary awareness and devote its focal attention to some other one.

Second, it is good in that goodness is shown to be the ultimate criterion grounding the critical intellectual dynamic that we call knowing. The attainment of Point S is, I think, nothing other than one's residence, however temporarily, within a good state of affairs. Here there is intellectual equilibrium between what one has paid focal attention to and how the real world is structured. Achieving

Point S or this state of equilibrium is not incidental; it is precisely the fundamental presupposition of all intellectual activity. And this presupposition is realized whenever goodness is instantiated. But if this is so, then the generic goal of all intellectual activity is the achievement of the goodness disclosed by any Point S attainment.[12] Goodness is thus the ultimate critical context within which knowledge operates, and truth is the judgment that our critical operations have rendered the best co-integrated conclusions that all of the relevant bits of information we presently possess are capable of yielding.

By "ultimate" here I do not mean important or significant. It is not the case that human beings are moral only when they are thinking about morally important objects. This is another flaw in the prevailing usage of the word. It arises from the confusion between what *moral* itself refers to. Popularly, the word seems to refer to, and metaphorically to reside within, the object of the sentence in which it is found. Thus, for example, when discussing these matters most of my students are quite happy to admit that the sentence "Mother Teresa is good" is somehow a moral sentence but are aghast when I suggest that the sentence "Coffee is good" is as well. But the word does not attach to objects in the real world, as though it were an objective property a given object either did or did not possess. It is instead a reflection of judgments made, hence of *critical* activity, and hence of the subject's critically active mind. Thus, a moral sentence is any which reports on that subject's critical activity. In the simplest of terms, a moral sentence is any that employs the word *good* or any synonym thereof, either explicitly within the sentence or else implicitly by reporting on a critical judgment that itself was grounded within goodness.[13]

This means, quite straightforwardly although to the puzzlement of some, that any sentence that reflects either directly or indirectly a subject's critical judgment is a moral sentence. So, the two candidate sentences in the last paragraph, while admittedly occupying different positions along the spectrum between importance and unimportance, are in a very real sense *equivalently* moral. They both reflect the same critical assessment and differ only to the degree that the objects of the assessment vary with respect to kind and degree of importance. The significance of this observation is that there are essentially no sentences that do not reflect critical judgments to one degree or another. And since critical judgments are themselves ultimately grounded within goodness as the condition of their possibility, we can see that the very structures of knowing and of language are laden with moral disposition.

Knowing, thus, both as an inward critical intentional activity and as reflected in the external event of language, is impossible to conceive of apart from moral judgments and (hence) categories. As our fundamental way of conceiving of the world,[14] the knowing mind brings to each new judgment about reality the presupposition and the expectation that goodness is present as the ultimate condition necessary for the possibility of knowledge. To participate within the structures of knowing and of language, then (and a being who cannot is not a *human* being),[15] is to be situated within a cosmic structure imbued with the transcendental possibility of goodness as well the historical actuality of it.

Moralness and the Capacity for Loving

Perhaps the grounding of knowing in goodness, and thus also in the distinctive and essential moralness of human beings, initially seemed obscure. If so, then the grounding of love in goodness might seem hackneyed. Regardless of whether or not we are religious, morally careful, happily married and/or settled in families or other relational communities, and so on, most of us are accustomed at the very least to thinking of love as the quintessential moral possibility of our lives. Fair enough. But we should at least examine the relationship between being moral and loving so that we do not carelessly presume upon it and thereby displace the opportunity to understand it better. Understanding it better will not necessarily make one an improved lover, because life does not arrive packaged in such tidy algorithms. But the opposite is quite likely: failing to understand love more richly will almost certainly desiccate our chances for being *in* it to our satisfaction or anyone else's.

Let me begin by offering a definition of love that I believe will fulfill the various needs we have of it (i.e., the psychological need for such a definition to align with our concrete experiences of being in love, the conceptual need for such a definition to be intelligible in and of itself, and the theological need for such a definition to be rooted in God). *Love is the gratuitous exchange of self-surpassing behaviors and intentions concerning a beloved's concrete existence.* There are several elements here that deserve attention as we try to see the relation between moralness and love.

First and perhaps most importantly, love is an *exchange* between beings of unspecifiable possibilities. I do not deny that love often appears much more one-sided than this implies. I would suggest, however, that those instances are not the paradigms of how we learn of love, but rather that reciprocal loving relationships are. The less actual exchange there is, in fact, the more we are inclined to modify our notion by words such as *unrequited, unfulfilled, frustrated* and the like. And then, when we do view one-sided relations as appropriate instances of love, such as that between parents and children, or between nurses and comatose patients, we typically view them as appropriate by stripping away from reciprocal relationships those elements that do not apply to these particular ones.[16]

To illustrate the point somewhat differently, the Catholic and Anglican identification of marriage as a sacrament is precisely a recognition of the greater appropriateness of this quintessential exchange relationship than of one-sided ones as images that help us to understand how God loves the world. I would certainly not want to claim that God's love of the world displays the balanced mutuality that sacramental marriages do. However, the *eros* (or self-enhancing) structure of reciprocal loving relationships is the appropriate starting point for the discussion of divine love. The one-sided structure of *agape* (or self-emptying) love is always a reflexive aspect, albeit an important one, within the larger context of *eros*. The characteristic Christian preference for *agape* in such discussions reflects an unrealistic and truncated understanding of the *self*-love of God in becoming human, as though in becoming human God eternally donates but never acquires.

There are other elements to reflect upon here as well. That love is a *gratuitous* exchange means simply that love and coercion are incompatible. It is not gratuitous in the strictest sense of the word, according to which nothing stands as the ground or cause within which a given action is taken. Instead, it is the voluntary and benevolent contribution of one's best to another who has indicated his or her willingness to receive it. Thus, it is an exchange that can be triggered only by the perception of this prior willingness. Such willingness may or may not be an expression of love on the part of the other; if this dynamic exchange were restricted to those in love, or, to say the same thing the other way around, if only love could count as this exchange, then persons would never be able to grow into it. Whether the recipient's willingness itself is love can only be determined by the other, *but it or something like it must be present*. Otherwise, not only have we stripped away the exchange or reciprocal nature of love, we have in addition (and far worse) violated what we all know is the fundamental psychological requirement of love, namely that we cannot love those who are unlovable. Any notion of love that insists that we can, I think, is absurd. I will say more about why in a moment.

Love is thus an exchange that intends, however softly, the self-transcendence of the beloved. By *self-transcendence* I mean nothing other than that the beloved is empowered to grow beyond his or her previous boundaries and limitations into a richer appropriation and appreciation of life, as a direct or indirect result of our contribution. *Life* is what is referred to in the phrase "behaviors and intentions concerning a beloved's concrete existence." Here I mean to reflect all aspects of reality that human nature touches upon, whether internal or external, psychological, intellectual, spiritual, or physiological. Wherever such an exchange is deliberately present, love is there.

It is not the case that love always accomplishes its transcending intention, of course; here, too, there are no algorithmic guarantees. This is noticed most obviously within persons who thought they were in love but were not, or else who were but then "fell out of" it. But it is just as true of persons who are in love. The most intimate of marriages and friendships endure isolated periods in which one or both of the lovers, on either the giving or the receiving end, experience no transcending intentions or results at all. We should not be surprised at this. It is the case, however, that the more such events stretch out next to each other, the greater the likelihood that the dynamic and reciprocal structure of love itself will dehydrate. If this occurs, we will begin to wonder not whether the other *can* enhance our existence, but much more fundamentally whether it is still his or her actual *intention* to do so. And because love must be triggered by the perception of the willingness for exchange, the posing of this question is a clear signal that the dynamic of love is becoming fragile.

As I said earlier, the actual contribution of love is unspecifiable in advance. This does not mean, though, that it is abstract. Without belaboring the obvious, we do not love concepts or possibilities but persons. Only persons can disclose their willingness to receive our expressions of benevolent self-transcendence, and only persons can reciprocate and respond in kind. Being in love is thus a fundamentally personal relation, and its presence discloses the presence of (at least) two personal beings. This is the significance, I think, of Ian T. Ramsey's thoughts above. If, entirely apart from the polemical intention to prove or to disprove the existence of God, one feels oneself grasped in love "by the cosmos" (i.e., not by an ostensively specifiable person), it is not unreasonable to say that the grasper is God. Of course, it might not be, too; such a feeling of being-grasped-in-love might simply be the ripple of an experience of love recently or even long ago vacated. (Even if this latter state of affairs is the case, though, more remains to be said about the grounding of *it* in God's love; I shall return to this in the next chapter.) But the point remains: where love is experienced, persons are present. The dynamic exchange of one's best values and intentions, combined with one's receptivity for another's, can only exist between and among persons.

Eberhard Jüngel discusses the Johannine interpretation of divine love in *God as the Mystery of the World*.[17] There he says that "love is not identical with absolute selflessness. Love is oriented toward a specific Thou. It desires *this* Thou and not [just] anyone."[18] I would take issue with Jüngel in this discussion only to the degree that he could be clearer about the self-transcending nature of both the erotic and agapic movements of love. When I go beyond myself in love, I do it *so that* my beloved's life will be enriched. And conversely, when I surrender myself to my beloved, I do it *so that* I can move beyond the limitations which the beloved's existence has shown as existing within myself, and which the beloved's existence invites and empowers me to transcend. Jüngel's discussion appears to be more interested in the bare dynamic structure of love than in the moral intentionality of this dynamic:

> Love is mutual surrender. . . . The exchange of mutual surrender
> means then, with regard to the element of having in love, that the
> loving I wants to have itself only in the form of being had by
> someone else. And it means at the same time that it wants to have
> the beloved Thou only as an I which also wants to be had. It can
> be put this way: in love one I and another I encounter each other
> in such a way that they become for each other beloved Thou's.[19]

This is good and helpful, but in a fashion that reminds us of Gerald
O'Collins, it lacks the *content* of what in fact transforms each "I"
into a "beloved Thou."

What accomplishes this transforming work, I think, is the essential possibility of being good, and hence the presence of transcendental Goodness within all human beings. And to return to a
thought suspended earlier, this is precisely what makes it impossible to love unlovable persons. This is not mere empty circularity.
Instead, to be unlovable is precisely to deny the presence of the
good in persons, nearly always within oneself and then usually
within the other as well. (Thus, I am using *unlovable* as shorthand
for the more complex process of this conscious denial.) But this in
turn negates the possibility of any self-transcending growth. Why?
Because such growth depends for its very possibility upon that
good. It does so in the following way.

Any act of subjective self-transcendence is a dynamic movement
from one state of existence to another.[20] Such movements are both
intentional and critical. On the one hand, they are intentional in that
they both foresee and intend a specific goal or terminus. This terminus may not be consciously known or realized from the start, and in
fact we often and even regularly adjust our goals better to reflect the
unforeseeable yet inescapable vicissitudes of life, but that does not
matter. What does matter is that we face our lives in such a way as to
presuppose that we *will* grow in maturity, or intelligence, or wisdom,
or physical strength, and in so presupposing lay the foundations for
actually accomplishing those ends. Human life is, among other
things, an alternating series of setting, revising, and accomplishing
such intentions. Conversely, such intentions are the dynamic by
means of which we move out of the present and into the future.[21]

On the other hand, such self-transcending movements are also
critical. Whenever we intentionally grow (for example, in any of the

four realms mentioned earlier), we do so because the goal or terminus toward which we direct our lives is judged to be better than our present state of affairs.[22] The decision-making process by which we discriminate among future possibilities of relatively equivalent likelihood, selecting one of them and thereby certifying it as our intention while rejecting the rest, is a process ultimately seated within our capacity to identify the good and move toward it. This capacity, universally and thus abstractly present within human beings, is what generically distinguishes us from nonhuman beings.[23]

It is this transcendental and universal presence of goodness within us that *we know* makes us different from nonhuman beings. Thus, another person who denies that presence in us denies what we know to be an essential constituent of our identity as a generic, but if so then also as a particular, human being. This is a miscalculation of such fundamental proportions that we cannot but be offended by it, and this offense makes it impossible for us to love that person.[24]

Is this a display of mere selfishness on our part? Perhaps; surely it would be hard to deny that this is often the case. However, this sense of offense is also a universally present phenomenon, a fact that requires us to inspect it more carefully in order to determine whether there is an essential condition of human being disclosed by its being triggered. Such an inspection here shows, I think, that its presence is as fundamental to us as is our inability (and unwillingness) to suppress it. We cannot eradicate the response of being-offended.[25] Why not? Because we know that the presence of abstract goodness in us—that is, the mere fact that we are human beings—places a responsibility upon others. And note that this responsibility arises not from our actual or historical display of good intentions and behaviors. Instead, it arises from a spring deeper and more fundamental than that: our transcendental or constitutive goodness, or what I have also referred to as our moralness. It is the presence of the *possibility* of goodness within us, and not only its historical expression, that we know is offended when the other deliberately refuses to exchange intentions of self-transcendence with us.

The presence of goodness in us, then, whether abstract and transcendental on the one hand or historical and categorical on the other, triggers responsibilities on the part of others toward us. (The obverse is true as well, of course, which is what generates our own responsibilities to them.) To put the matter more axiomatically, "goodness beckons enduringly." Philosophers and ethicists from Aristotle to our own day have recognized this dynamic and tried to come to grips with it, an observation that ought not pass us by since it discloses the perduring universality of the recognition and thus of the reality it discloses. Those who deny our goodness offend their responsibility to us as *bearers* of goodness and thereby make it impossible for us to love them precisely because in denying that responsibility they have shown themselves to be unwilling even to begin participating in the exchange that is the essential structure and precondition of love. They stand toward us as though we were nonhumans.

In the next chapter I shall resume this discussion at the point of saying how moralness and love are grounded in God. Here, let me simply indicate the connection point between the two discussions. If human beings are, as I suggested earlier, the highest expression of the material universe of which we know, and are in fact that material universe come to self-awareness and self-expression, then the goodness that is correlative to the moralness of human beings calls for an accounting that itself reflects the structure of that goodness. But we have just seen that goodness beckons, that it intends an effect outside of the person in whom it resides, whether abstractly or concretely, and correlatively that it invites responsibility from outside as well. We can therefore say that goodness is constitutively personal and social—personal because it constitutes the crucial distinction between personal and nonpersonal beings, and social because it both intends and invites effects beyond or outside of itself.

To return to our question, then, the inquiry we raise concerning the presence of goodness within the material universe must reflect the same structure of "beyond or outside" on this macro or transcendental scale as it does on all of the micro or historical scales that we are better acquainted with. And further, if we insist upon complete reflectivity between these two scales, which we should because we have no warrant to inaugurate a different structure when we are thinking on the macro scale, then the "beyond or outside" to which historical expressions of goodness are responsible must itself be a "who," that is, personal. This is nothing other than

Ramsey's insight attained from the other direction. Not surprisingly, I think that this "who" is God.

I can complete this short discussion of moralness and love by saying more precisely now what I felt was lacking in O'Collins's account of divine revelation. There I continually mentioned that although I greatly appreciated the form and structure of his account, it was avoidably weak at the point of filling in the content of this structure. Now we can see that the ultimate content of divine revelation, and thus the universal expression of it as well, is the goodness within which all that is distinctively human is rooted. Strip away the possibility of consciously and deliberately participating in this goodness, and *human* beings would be indistinguishable from other sorts. On the other hand, God's goodness, graciously present within the universe as the beckoning pole that elicits the self-awareness and self-transcendence that are distinctive of human beings, is that to which we ultimately respond when we function distinctively as human beings.[26] Everything that we either intend or do that is "good" is thus an historical expression, from our end of things, of God's ultimate and transcendent goodness. Or to say the same thing the other way around, God's transcendent goodness is historically expressed by that part of the material universe that has come to self-awareness and self-transcendence. And expressed goodness *is* divine revelation.

Moralness and the
Capacity for Hoping

It should not surprise us that theological treatises on the notion of hope tend to settle around political theology as its primary vehicle. This concentration is not a mere accident of history, as though the seminal works of Rubem Alves and other liberation theologians usurped a stage that other nonpolitical theologians would rather have occupied themselves.[27] As a matter of fact, the more one thinks about it, the less surprising it is that hope is usually contextualized within a political framework. My interests, though, are not so much in the precise content of such political hope but instead in the prior discussion of the nature and shape of hope itself.

As I have already indicated, I think that hope is a constituent feature of what makes one a human (or moral) being. And as we have seen thus far with respect to knowing and loving, to be moral implies giving expression. Something is not knowledge in any meaningful way until and unless it can be expressed in language, and likewise something is not love until and unless it can be expressed to and with another person. So too here. As I shall try to show, hope is essential to one's moral capacity and thus requires (or, better yet, presupposes) expression in order to become what it truly is. And as I shall also try to show, the arena of hope's expression is temporal and communitarian in a way that completes the temporality and communality of knowing and loving. If I am successful in establishing the ordered relations between and among these features of moralness, then I shall have shown both how they and their product, the community, are essential to the notion and the possibility of being moral and thus of receiving God's self-revelation.

An adequate introduction to the notion of hope as a moral feature needs at the very least to include the following three aspects: the capacity for memory, a relatively indeterminate feature, and the capacity for confident commitment. The first and third aspects draw our attention to specifically human possibilities; the second locates those possibilities within a cosmic context of a certain shape.[28] The removal of any of these three would, I believe, effectively eviscerate the notion of hope as we experience and participate in it.

The recognition that human beings can abstract from experiences and observations and project them (i.e., hold those abstractions as objects of experience and critical inquiry themselves) is scarcely unique, either to me or to theology as a whole. In fact, this recognition is so basic to cognitional theories in general that we can simply bypass its detailed explication and defense. Instead, I wish to draw attention to the forward or future thrust of this cognitive movement. When I am involved in a present-time experience, such as the experience of sitting here at my desk and looking out the window at the building outside, an inescapable feature of that experience for me is its passage through my senses and into my mind, where it is held as a datum (in this case, an image) in my memory. When a sufficient number of such experiences have been repeated and stored, I become increasingly comfortable that the next such time I sit down here, I will see the same building that I have in all of the past similar experiences.

Note the bidirectional dynamic of memory here. On the one hand, its most apparent function is to collect the incoming stream of images of present-time experiences and store them in a roughly chronological stack (however it is that the neurochemistry of our brains accomplishes this) in order to reacquaint us with the past whenever we need it.[29] Hence the relation of memory with the past, as most of us are accustomed to think. But there is also a future orientation of the memory that is implicit within its past orientation and thus hidden or obscured by that more aggressive one. This future orientation has in fact just been illustrated: we reach back into our memories "so that" or "in order to" or "because we intend" some purpose with the memories thus recollected. As of the instant that we conceive of and intend that purpose, it is future to us. Thus, the *intentional* function of memory is, as with all intentional acts, so to orient us toward the future that we come to exist in it in a manner that critically appropriates the past and renders that future comfortable.

Memory, then, serves a critical function in that it not only collects and stores[30] but in addition may be called upon to contribute usefully, pragmatically, judgmentally, beneficially, savingly, and the like, to our stance toward the future and thus in principle to our existence within it. Our minds sift through the stored data[31] and utilize those bits they judge will best serve our purposes, even when (and of course this is true by definition) those purposes have not yet been realized or instantiated. *Memory* is thus the name we give to the dynamic capacity of our minds to do these two things: to collect on the one hand and to sift with respect to (or in alignment with) designated future intentions on the other.

We have already seen how cognition[32] presupposes and thus discloses the dynamic presence of goodness. Here we see the same thing, except with respect to the future in addition to the present and past. In order for memory to be able to collect, to sift critically, and to identify the aligning intentions, goodness is required as the ultimate specifiable condition of its possibility. That is, the innate capacity to distinguish between better and worse alternatives in the future and to select (even if only temporarily) one over the other presupposes the operation and the deliberate application of goodness as the yardstick by which this critical segregation occurs. And if I am correct in suggesting that hope reflects the triadic structure mentioned above, then hope is a fundamentally moral stance or intention as well, since it depends fundamentally upon a mental operation that presupposes and utilizes goodness.

The second constituent component of the notion of hope draws attention to a structure of the real world beyond our minds, thus including them but not limited to them in the way that critical intentionality is. This has to do with time itself. In the appendix to this book, I shall define and discuss a concept of time that I believe is both notionally correct and religiously correct or usable as well, so here I shall simply presume what I will present in more detail later on. When we hope (and here my language presumes as well upon the third component to be discussed shortly), we commit ourselves to a state of affairs that is not *and may never be* but toward which we stand nonetheless as though its coming-into-being were both quite likely and influenceable by our personal efforts. The point to notice here is not whether or not we turn out to be correct with respect to the coming-into-being of our hope. It is instead that the very possibility of such a stance toward the future presupposes that that future is not set or determined.

Whether the state of affairs our hopes intend occurs historically or not, before it or any alternative becomes reality, we stand toward the future as though it were influenceable. The exact shape of our hope *is* our recipe for how we would like that future to turn out, of course. That shape is itself subject to the length of time between "now" and "then" and the growing welter of additional and unforeseen possibilities that will arise with any and all increases in that length. It is subject as well, at least in part, to the degree of deliberateness or commitment that we have to the coming-into-being of our hope; we will certainly invest more energy into assisting a strongly held hope into historical reality than a weakly held one. But the formal point remains: the notion of hope presupposes that the future is influenceable and thus not determined.

We observed after discussing the first component of the notion of hope that it presupposes goodness as the condition of the possibility of being what it is, namely a critical stance toward the future. Here we can add to that description the observation that standing this way toward the future discloses our rather strongly held belief that we can help to shape that future in ways that reflect our own intentions and desires: that we can change the future entails that the future is changeable. "Our own intentions and desires," in turn, are the subjective and historical expression of what we would take to be goodness concretely instantiated in the world. Thus, as I hinted earlier and shall return to in more detail in the appendix, the coming-into-being of our intentions is not only the dynamic mechanism by which we move from present to future, but more importantly for our purposes here, the dynamic mechanism by which we also try to instantiate goodness into that soon-to-be-present.[33] The aphorism "when we hope, we hope for the best" is more than mere platitude; it expresses our belief that things could be improved and that we can identify, at least provisionally, how that could be.[34]

The final component of the notion of hope is more than likely what we most readily think of when thinking of hope: confident commitment. Here there is not a great deal to add to what I have already said except to note that hope is not abstract, either in the degree or in the object of our commitment. Of course, we often experience objects of hope abstractly, but that has to do with the unspecifiable and ungovernable possibilities that surround that object and not with the nature of hope itself. The notion of hope is a psychological and, I think, spiritual stance that the future will turn out in a certain way. Thus, it is at root an interior expectation. Whether or not the future actually does turn out that way is a complex combination of interior expectations on the one hand and exterior causes and factors on the other.

Hope is one's adaptable commitment that the future will embody a greater amount of concrete or historical goodness than does the present. It must be adaptable because of what we just saw, namely that the future is relatively open or undetermined by definition. We can never antecedently know, much less corral, all of the relevant causes that will terminate in a given event or state of affairs; that is, we never stand toward tomorrow as we stand toward yesterday. However, and even more fundamentally, we can never *not* stand toward tomorrow.[35] We must take *some* critical perspective toward the relatively open and undetermined future, and hope is precisely our way of displaying our belief that it will be a positive and worthwhile one.

If this is true, though, then when viewed from another direction and in concert with everything else we have just seen, hope is a rather complex human behavior. Its complexity reflects a negative evaluation of the present ("things need to improve"), the positive possibilities of the future ("things need to improve in this or that way"), and our commitment ("I am going to influence the present in whatever way I can to bring about those positive possibilities").[36]

I would insist that hope is a behavior and not merely an interior expectation, although it is that at root, because we ourselves can act in such a manner as to contribute to the causes that would help to instantiate our hoped-for desires. This means that we can refrain from acting in that manner as well, and it would be ludicrous to accept a definition of hope that would approve of an interior expectation to survive as "hope" in the face of one's conscious refusal to do something which would help to bring it about. That is, it is morally indefensible to want the good and yet refrain from doing what we can to accomplish it, because *goodness beckons us.* We may not be able to do everything to bring about our hope, and we certainly may not know everything necessary to do so, but we cannot deliberately reject an opportunity to accomplish a good intention without trivializing the confidence and the commitment that constituted our hope in the first place. Such an action would contradict either our confidence, which is the added degree of goodness we believe will attend the attainment of our hoped-for object as over against the present state of affairs, or our commitment, which is our response when goodness beckons us, or both. In either case, though, hope is rendered moot. And if it is not to be rendered moot, then hope, like knowing and loving, requires concrete historical expression.

Hope is thus the temporally enduring expression of goodness. Acts of knowing and loving reside "within" time, of course, simply because we as knowers and lovers do. But hope is that feature of being moral that most clearly and historically carries goodness from the present into the future and thus brings the future into the present. It is not more laden with moralness than either of those other two capacities, but as we shall see it is that which is most enduring over time, and that will turn out to make a profound difference to the meaning of the Christian community.

Moralness and the
Capacity for Community

In one sense I have now said in outline form all that I believe needs to be said about the distinctively moral nature of human beings. To be a moral being means that one is rooted and grounded in goodness. This grounding is abstractly present in the possibility of knowing, of loving, and of hoping. The actual expression of each of these in turn displays *how* we are moral as assessed by the criterion of ultimate goodness itself. Those concrete expressions of knowing, loving, and hoping that align with goodness (i.e., that are "true," "transcendently enabling," and "confident commitments" or, which negatively put, serve to overcome ignorance, autonomy, and anxiety) concretely express divine revelation in the historical realm. The next chapter will discuss the relationship between these and God, and so for the time being we may understand God as the ultimate Personal Goodness who grounds and thus initiates each of these personal possibilities.

Before embarking on that discussion, however, I wish to pay closer attention to a feature of moralness that each of these three capacities presupposes, but so softly that we are likely to overlook it. (To be more accurate, if less polite, Protestants often tend straightforwardly to overlook it, while Catholics often tend so to assume it that its grounding in human moralness is missed and thus functionally overlooked.) This feature is the communitarian nature of human moralness. I shall discuss "the community" in two stages: (1) the explicitly communitarian nature of knowing, loving, and hoping, and (2) the nature of the community rather than the individual as the fundamental location of the expression of moralness and hence of divine revelation as well.[37] If I am correct, then this would contrast with theories of divine self-disclosure that locate (or identify) revelation within such nonmoral and nonpersonal entities as the Bible, the Gospel, miracles, the death-resurrection-ascension of Jesus, the human intellect, and the like.[38] And also, if I am correct, then the community as fundamental location of moralness would constitute the testing ground for assessing putative expressions of divine revelation within itself and other communities. The community exists in time as the concrete medium of God's self-revelation, as may be discerned by the largely past orientation of knowing, the largely present orientation of loving, and the largely future orientation of hoping. Thus, it summarizes and symbolizes what it means to be human.

In addition to what I said earlier, the communitarian nature of knowing can be demonstrated by returning to the distinction between belief and knowledge. The usual distinction here is that knowing refers to convictions about reality that in principle could be wrong but that we in fact do not have any reason for doubting at the present, whereas believing refers to convictions about reality that we do in fact have reason for doubting, even if such reasons are not strong enough to inspire us to jettison or even revise the convictions at the moment. The significant distinction between the two is thus not of kind but rather of degree; the same mental act is at work within each, with the difference located in the degree of surprise we would experience if the conviction turned out to be wrong.

Furthermore, and more to the point in the present discussion, knowledge and beliefs are always concrete in that they are always about this or that feature of reality. This or that feature might itself be abstract, of course; there is nothing especially illicit about knowing about "marriage" as over against knowing about "Bill and Brenda," for example. But those differences have to do with the objects of our mental acts, and not about the specificity or particularity of the mental acts of apprehension themselves. *Those* apprehending acts are concrete because they are acts of our minds.

So, we can now refine our original question concerning the difference between knowing and believing by asking how the one concrete mental act of apprehension issues forth and embraces its object either unhesitatingly (knowing) or more hesitantly (belief). Here the difference is finally able to be located, but it is neither exclusively in ourselves, since one mental act constitutes the dynamic of both, nor exclusively in the object, since it is a category mistake to think that objects in the real world can "possess" attributes such as certainty or doubt and "reflect" those attributes back onto our minds. Instead, I think, the difference here is located in the group or the community in which we learn about the object itself, and thus ultimately in which we learn about learning itself.

Bernard Lonergan invites us to think of how we interpret maps in this connection. When we read a map in order to determine how to drive from California to Indiana, for example, practically speaking we have almost no opportunity at all to assess the adequacy and accuracy of the map before starting our trip. Instead, we depend upon a great and largely inaccessible number of persons to have done their jobs correctly, from pioneers to surveyors to cartographers to printers. The only concrete and practical way *we* have to assess the accuracy of the map is to begin driving and see if following the map does in fact get us to Indiana. But, of course, our decision to get into the car and begin driving in the first place reflects our prior decision that the map *is* accurate, and it is *this* decision that is of interest to me here. On the one hand, this decision is a decision of at least belief and more typically of knowledge (and the distinction is irrelevant because it is the more basic apprehending act I am looking at), *and* it is belief or knowledge that is rooted in the experience of many hundreds of inaccessible persons that in fact the map is trustworthy. "It is that belief, that dependence on countless others, that is the real basis of one's confidence in maps."[39]

This illustration could be spun out in innumerable ways about even more innumerable and inaccessible persons. The conclusion from any and all such reflections, it would seem, is that the very possibility of knowledge as we experience it presupposes the contributions of relevant communities of persons over time to us: the community of pioneers, surveyors, cartographers, and printers with respect to knowing where to drive; the community of miners, loggers, engineers, blast furnace operators, assembly-line workers, packers, and drivers with respect to knowing whether we can sit down in a chair without its collapsing on us; and so on.

Furthermore, not only do we presuppose a "mere" contribution from the various members of these communities to ourselves, but more to the point, we presuppose a *truthful* or *trustworthy* contribution from them. That is, we expect for them to have done their jobs well, integrating their diverse experiences with reality and expertises over reality in ways that allow the two to line up rather than to compete or to conflict. Ultimately, I think, at least in its historical aspect, the concrete possibility of knowledge presupposes this voluntary and "truthful" interplay between experience and reality on the part of each one of those usually inaccessible persons. Apart from such a presupposition, quite literally we would never get out of bed in the morning—or climb into it the night before.

Some relevant community of human beings, which we presume to be committed to the truthful interchange between bits of information on the one hand and reality on the other, exists as the historical possibility of our knowing in the concrete ways that we know. It is fundamental to this aspect of knowing that moralness exist as the basis of our confidence in that community and of their contributions to our knowledge about the world.[40]

It is not quite so difficult to perceive the communitarian nature of love, and thus I need not spend so much time on it. It is clear that the specific structure of this relationship presupposes a community of (at least) two persons. Seen from the perspective of the donor, the essence of love is so to embrace a beloved so that his or her concrete existence is enhanced or enriched. From the beloved's perspective, then, the essence of love is the actual willingness to receive such enrichment and to reciprocate from the well of his or her own resources and gifts.[41] From either vantage point, however, the other enters into the very essence and definition of love and thus, too, of what it means to be a moral or human being. In both instances, goodness constitutes the ultimate yardstick by which the likelihood of the giving act is assessed *as* enhancing or enriching.

Finally, then, we can consider the communitarian aspects of hoping. Here, too, goodness is transcendentally operative in that hope intends for something better in the future that, by definition, does not exist at present. But it does not do this abstractly, either in terms of the actual goodness which hope intends or in terms of the objects to which it applies. It is especially this latter observation that is relevant here, because the objects of hope are typically either individuals or else communities of individuals. But even in the first instance there is a community present, bare as it is: the community of oneself and that other individual.

When we hope, we typically hope for *this* person to get well, or for *this* war or *this* suffering to cease, or for *this* unemployed person to get a job, or for *this* oppression to be alleviated. In nearly all instances, hope is an expression of future-oriented goodness whose subject and object are personal.[42] The presence of hope is thus a signal not only of our capacity for the abstraction of goodness and its application to a future state of affairs but in addition an expression of goodness that links us with the individual (or the larger community) in that future. Thus, it constitutes a community over time, and this, as I have suggested already, is how the future is dynamically brought into the present.

Now we can see the reason why most theological treatises on hope have tended to concentrate on the political arena as the expression of hope. Politics is typically the most obvious area of the need for hope (i.e., of "the negative evaluation of the present" discussed above) and is thus the most obvious area of its salvific application as well. Politics is, among other things, the art of community construction; a more accurate if more turgid description would be that it is the art of communities construction. If this is so, though, then the inevitable competition between and among the values and interests of these various subcommunities cannot but result in the suppression of some of them, and this suppression is the historical bed of both the negative assessments and positive commitments of hope.

The special focus of the theology of hope upon the political arena should not blind us to the fact that this focus is a deliberate reduction, understandably grounded within what I just referred to as the obviousness of its need and application within that arena. But it is just as important to discern and apply within smaller communities as well, if not perhaps more so: one of the features that relativizes hope, as we saw, is our assessment of the likelihood of its coming-into-being with respect to competing possibilities. When smaller groups of persons are involved, and certainly smaller numbers of subcommunities, the total number of such possibilities usually decreases, and the likelihood of our hope coming-into-being correspondingly increases. This is the rationale, I believe, for what Catholic social theorists call the principle of subsidiarity: "a principle in Catholic social doctrine which holds that nothing should be done by a higher agency which can be done as well, or better, by a lower agency."[43] This principle enshrines more than simple pragmatism. In addition, it enshrines the critical and hence ultimately moral alignment between our hopes and intentions on the one hand, and our assessment of the most likely path from the present to its achievement that we can envision and pursue. This goes beyond simple pragmatism because, once again, *goodness beckons.* When it does, we cannot justifiably sidestep the responsibility to pursue it deliberately, behaviorally, and historically.

While the community exists on the one hand at a level more abstract than the individual, it is also, and on the other, the most tangible location of all three aspects of moralness and hence the most tangible medium of divine revelation. The community collects goodness from the past (knowing), distributes it within the present (loving), and projects it into the future (hoping). It does these not accidentally but essentially, and not capriciously but critically. There is a fundamental sociality to human moralness that echoes, I believe, the fundamental sociality of God. This chapter has outlined both the form and the content of divine revelation which, in a nutshell, is "expressed goodness." The next chapter will ponder this in more detail, but from the perspective of God as the ground and initiator of goodness rather than human beings as receivers and expressers of it. Its completion will in turn complete the core of my proposal regarding divine revelation.

4

God as Source and Object
of Divine Revelation

Gerald O'Collins notes that ordinary language regularly reduces the meaning of *revelation* to "unexpected and important pieces of information which may significantly change [someone's] attitude."[1] He goes on to say that while we may not wish to take issue with this meaning, it is clear that its restrictiveness obscures the way revelation reveals. The last chapter attempted to say *what* revelation is, and so it remains the task of the present one to try to say *why* it reveals. Here we shall follow the approach of that chapter so as to indicate how God is the source and ground of the moralness that is distinctive of human beings, and further how God is the source and ground of the specific expressions of moralness we considered there: knowing, loving, hoping, and community.

Here, then, is our question: Why is revelation revelatory? Why is it not simply normal, or natural, or usual? Why, in addition to those, does it also disclose in ways that we need the category of revelation to help us to understand? So far as I can determine, traditional treatises on divine revelation regularly overlook this question. At worst, the reason for this might be that their authors did not perceive the need to address it and perhaps in some cases did not even see it as a question.[2] At best, the reason might be that those authors felt free to presume the question because in their view it reaches to the heart of the integral relationship between God and human beings; if so, then addressing other questions in the divine-human matrix would address this one along the way.

I am inclined to resist, and in fact to move beyond, both of these alternatives. As I have already stated at various points, I believe that revelation constitutes the ground of the possibility of being human, and thus that we need to pay extremely careful attention to the matter of identifying both its initiation by God and its reception by human beings. Revelation is integral to being human but also, I would claim, to being God as well. I can state my understanding of this relational matrix in the following axiom: *Just as it is impossible to conceive of divine revelation apart from God and human beings as the initiating and receiving poles of revelation, so, too, it is impossible to conceive of God and human beings apart from the relationship of divine revelation.*[3] If I am correct in this, then revelation is in fact (1) a relationship (2) that is so constitutive of both God and human beings that we might call it an ontological relationship. It remains to be said, of course, exactly how revelation is constitutive of divinity, although Chapter 3's discussions concerning how it is constitutive of humanity give us plenty of hints toward an answer.

The target answer here, I believe, is that goodness is the proximate ground of the possibility of being human or moral; that is, to be human is to be moral in the ways discussed in Chapter 3. The remote ground of this possibility, then, is the self-revealing God who is (among other things) the Goodness that moralness presupposes and revelation conveys and expresses. To those whose hearts incline them to the pursuit, revelation reveals because goodness beckons them to itself, not as an abstract or lifeless thing, but instead as the ultimate Personal Goodness of reality whom believers call God. The possibility of moralness is our contact with God, and expressed goodness is our response to that contact. And since our response is itself shaped by the possibility of moralness, and hence of goodness as an existential condition of the universe, our being good is both a response to divine revelation and an ongoing expression of it. God is both source and object of revelation, of expressed goodness. All that is good comes from God and further discloses God. And this is not extrinsic on God's part, but inherent in what it means to be Father of Jesus, that is, relationally identified with humanity.

It now falls to us to consider in more detail how God grounds the possibility of being human. Some readers might not find much of creative insight in these words. If so, I would be neither surprised nor disappointed since we have already aired the relevant topics considerably in Chapter 3. My words here will echo what was said there, not in a mechanical or repetitive way but instead in the same way that causes are echoed in their consequences and questions in their answers. Keeping in mind what was said earlier, then, we now begin to shift our focus from those who receive divine revelation to the God who initiates it.

God's Goodness as the Ground of Knowing (Father)

Knowing is a moral activity in addition to being an intellectual one. Knowing, that is, presupposes the existence and the applicability of goodness as the ultimate condition of the possibility of distinguishing between what is, and is not, the truth. Truth is a state of affairs in which objective reality is perceived and held by the mind in a way that satisfies the mind's curiosity or intellectual dynamism (at least in this or that particular area) and thus discloses the mind's contentment that what is known corresponds to what is in fact. Lacking a more imaginative name, I called this contentment Point S, signaling that when the dynamic intentionality of the mind is critically satisfied, truth has been attained. Point S might well be a temporary attainment; there is neither any guarantee nor any metaphysical necessity that a particular bit of information may be called truth only when it is never again subject to revisability. Given the advances of human knowledge that we are privileged to enjoy, and those to which we yet hope to contribute, not much more could be asked.

But how is this grounded in God? How does human knowing or intellection reflect and in fact participate in God's knowing? When proceeding toward an answer here, the danger is that we are immediately tempted to construe God's knowing as analogous to human knowing rather than correlative to it. That is, we are tempted to think of God's knowing as a series of divine mental acts whereby bits of data stream into God's mind and constitute a growingly comfortable unity, a sort of divine Point S. That we regularly fall to the temptation to think this way about God is not surprising; after all, it is difficult to conceive of thinking, much less knowing, in any other way. But doing so leaves unanswered the question that we are here faced with, namely the ultimate origins of the possibility of human knowledge and knowing. All of the medieval controversies concerning unmoved movers, uncaused causes, and the like, were nothing other than attempts to encourage us to see that when we are faced with the question of God's activities, we must massage our grammar carefully enough so as to ground human activity in the divine and thus account for it in religiously and metaphysically satisfying ways, but also clearly enough so as to avoid simply making divine activity an arbitrary first step in the chain of activities that eventuates in our own. That is, we must reside between the traditional polarities of utter transcendence and utter immanence, otherness and identity, and reside between them in ways that appropriate the insights of both poles rather than shrink from either. With respect to the present topic, then, I believe that this proper residence is named mystery.

Here, too, we are faced with misunderstanding borne of ambiguity. In scientific and other quantifiable regions of human knowledge, *mystery* nearly always connotes enigma, conundrum, or secret. The operative metaphor of this common definition is thus either an incomplete or a defective intellectual apprehension of reality. Potential resolutions of this kind of mystery are achieved by persistent intellectual inquiry. When seen in this way, mystery is also provisional rather than constitutive, as reflected in the widespread assumption that all intellectual problems are ultimately solvable.[4]

Although it must be admitted that mystery functions much like this in a great deal of theological literature, it is unfortunate that it does so. The real point behind calling various aspects of theology mystery, or calling God ultimate mystery, is not to imply that someday some sort of messianic detective will uncover the final clues to the Ultimate Puzzle and bring about a Point S condition with respect to our understanding of God. It is instead to remind ourselves that God is the ultimate condition of the possibility of knowledge (hence the intellectual overtones in the word *mystery*) but not merely as the first mental actor in an entire series of mental acts. As Mystery of the world, God is that which our knowing capacities presuppose as both source and target of knowing itself. How can this be more fully understood without invalidating its essence as *Mystery*?

A proper theological development of this notion, I think, proceeds in two stages. The first is the stage of reflection upon the subject of mystery (human beings), and the second is the stage of reflection upon its ultimate or remote object (God). I have already suggested a few things about this first stage in Chapter 3, so here I shall add to that and then proceed further into the second stage which is of specific interest here.

The word *mystery* is especially and appropriately laden with intellectual overtones. (Thus, my criticism earlier of this fact as reflected within theological treatises is not against it per se but instead with the unwillingness to proceed beyond this fact and inquire into the nonintellectual conditions to which it invites attention.) In a word, that there is a condition of intellectual mystery implies without possibility of denial that human knowledge is finite. To say the same thing the other way around, as human beings we encounter the finiteness of our knowledge whenever we inquire into matters that are (presently) enigmatic, hidden, confusing, and the like—that is, whenever we inquire into matters concerning which we are not in a Point S condition. And since it is not a culpable failure not to be in a Point S condition, but is in fact a natural and foundational condition of our intellectual existence, it may thereby be seen that knowing intends to move from the more finite to the less finite, from that which is presently mystery to that which is not.

Knowing, therefore, is more than simply a cognitive act that perceives and transfers data from the external world of facts to the internal world of knowledge. More fundamentally, and in fact giving rise to the possibility of such acts of perception and transference, knowing identifies human beings as existing on the boundary or cusp between the realms of the finite and the infinite. But these two realms are not identical; they are different. Granted, they are *differently* different for each human being; what is known to one person may not yet, or in fact ever, be known to another. But over and above these concrete and historical differences, the two realms of the finite and the infinite are themselves of different orders.

Humankind as a whole exists within the one and perpetually strains toward the other.

This is what many have referred to by the name of transcendence, that human beings may and in fact do transcend cognitive limitations whenever they come to know something they previously did not. But *transcendence* is itself a relational term rather than a static one, because it refers to the relationship not simply between the less one knew in comparison to the more one knows, but more fundamentally still to the relationship between the two realms of the finite and the infinite, two realms disclosed by the inescapable observation that human knowing always intends to move from the former to the latter. And the latter realm, the realm of the mysterious or the infinite, always exists (by definition) as the beyond that is not *so* beyond that it is unreachable or inexperiencable. Granted (again, by definition), we never exist within it, but we exist always on its very edge or boundary by virtue of regarding it as the source from which knowledge will come, from which problems and enigmas will be resolved, and thus *toward* which we are intellectually heading. And because any and all acts of knowing presuppose this orientation, we experience the realm of the infinite or the mysterious whenever we experience ourselves on its boundary.

From the perspective of the human subject, then, knowing demarcates the possibility of a transcendence from the known to the mysterious. Because this possibility is not optional or elective but instead constitutes a given condition at the essence of what it means to be human, it is also inescapably relational. The intrinsic possibility of knowing relates us intrinsically to that which is not (yet) known, which is the unknowable. The truth of this statement can be tested by supposing its opposite: were there no such existing condition that I have just called the unknowable, then in principle and historically someday in fact, all things would be known to human beings. If that sounds improbable, as it does to me,[5] then the only alternative is to presuppose the existence of some condition or state of affairs more or less coincident with what I have called the unknowable.

We can now shift our gaze from the finite or known to the infinite or unknowable, and thence to God as the ultimate object of our knowing. We cannot turn our gaze to it as something definite, or concrete, or knowable, of course, since that would not be faithful to its nature and definition.[6] But that does not mean we cannot say anything at all about this unknowable. Even without being able to name it or define it, we can say that from its perspective, it perpetually approaches us[7] in a manner that I referred to in Chapter 3 as "the beckoning of goodness." That is, precisely because the phenomenon of knowing itself is a relational phenomenon, both poles or parties to the relationship actively engage it and participate in it.

Of course, the *how* of this engagement or participation is relevantly different from each of the two sides. From the finite or the human side of things, we engage in the relationship by grasping and straining toward the infinite unknowable in movements that define themselves by acts of perception, categorization, thematization, and the like. From the infinite or divine side of things, the movement is very different while yet remaining active. Its activity (or activeness, if *activity* appears to be too located within the finite or categorical side of things) is precisely its constituting the ground of the possibility of finite self-transcendence itself in the act of knowing. And even though we are not accustomed to thinking of grounds as being active, there are two reasons to view this as an exception: first, it is the ground of a *relation*, and, second, it is the ground of the specific relation of *knowing*. Neither relations in general nor knowing in specific are static or motionless. Instead, they are dynamic and intentional, including within themselves that which is not themselves, as the very concept of relation makes clear.

The unknowable, therefore, makes possible the known, even as the known presupposes the unknowable. And the unknowable makes the known possible precisely in that it exists as more fundamental than the known. This more fundamental is "more" not merely chronologically but beyond that in logical ways as well. This can be seen in the ordered nature of the relation we have already discussed: the finite transcends itself by incremental acts of knowing toward the infinite, acquiring in the process not simply another datum of information but in addition a greater familiarity with the infinite unknowable itself. Things do not move in the same way in the opposite direction, though. The infinite does not transcend itself in historical movement toward the finite by incremental and faltering steps, or any steps at all, precisely because it includes the finite within itself since it is the ground of the possibility of that finite. Thus, the activeness of the relation of the infinite toward the finite is not an historical activeness, as is the case with the activity that transcends from the more finite to the less finite. It is rather a movement that encompasses and summarizes the differentness of the realms of finitude and infinitude, a differentness in which infinitude includes within itself that which it is not, making it in fact possible, while yet remaining the ever-infinite or ever-unknown.

Thus, from its end of things the unknowable, too, is relational, but in a manner we cannot identify with the relationality of any two objects within the universe precisely because *this* relationality constitutes the very ground of the possibility of all of *those*. We cannot expect it to be formally like them since that would make it one of them, and we would merely have extended our quest one step further rather than answering and resolving it. Rahner says in this regard:

> And so the distinction between God and all finite beings is not only clearly called for: it is even the condition of the possibility for any distinction at all, both between objects in general and the horizon of transcendence, and between object and object. . . . The horizon cannot be comprised within the horizon, the whither of transcendence cannot really, as such, be brought within the range of transcendence itself or be distinguished from other things. The ultimate measure cannot be measured; the boundary which delimits all things cannot itself be bounded by a still more distant limit. . . . So this nameless and indefinable being . . . is seen as absolutely beyond determination. It is only there in so far as it determines all, and is not only physically but logically beyond any determination on the part of the finite subject.[8]

What I have called the infinite, the unknowable, the ultimate condition, and so on, Rahner here calls God. As a distinctly human activity (and hence relation), knowing is personal. And if the ground of knowing is itself relational, which I have tried to indicate, then that ground must itself be personal (or Personal, since it makes possible the personal dynamic of knowing) in ways that are appropriate to it as the condition rather than the conditioned. The personal nature of God will become somewhat more clear in the next section, where we will discuss God as the ground of love, than it may have been in the present one. But here we should at least recognize that the reason for this greater clarity probably lies in our callousness toward the personal nature of human knowing, as though it were not moral but merely natural, like moving our little finger.

We have now completed the first part of the attempt to ground a specifically moral activity within its larger transcendent context. In Chapter 3, I advanced the thesis that knowing is a moral activity because it is made possible only on the supposition that goodness exists as the condition distinguishing truth from falsity. Here I moved beyond that arrangement and tried to show how God, known here and always as Ultimate Goodness, grounds the dynamic intentionality of knowing by being the other pole of the moral, and personal, act of knowing. As that other pole, God is knowable in relation to us as the ultimate Mysterious target of all knowing and of all knowledge. But it is more accurate to say that as that other pole, God is unknowable since that which makes something possible is clearly distinguished from that which it makes possible. God is the eternally unknowable, experienced as such in two ways: first, as that toward whom we *intend* in our self-transcending critical activities but do not ever *attain* since that which is attainable cannot by itself account for its own attainability, and, second, as the ultimate goodness whom we experience indirectly as the condition of the possibility of the Point S relaxation that we directly experience whenever we hold a datum of knowledge as true. It is in these senses, then, that it is meaningful to speak of God as the ultimate and perpetual Mystery of the universe.

God's Goodness as the Ground of Loving (Son)

By now I may well have exhausted the patience of the reader who picked up this volume expecting a more or less traditional account of divine revelation within the Christian religion, especially one that italicizes the role of Jesus. Of course, by now I also hope to have made clear why I do not start with Jesus in my understanding of revelation: doing so looks more like an arbitrary stipulation than a genuine *re-cognitio*.[9] I have argued instead that we need to approach the notion of revelation from the outside, as it were, from the perspective of what divine revelation is in the abstract, and only then move to discuss the specific ways in which Christians have recognized this notion displayed concretely in history and especially in Jesus.[10] This is the only route, I believe, that avoids the problem of circularity both in general ("divine revelation is what we say it is because we say so") and in particular ("Jesus is the revelation of God because we say so"). And this problem is a good one to avoid if we wish to understand the concept in its richness ourselves, much less if we wish to be able to converse about it ecumenically.

However, I also write from a particular perspective myself, one that is Christian and evangelical and ecumenical.[11] It is thus essential to consider *how* Jesus has come to be recognized and confessed as (among other things) the revelation of God. If we do not, then we simply exchange one kind of Christian blunder ("Jesus is the revelation of God because we say so") for its opposite ("divine revelation is fully understandable apart from Jesus"). The thesis I shall advance here, then, is that the human capacity to love is grounded in the self-transcending act of God whereby God grasps in love that which is not God and thereby renders it lovable. The specific and concrete historical demonstration of this divine act is the love of God for Jesus of Nazareth, and thus the present section deals with christology, or the study of the religious significance of Jesus. But it does so within the framework of the entire book itself and not merely as the apex or goal of the book. That is, as an expression of the self-transcending God, even if its clearest and most definitive expression, christology is a moment within soteriology and not identical with it. This point is regularly overlooked by Christians but is entirely consistent with the Johannine affirmation that "God loved the world so much that He gave His only-begotten Son" (John 3:16). In this statement, God's love of the world is the condition from which the sending of the Son ensues. We shall accordingly consider the ordering of the divine love on the one hand and the sending of the Son on the other in the pages that follow.

Perhaps the best place to start our reflection in christology is to try to say what it is *not*. Here there are two extremes to avoid. First, christology is not an attempt to "prove" that Jesus is God; that is, it is not Jesus apologetics. As I have just stated and shall try to show more clearly below, christology is ultimately a confession about God and not about Jesus of Nazareth; only secondarily is it about Jesus the human being. It is primarily a confession about the radical extent of God's love—so radical, in fact, that once one understands the presence of God in Jesus, no greater thing can be said than God *is* love. This confession is not an identity predication along the same lines as "Mary is a teacher," for in this latter predication it is clear that the subject might well not be the predicate—that is, a teacher—and thus the point of the sentence is to tell the audience that she is. But in the sentence "God is love," no such distinction between subject and predicate is envisioned. It could be stated the other way around ("Love is God") with no loss of meaning or significance, and no need for recourse to poetics, metaphor, or predicate nominative, in a way that the other sentence could not be ("A teacher is Mary").[12]

Second, and to the extent that christology draws our attention to Jesus, it is also not a way of saying that in Jesus of Nazareth the world discovers a maximal but historically accidental convergence between religion as conceived by God on the one hand and religion as conceived by human beings on the other. To be clearer, a transcendental christology is not especially interested in arguing that Jesus was the most fully authentic human being who ever lived, as liberal Protestants in the nineteenth century proposed, following the lead of Nestorius in the fifth. It might well be the case that He was such a human, but that is not what is at stake.[13] The reason it is not is (once again) that this is a statement not about God but instead about Jesus of Nazareth, and a comparative one at that. The best, if not only, way one could really understand this statement would be to follow accepted historical methods and compare the claims of the full authenticity of Jesus against any and all other candidates.

Initially there seems to be little difficulty for anyone who wishes to do such a comparison. The difficulty arises, however, once one begins to ask about the nature of the criteria by which the authenticity of Jesus and the other candidates is to be assessed. Where do those criteria come from, and how are we to know that they apply fully to the project at hand? Either, on the one hand, those criteria are fully compatible with what Christians believe about God as grounded in the loving self-expression of God in the person of Jesus of Nazareth, in which case Jesus is the assessor rather than the assessed, or, on the other hand, they are somehow external to what Christians believe about God, in which case Jesus has already been judged to be both less than central and less than ultimate in our understanding of God. In either event, regardless of how fascinating an inquiry it might turn out to be, it is not of very great interest to traditional christology to show merely that Jesus was the best available model for how to live a good human life. And it is certainly not of very great interest to traditional christology to affirm a possible consequence of such an historical comparison, namely that in principle an even more authentically human being might come along, leaving both Jesus and all other candidates in the dust.

What this means, then, as I have suggested both directly in the preceding paragraphs and indirectly by locating christology within the larger discussion of God as ultimate source of human moral capacities, is that christology is first and foremost a Christian confession about *God*. It is a confession that God is love, that love always reaches out beyond itself in order to intend and to exchange goodness with the beloved, and thus that God is radically relational. And furthermore it is a confession that God is love not abstractly but concretely and historically: in Jesus of Nazareth, God shows us that to be God is to be essentially and radically open to the exchange of goodness with others. It is for this reason that Jesus is confessed by Christians to be the revelation of God—not as though in Jesus we learn what God wants for us to know about what Jesus was like, but rather that in Jesus we learn what God wants for us to know about being loved by God and thus enabled to be faithful to God. It is in learning this about God, then, that we co-learn about being human.

This is, then, the reason why the Christian community came relatively early on in its existence to think of Jesus not only as a child or "son of God," not only as a heavenly redeemer figure or "son of man," not only as the embodiment of a paradigmatic human being or eschatological "last Adam," and not only as the "Wisdom" or the "Word" of God historically available to historical persons. In addition to and beyond all of these, by the end of the first century, Christians came to think of Jesus as God-in-the-flesh.[14] Once again, however, we must caution ourselves against thinking that the ultimate motive for such thinking was to think of Jesus Himself, as though He were the ultimate target of their theology. He was not. Instead, they were interested in clarifying who God was and how their knowledge of God had been significantly revised and enriched in their encounter with Jesus, which is why we need not be dismayed by the lag between Jesus' death and resurrection on the one hand and the earliest confession of Him as God incarnate on the other. All of the titles and images we have from these early centuries, especially the first, indicate that Jesus was the avenue or means to God. In traditionally systematic terms, christology then was located within soteriology, neither competing with it on the one hand nor becoming relativistic and peripheral on the other.[15]

How, then, should we understand the significance of Jesus in a way that avoids the extremes we have thus far identified and yet warrants His permanent and unsurpassable significance in the Christian understanding of God? To begin an answer here which this study can suggest but cannot complete, we turn first to the notion of human beings as radically open to self-transcending and then to God's self-transcendence as the ultimate condition rendering that human situation possible.[16]

Human beings are able to become other than what they originally are. Given everything we believe about the evolutionary provenance of all forms of existence, including the human, this is not exactly startling. What renders it significant for this study, however, is that human beings are able *intentionally* to become other than what they originally are. That is, while the rest of cosmic reality self-transcends in what we can only call a passive form, moving toward higher forms of differentiation and life as an expression of the formal and gracious nature of the cosmos itself working upon each part of the cosmos from the "outside,"[17] human beings actively and internally grasp what is only passively present to everything else and *deliberately* identify, intend, and achieve occasions of physical, intellectual, psychological, and spiritual growth. So far as we know, human beings are the only cosmic beings so constituted as to be able to do this.[18]

This affirmation is itself a recognition and in fact a summation of innumerable human observations. If it is a true affirmation, though, then it is at the same time an articulation of a universal condition in which humans find themselves and over which they have no control. In more classically philosophical terms, it is an *a priori* truth discovered *a posteriori*. It is *a posteriori* in that it reflects and summarizes what observations tell us about the things human beings do, and it is *a priori* in that such observations, if accurate, reveal and display the condition that initiates the possibility of human beings doing those things in the first place. I believe that this is the ultimate way to refer to the condition of "grace" since we do not have control over it (and, as a theological statement, God does) but since it allows us to be what we are: morally free and responsible.

This latter point is not unimportant, because it has to do with a condition that exerts some kind of influence upon human possibilities. Typically, I think, we view human possibilities as *un*conditioned, or as free, limited only by the boundaries that face us at the far edges of human existence itself.[19] The language of "conditions" thus always appears intrusive, colliding with what we take to be fundamentally true of human existence, that is, its freedom. But this alleged collision is illusory, not because "conditions" would not somehow impair and impede our freedom but instead because *freedom* is the ultimate condition governing and bounding human existence. Aside from directly theological statements about God, then, the most fundamental thing that may be said about human existence is that it is free. Said the other way around, except for explicitly theological ones, the most fundamental and universal condition of human existence is that of freedom.[20]

Why is this an important constituent within the proximate discussion of christology and the more fundamental discussion of God as the ground of loving? Because when conceived as all-but-radically free,[21] human beings are *thereby* conceived as all-but-radically open to self-transcending possibilities. Foremost among these in this particular context is the possibility of being open to God. In no way is it derogatory of human freedom to be open in faith to God so that one's concrete human life expresses in halting fashion what God intends of human life. But if this is true (i.e., possible), then in no way is it derogatory of human freedom to be so open in faith to God that one's concrete human life expresses fully and completely all God intends of that human life in its historical context and culture. Granted, it may be unlikely and improbable, but it is nonetheless fully compatible with what we have observed about human life that it is *possible*.

Once this point is grasped, then it is only a small step to link up this abstract but real possibility with the concrete and historical life of Jesus of Nazareth as Christian faith conceives of Him. The whole point of the murky and at times conceptually convoluted christological language of person, nature, hypostasis, prosopon, homoousios, and all of the rest, is to translate this point into intellectual precision: if human beings are essentially open to the possibility of self-transcendence, then it is historically possible for this self-transcendence to be so actualized that one in fact lives a life concretely reflective of everything God both intends for human beings on the one hand and graciously offers to them on the other. For Christians, at least, Jesus was that person.

I said earlier, though, that christology is proximately but not ultimately concerned with Jesus, and that its longer-range target is God. To make the same point more clearly now, it is not of ultimate interest to christology to claim merely that Jesus was what God wanted us all to be. Considered by itself, this would be historically fascinating and perhaps even transfixing but not much else.[22] In specific, it would not be *theological.* Grammatically put, all of the traditional christological titles (for example, Son, Word, Wisdom, Messiah-Christ)[23] are *genitives*; that is, they focus our attention eventually upon the God whose Son (or Word, or Wisdom, or Christ) Jesus was. Thus, we need to pay attention to *God* in this context, not only as a nice or expected thing to do but precisely as our way of echoing the earliest christological insistence that in Jesus of Nazareth the very presence of God is encountered on earth.

If this early insistence is to be understood, and more importantly if it is to be maintained in our day, then what christology confesses about Jesus must be able to be true only as an expression of what God was intending and accomplishing from the divine side of things. That is, if it is true that in Jesus of Nazareth we encounter the very presence of God, then, unless this presence was a sham (or, even less likely, the presence of another god), it is possible for God so to transcend the conditions of divinity itself that God became a human being in concrete history. Not surprisingly, this is what the earliest Christians believed about their encounter with Jesus: "in [Christ] the whole fullness of deity dwells bodily, and you have come to fullness of life in him."[24]

This is, I think, the fundamental theological inclination that frames the traditional Christian confession that God is love. In love, especially that form displayed by God which thus characterizes our possibilities as well, the lover does not simply exchange things with the beloved, regardless of how sophisticated and spiritual those things are. Instead, and far beyond this level of exchange, the lover offers up his or her own *presence* to the beloved in intense and deliberate invitation, promising to accept the beloved's reciprocal offer in turn. But such an offer cannot be made and accepted without both lover and beloved becoming permeated with the other, charged by the other's resident presence, and thus a new person even though in the same formal identity as before. All other expressions of self-transcendence pale before this one, not as though meaningless but rather as symbolic, pointing to that ultimate Self-becoming-other that gives possibility and hence substance to the lesser expressions of the same.

The self-transcendence of love is thus at the same time a self-transformation, for the "new" presence of the beloved cannot but make a difference in the life of the lover. And for precisely the same reason, it cannot help but make a difference in the life of the beloved as well. In loving one who was other-than-God, God became other-than-God and thus beckoned that other-than-God to the new kind of existence we all too blithely call human. The newness of that new existence was precisely the presence of God within it, generating for the first time in the cosmos the historical possibility of material reality able to transcend itself in knowledge, love, hope, and community. That is who Christ was definitely and thus what God intends for all of humanity. Hence it is also what christology is: the Christian community's faltering attempt to articulate the self-initiated outward movement of God whereby materiality itself became the vehicle for God's very presence and thus became human. To be human is to *be* the presence of the immaterial God in material form. That is, human beings are the self-expressions of God. We are human only because of the prior self-transcending movement of God whereby material life was grasped in love by God and thereby rendered the material presence of God in the world. The possibility of receiving God's presence, which is nothing other than God's self-revelation, presupposes an affinity between the giver and the gift. But since in this case giver and gift are both persons, the material must be constituted *as* person in order to be able to receive the gift. Putting the matter quite ungrammatically, human nature *is* what God has revealed it to be—

come: to be human is to be the divinely constituted vehicle of God's presence.

It is not simply the case that God's self-transcendence in love initiated a change in material being. It also rendered a change in God. It is this "newness" in God that serves as the ground-level experience that the doctrine of the Holy Spirit tries to look back upon with some kind of intelligibility.

God's Goodness as the Ground of Hoping (Spirit)

We may now return to the notion of hope, first recalling a few features discussed in Chapter 3. There I noted that hope conceptually presupposes certain things about the way we are in the world: that we exist here as beings capable of drawing upon the past in order to influence the future for good, that the reality of such existence presupposes the relative changeability of the "future,"[25] and that our commitment to influence the future for good is in itself an expression or function of goodness residing concretely in the world. Not surprising, it is the specifically personal expressions or objects of hope that will be of greatest interest to the discussion of hope and the Holy Spirit.

If love is, as defined in Chapter 3, the gratuitous exchange of self-surpassing behaviors and intentions concerning a beloved's concrete existence, then hope is a constituent element of love itself. This is because we cannot intend the self-transcendence of our beloved without thereby having an image of what we wish for him or her to become. By definition, this image differs from the beloved's present to the degree that it is presently-hoped-for; that is, we do not hope for what is but instead for how that "is" may be improved or transformed and thus made new.

That future transformation, though, or what we presently hope for in the life of our beloved, cannot occur without our participation, for we noted as well in Chapter 3 that it violates the moral character of hope to hope for something but yet refuse to do whatever we can to bring it about. It does this, once again, because goodness is dynamic; "goodness beckons." Thus, when the beloved's life is transformed in the ways we had hoped, under normal circumstances that transformation occurs at least in part because of our specific and concrete contribution to the other's life.[26]

Thus far, this analysis seems fairly tame, perhaps even commonplace. If so, then the addition of one more commonplace observation might well precipitate one that is not, namely how both the lover and the beloved are changed in the specifically personal expression of hope called love. Thus far we have looked at things from our own perspective in the present rather than the beloved's perspective in the future. Approached from the latter perspective, though, things appear somewhat different. Shifting our gaze to the actuality of fulfilled goodness and away from the initiation of intended goodness, we see that fulfilled goodness or realized hope has been made actual only by the participation of the lover in the beloved's life. I (the beloved) am now different, once again, to the degree that the lover's hopes have been realized in me by the actual donation of goodness that constitutes the difference between then and now. And when this transformation is viewed within specifically moral contexts, I am not only different but also *new*, precisely because I have been changed by goodness at the very core or center of what it means for me to be human.

Without meaning to be either trite or melodramatic, then, one of the constitutive purposes of hope is the coming-into-being of a new person. And because love is itself constitutively reciprocal, we can say that an even larger purpose of hope is the coming-into-being of new persons. And finally, we can go one step further: because love has as its usual shape not just the abstract desire for self-transcendence but in fact the historical actuality of self-transcendences as well (i.e., realized hope), then we can say that under normal circumstances love is not present where concrete expressions of self-transcendence are not. Where a new person has not been brought into being, there love is not.[27] Conversely, where there is a (morally) new person, regardless of the incremental degree of the change, love is present.

The doctrine of the Holy Spirit as Christians have understood it (especially, if we are to be honest, more recently)[28] insists not only that God is not immune from this same process of self-transformation and change but in addition that God's own self-transformation is the very ground of its possibility. In freely and lovingly becoming embodied, God not only became the ground of the possibility of human being itself, as we saw in the discussion of christology above, but in addition became a "new" God.

What we are tempted hastily to add here is not so much that God became new, but rather that our notion of what and how God is became new. This is understandable; it is neither mere fundamentalism nor mere skittishness that insists that one of God's attributes is unchangeability. But we must recognize as well that the enormous difficulty into which the Christian tradition deliberately entered concerning the threefoldedness of the one God had as its ultimate intention more than mere notional or doctrinal development. The tradition had this intention, but precisely and only because of its experience of God now known as Father of Jesus. Once the early Church came to the realization that Jesus embodied what Jewish tradition had called the Word of God and the Son of God, and embodied them in the same person, and in fact embodied them precisely as God incarnate rather than as historical or personal accident,[29] then the stage was set for the insight that God's coming-into-flesh was itself not historically bound but was instead a permanent feature of the God whose love of the world was permanent, whose presence in the world was permanent, and thus whose desire to be loved by the world was permanent as well. That is, the early Church discovered what had been true of God all along: God is ultimately relational. The change signaled by the emerging language of incarnation resided not just in the minds of the early Christian believers but more fundamentally in their inspired discovery that God's self-transcendence itself grounded the very possibility of their love and faith to begin with. "We love because He first loved us" (1 John 4:19).

God's relationality is expressed not merely with respect to the world but intrinsically and eternally as well, and thus as a permanent feature of the very being of God. Rightly or wrongly, the early Church came to articulate this insight as the only expressible ground of its experience of salvation through Christ. Its best-known confessions were themselves attempts to distill this relationality into words: God is love; God is good(ness); Jesus is the Son of God. Of course, each of these faltered in saying precisely what was intended. Why should we expect otherwise? However, each also succeeds in uncovering another facet of God's dynamic and self-expressing relationality.

One cannot enter into relationality without thereby entering into the possibility of newness and change. If this is true on the "horizontal" or historical plane, then it certainly cannot be less so on the plane that constitutes the transcendent ground of the possibility of that historical one. This is nothing other than a conceptual or metaphysical rephrasing of what the early Christians said about God more concretely: "in [Christ] the whole fullness of deity dwells bodily, and you have come to fullness of life in him" (Colossians 2:9); "in Christ, God was reconciling the world to Himself" (2 Corinthians 5:19); and so on. Here, even before the crystallized incarnational language of the later first century, we see the early insistence that God acted in a new (but still saving) way in Christ. In so loving the Son that the very self and character of God could be identified in Him, the Father became new.

In our day, we are constantly inclined to interpret these and similar statements in specifically and anthropologically soteriological ways, preferring to think first and last about ourselves as receivers of grace and salvation. In particular, we are inclined *not* to interpret them in specifically theological ways, that is, in ways that reflect upon God as initiator of grace and salvation. One should not separate too surgically between these, of course. I prefer to think of them as opposite sides of the same coin—opposite and thus permanently attached. And it is precisely as statements about God that we see the self-transcending and becoming-new aspects of God's self-revelation. On our end of things, we are not made new creatures in Christ apart from a corresponding newness in God.

How is this newness on God's part to be understood? Certainly we are wise to avoid the language and also the thought of what philosophers call formal causality here, the thought that the creature's love of God causes a change in God's essence or (to use the scholastic equivalent) God's subsistence. I think that the best reason to avoid such language is that it envisions an inadequate image of God: as autonomous and utterly self-reliant Being who from a grace that is distinguishable from God's very essence created and therefore loved the world.[30] Better than this is the view that God's very essence is to be the "to-be" of all existence.[31] Thus, because

God *is* love—that is, because God's to-be is love and love is essentially reciprocal—God is essentially related to the world as the beloved or the receiver of that love.

Here we get to the point: if it is of the very essence of God to-be-related, then that relationality is not "begun" or grounded at the point of the creation of the external world but constitutes instead an interior function of God's very Being. This is the embryonic truth wriggling into intelligibility in the Johannine claim that "God so loved the world that He gave His only-begotten Son" (John 3:16). In more formal trinitarian language, Thomas later expresses the thought that "the Holy Spirit is the love whereby the Father loves the Son."[32] The Holy Spirit is the Father's love for the Son and vice versa, not something that merely relates the two or something that is externally created out of this love, but precisely as a "new" Person in God who is constituted *as* the personal love of Father and Son for each other. And further, this newness is not merely a personal relationality within the divine Godhead but is constitutive of creaturely love as well. That is why Thomas can go on to say in the same breath that "the Holy Spirit is the love whereby the Father loves the Son, and also the love whereby he loves the creature." When viewed from the perspective of humanity, spirit is that divine gift, that donation borne of love, whereby we as material beings are constituted toward spiritual self-transcendence and thus toward moral growth and newness. When viewed from the perspective of divinity, Spirit is the dynamic ground of that possibility, the intention of the Father to love the Son and of the Son to love the Father. Out of that love was constituted a Being so essentially personal that we could never be in the presence of God without thereby being in the presence of love, and we could never be in the presence of love without being in the presence of (the Spirit of) God. It is in this sense and for this reason that earlier I did not hesitate to say that "love is God."

William J. Hill considers the newness of God in a passage so moving that I think that it is worth citing at length:

> Intersubjectivity is thus dependent upon the degree to which persons unveil, communicate, and commit themselves to others— as well as choose to respond to the self-bestowal of others.[33] There is surely no reason why such personal becoming cannot be under-

gone in relationality to the three Persons of divinity. But is there any reason to deny that God himself, remaining immutable in his nature, can choose *to become on the level of personhood*? May not God choose to relate as he will to a community of finite persons with the free intentionality of intimate knowing and loving, becoming towards men the kind of God his love elects? God's love lets the finite person be in its very otherness, in its freedom and becoming. As it enacts itself, God's awareness of it must alter; he must come to know and love what he did not know and love before as actual in a finite way. This seemingly bespeaks a "becoming" in God within the domain of intentionality analogous at least to the personal becoming of men—once again, however, without implying acquisition by God of intrinsic perfection previously lacking to him. Perhaps to try and speak of becoming in God in this fashion . . . is to attempt to say too much. . . . But at least we can say: should this loving exchange be at all a possibility, its language will be rooted in a symbolism of person rather than a metaphysics of being. Such language is at bottom prayer; it is the speech of mystics and prophets rather than of theologians.[34]

Earlier in this chapter we saw that hope is love intended in the present and expressed in the future. When thought of only at present, it is precisely hope. When thought of as realized in the future, though, it is also goodness, transcendentally and communitarianly actualized. It is the former because of the nature of hope, which is to criticize the present and strain toward its improvement in the future. It is the latter for two reasons: first and more obviously because we usually hope with other persons in mind,[35] second and less obviously because the person in whom our hoped-for intention is actualized, whether that be ourselves or the other, is then constituted as a new and thus an "other" person precisely to the degree that goodness has flowed into that life and brought about its transcendence.

God's Goodness as the Ground of Community (Trinity)

Chapter 3 began with a reference to the difficulty St. Augustine faced in his attempt to render the experience of the Trinity understandable without obscuring either the experience itself or God's presence within it. It is not a gratuitous criticism of the theological reflection on God the Trinity since then to suggest that Augustine's task has yet to be completed. I shall not complete the task within this book, either. I can, however, offer some clues to how the experience of God as Trinity (Father, Son, Holy Spirit) grounds the experience of humanity as a community existing within the conditions of time and history. My target here is not to summarize all of contemporary theology concerning the Trinity or even to show how the Christian doctrine of the Trinity[36] is more than mere speculation about divinity. Far more importantly, I would claim that this doctrine grounds the part of Christian tradition that insists that the community (rather than simply the individual within it) is both the effect and the goal of divine revelation. The Trinity is God acting personally and communitarianly within history, not abstractly but concretely, constituting the possibility of the human community's response in faith and commitment, and thus rendering that community a community of God.[37]

It is by now a theological commonplace that trinitarian doctrine developed out of christological reflection. (This is not, of course, equivalent to the claim that God *became* Trinity.) To put the matter only a little too bluntly, the early Christian communities did not begin to think about the third Person of the Godhead until they had achieved comfortable conformity in their thinking about the second. The reason for this delay is also well known: the Jewish provenance of Christianity insisted upon the undifferentiatedness of God regardless of the extent of differentiation present within human reflections upon God. In this respect at least, Christianity did not intend to be explicitly anti-Jewish.

It did have to come to terms, though, with its own experience of God in Jesus, whose *abba*-consciousness formed the basis for the later confession of Jesus as Son. As this confession took hold, emboldening further and deeper reflection upon Jesus as divine and as God, there naturally arose the suspicion that the Father and Jesus were different gods. This may be seen in Origen's dialogue with Heraclides. The latter was so careful to distinguish the Father (as God) from the Son (as God) that he affirmed that their "unity is a unity of two Gods [whose] power is one."[38] The orthodox or centrist response to this suspicion ultimately insisted that that which related the Father and Jesus was itself fully and coequally divine. This avoided the problem of a primal God (what Heraclides here names "power") existing prior to the Father and Son and granting their divinity to them, while avoiding the opposite problem of two utterly unrelated gods. We have already seen this orthodox resolution, articulated by Thomas but resident within Christian theology long before: "the Holy Spirit is the love whereby the Father loves the Son [and the Son loves the Father]." With this step, further enumeration concerning the "persons" in the Godhead came to rest.

It is tempting at this point to rehearse the long and often contorted process whereby the actual relations between and among the persons of the Trinity nestled into conceptual canonicity, focusing on (among others) the terms *mission, spiration, hypostasis, perichoresis, appropriation, subordination*, and the like.[39] What is more useful for our purposes here, though, is the reminder of a few paragraphs back, namely that the doctrine of the Trinity is first and foremost a doctrine of the mystery of divine salvation experienced in Jesus and thus in history. That is, in Jesus the early Christians experienced God (Yahweh) in full and in flesh, whose presence now perceived as a human person triggered an experience of salvation that was continuous with but also incomparably more affectionate than that enjoyed by their Old Testament ancestors. Being loved by Jesus was, for them, indistinguishable from being loved by Yahweh, and the guarantee of this identity was that "God's love has been shed abroad in our hearts through the Holy Spirit which has been given to us," enabling us to call God *abba* as well because it is "the Spirit itself co-witnessing with our spirits that we are children of God."[40] The Holy Spirit is love existing between the Father and Jesus, grasping us in that same love (indeed, could there be any other?), bringing us into the very communion of God, drawing us out of the historical realm and into the divine just as surely as that same love drew the Father out of the divine realm and into the historical. "Trinity" is God revealed and experienced in history as knower and as known, as lover and as beloved, as hoped for and as constituted new.

As human beings, we experience the world in knowledge, love, and hope, and thus in community. Ever since the Enlightenment, Western philosophy and theology have struggled to think of human beings as individuals, at times even as autonomous ones. That has been a tragic struggle, for as autonomous we are least, not most, the image and likeness of God. When we are ourselves, we reflect God—as images, to be sure, but nonetheless as images of the threefold and communitarian God. The Christian tradition has long insisted that that *is* human existence. Faith recognizes and willingly grasps, but does not create, this structure. Instead, God's self-bursting and self-transcending revelation creates it, bringing human beings into existence as embodied spirits able to know, to love, to hope, and to live in communion with God and with the world.

Conclusion

We arrive at the end of our journey, having addressed ourselves to both of my original intentions. The first was the negative intention of pointing out what I believed to be weaknesses within representative and influential theories of divine revelation. Those weaknesses ranged from the extreme to the subtle: from James I. Packer's rather arbitrary designation of certain bits of information (i.e., biblical ones) as revelation, echoed by William J. Abraham's arbitrary designation of certain bits of historical events (i.e., miraculous ones) as revelation, to Gerald O'Collins's seeming resolve not to think of the content of divine revelation but to pay strict attention instead to the formal christological and trinitarian elements in what was handed down to him in tradition as divine revelation. The theologians surveyed in the first part variously displayed the posture of impersonalness, the inability or unwillingness to consider how the believing human being was a constituent element within the relational notion of divine revelation, preferring instead to view those human beings as spectators or observers in the very process those same theologians insisted was intended to bring us to salvation. The theologians surveyed in the second part variously displayed the posture of circularity, the inability or unwillingness to consider the material criteria by which certain things were, and other things were not, able to be trustworthily defined as revelation, but also not addressing the question of the notional criteria of "revelation" lest, perhaps, those criteria were met by persons and traditions outside of the Christian one.

I tried to wend my way through these various obstacles. I began this venture because of my initial uneasiness with most traditional theories of revelation. This book offers, I trust, a serious if admittedly incomplete attempt to suggest why it is that revelation reveals. Philosophers would say that I am indulging in meta-critical revelational conceptualizing, a description that is not bad in spite of its turgidity. That is, I have tried to suggest in this book where I think that future (Christian) treatises on divine revelation should go, not in contradistinction to what the Christian tradition has accepted as revealed but instead precisely in view of it. It is only *because* revelation reveals that we can ask *how* it does so. But answering the *how* question by definition takes us beyond the *that* one, and into waters that are relatively uncharted by Christian thinkers.

My second overall intention was the more constructive one of suggesting how a Christian theory of divine revelation should proceed if it were interested in avoiding these same difficulties. In trying to avoid the first weakness of arbitrariness and impersonalness, for example, I tried to show that revelation (in its Christian sense) constitutes or grounds the possibility of certain historical beings as *human* beings. Something exists by which to define what humans are and how they differ from nonhumans, and whatever that something is must be identifiable either intrinsically or organically with divine revelation if the latter is not to be seen as arbitrary (and thus legitimately avoidable; only a thing within human consciousness rather than the very constitution of that consciousness itself) or impersonal (and thus humanly irrelevant). In trying to avoid the second weakness of circularity, I tried to show that what the Church has experienced as revelation was experienced and called that because of the ultimate grounding of those experiences in the trinitarian God. Certain kinds of experiences, that is, while occurring in the natural world of time and space and regularity and materiality and the like, nevertheless mediate the presence of God to persons within that world. When looked at from this perspective, clearly it seems hopeless (conceptually and not simply historically) to try to compress all revelational experiences into a categorical or canonical list. This is the mistake that in my opinion most Christian thinkers committed: in trying to come up with such a list, they presumed the criteria for its construction and thus have not been of much critical help. In place of that list, they simply rehearsed what believers in the past took as revelational events and experiences. That might have been appropriate for believers in earlier ages, but

for better and for worse we live in a critical age and ought not rest
content with uncritical accounts. What is needed instead, I think, is
to try to say how it is that God acts in the world in ways that
Christian believers have experienced as revelational and then determine what the general and thus most basic effects of those experiences have been, never forgetting that those effects were divinely
produced and hence divinely disclosive.

Human beings are, I concluded, the earthly beings most fully
capable of knowing, loving, and hoping, and thus of existing within
community. While it is increasingly difficult to define a human
being in airtight categories, surely at the very least humans display
these relational features most fully and completely. What each one
of them presupposes, however, is goodness and, specifically, a
personal involvement (or relationship) with goodness. But *goodness* is how Christians have characteristically described God, not as
one attribute among many but instead as that which fundamentally
designates God's moral essence and (lest that word seem too static)
disposition. Thus, in being what humans are most fully, we are
thereby relationally affiliated with God in an experientially unavoidable (although consciously deniable) fashion.

In my final attempt to define revelation as Christians encounter
and experience it, I tried to say what was trinitarian about it. The
general failure to tackle this problem is the most obvious weakness
of traditional Christian theories of revelation, even if it is not the
most important one. Seen in this light, is it not somewhat bizarre to
say (for example) that certain inexplicable or miraculous events are
(by stipulation) divine revelation, when one has not yet even tried to
say anything about the God who is allegedly revealed through
them? The ancient Israelites were convinced that many gods ex-
isted, for example, and that all of them could speak and act in
history, and that those speeches and acts were therefore inexplicable except by recourse to the gods. We are not much different in our
day. We, too, believe that certain historical events are inexplicable,
and the only difference is that in place of their "except by recourse
to the gods," we insert "in view of the limits of natural laws and
scientific hypotheses." But if it is not the case that everything
inexplicable is caused by God, it is even less the case that everything
inexplicable reveals God, as anyone who has taken the time to track
the post-Enlightenment "God of the gaps" has discovered.

What was needed here, then, as before, was some kind of linkage between the experience of human beings on the one hand and the trinitarian God whom Christians confess on the other. And this linkage needed to surpass both the arbitrariness and the circularity of traditional theories of revelation so that, again as before, we would not be left with a theory that made sense only to Christians and not to anyone else. Doing our homework only this far would itself be a denial of a part of God's revelation, in particular the part that discloses to us the insight that God is creator of heaven, of earth, and of all human beings in both.

As before, then, we discovered that it is possible to observe this linkage in the same features of human beings, namely that we are capable of knowing, loving, and hoping, and that doing these locates us in a community of persons. In view of this observation, it is appropriate to inquire one step further: how, if at all, it is possible to ground it in (the trinitarian) God. And this is what Chapter 4 addressed. This grounding is religiously satisfying both because it is true to the nature of religious observations concerning the world (and especially that which situates them between mere coherence on the one hand and metaphysical or logical necessity on the other) and because it relates God as Father, Son, and Spirit to human beings as knowers, lovers, and hopers.

Now, what has all of this to do with divine revelation? The usual definition of revelation is that "God speaks to us" or "God discloses to us." But that definition completely takes for granted, and pays no deliberate attention at all to, the fact that we are beings to whom God *can* speak, to whom God *can* disclose. And paying no attention to that fact left unaddressed the question of why God does not do the same thing with rocks and paint cans, which none of us wants to believe. Divine revelation cannot simply refer to *what* God says or discloses to us, therefore. It must refer instead, at its heart and at its deepest level, to how God has made us—what God has brought into being precisely in order to receive God's gracious self-expressions—what human beings are as the highest and best expression of life currently on earth—that is, beings with whom God can relate. It is in those beings, we human beings, who can know, who can love, who can hope, who can live in relational community, that we see who the God is who has made us and whose self-disclosures we are.

In this sense, then, I hope that I both have and have not suggested a new way of thinking about divine revelation. On the one hand, there are references and connections made above that, if not strictly new, are most likely unusual. The clearest example of this is the extension of the notion of revelation itself to include not only the overcoming of sin but in addition the very existence of material beings capable of self-transcending moral decisions and activities. This is not intended as a direct or frontal attack upon that part of the Christian tradition that has interpreted the place of revelation in more narrowly soteriological terms. It is instead intended to say how the self-disclosing act of God that we call revelation functions on a much more fundamental level than sin by itself, a level presupposed by the mere possibility of moral behavior. If moral behavior were not possible, sin would not be, either (which is why the Christian tradition does not apply the effects of salvation to animals). But if it is, then revelation must be directed to that more fundamental or presupposed realm of behavior, lest it be untouched by God's self-revealing love.

It is in this respect, then, that I hope that I have not said anything new about divine revelation. If God is Trinity, that is, self-transcending knowledge, love, and hope, expressed and received within the divine community of the Godhead, then the mere possibility of human beings constituted as knowers, lovers, and hopers in community is best accounted for when it is grounded in the divine community. But clearly human beings are thus constituted, and thus grounded as well. It in this sense, then, that a theological account that says so is not new but instead old—as old as the emergence of human being itself.

That is what I hope to have accomplished here. If God is as central to the existence and the constitution of human beings as the Christian tradition has insisted, then theories of divine revelation should not rest content in simply presenting a God whose presence is morally optional as the ground of human existence. Human beings are free to deny their groundedness in God, of course, because the freedom in which God approaches us finds its complement in the freedom that is ours to respond in either faith or unfaith. This book has examined that foundational groundedness and has suggested that it is what constitutes divine revelation.

APPENDIX
GOD'S KNOWLEDGE OF
THE FUTURE: PRELIMINARY
AFTERTHOUGHTS

What I have written thus far is based on a certain assumption concerning God and time and, more particularly, God's knowledge of the future. My own view is that God cannot know the future in anything approaching the way God has traditionally been said to be able to. This contends with the vast bulk of the Christian tradition concerning this question, in particular the two theologians who have been the most significant in my own formation, Thomas Aquinas and John Calvin. And it surely contends with the group with whom I most readily associate myself, American evangelicals. Thus, it is not advanced, or held, lightly.

The following does not constitute a full-blown defense of the position that God cannot know the future but is rather a preliminary outline of the various kinds of warrants and arguments I believe can and should be marshalled in such a defense. From the outset I would insist that the probable effect of the following upon a "traditional" believer will be logically unpersuasive. But I do not believe that it will be rhetorically unpersuasive, especially if that believer pays close attention to how he or she functions as a believer in the world and then checks out the arguments and experiences that form the grounds discussed below concerning the question of God's knowledge of the future. If this is done, it will be seen that a wide slice of one's normal religious experience has been addressed. More negatively put, it will be seen that not much room remains from which to continue to defend the traditional view. It is my hypothesis that Christian believers routinely assert the traditional belief concerning God's knowledge of the future but routinely behave just the opposite. The following is offered as a catalyst to bring this ambivalence to the surface.

I. The Traditional View

A. Traditionally, the question of God's knowledge has begun and ended with the question of divine omniscience. The property of divine omniscience has been taken to mean that God's knowledge is comprehensive and infallible. That God's knowledge is comprehensive means that God knows everything, whether that thing refers to an event (etc.) in the past, the present, or the future. Thus, God knows *right now* (2:13 P.M., March 13, 1991) with the same degree of unmistakability what *did* happen at 2:13 P.M., March 13, 991, and what *will* happen at 2:13 P.M., March 13, 24,991. That God's knowledge is infallible means that God cannot be wrong in what God knows. That is, God cannot know something that did not occur in the way God's knowledge says it did, nor can God fail to know something that did occur.

B. Both of these are essential elements in the traditional assessment of God's knowledge of things. The combination has led most theologians and philosophers to conclude that God is not "in" time but is rather outside (or beyond) time, since clearly we human beings are "in" time and we cannot know the future in the same way (much less with the same degree of certainty) that we can know the past. The word used to describe this is that God is *eternal*. The word *everlasting*, which might appear to be synonymous, is used instead to describe things that exist without beginning or end but clearly within the conditions of time and history, such as the number 3. Thus, 3 is "everlasting" whereas God is "eternal."

II. Negative Assessment of This View

The question is whether it makes any sense at all to say that God knows *right now* (2:13 P.M., March 13, 1991) with the same degree of unmistakability what *did* happen at 2:13 P.M., March 13, 991, and what *will* happen at 2:13 P.M., March 13, 24,991. (To remove the well-known problems of verb tensing in this example, we can replace "right now" with "T_1," defining T_1 as any time subsequent to 2:13 P.M., March 13, 991 but prior to 2:13 P.M., March 13, 24,991.) The problem is not with God's knowledge of the past, of course, but instead with God's knowledge of the future. That is, does it make any sense at all to say that God can know something that has not yet happened? Three negative answers suggest themselves.

A. *The argument from physics* begins with the notion of time itself. What is time? Is it simply and completely what our watches and calendars ultimately measure, the movement of the earth around the sun? Is time the title for a movement of physical bodies in proximity to each other? There are reasons for and against this understanding. The latter seem persuasive enough to come up with another definition of time.

1. Reasons for:

a. This *is* what our clocks and calendars tell us, and that counts for something.

b. This "gets us where we want to go" (is pragmatically beneficial) for 99.9 percent of the contexts we think of when we think of time.

2. Reasons against:

a. What about when we travel to other planets? Since they move at different speeds around the sun, whose time will register on the clocks and watches that interplanetary (let alone intergalactic) travelers take with them? (This is the basis of Einstein's theory of general relativity.)

b. What about the subjectivization of time registered by different bodies at different gravitational proximities to the same massive body? Einstein also showed that if my son Mark and I live (respectively) on Mount Everest and on the shore of the Dead Sea, he will age more quickly than I. Granted, in our lifetimes the final differential will probably be negligible, but what if he travels off into space for a while, vastly accelerating that differential? When he returns, he will be older than I. What should I then call him— Son? Dad? What happens to the notion of children when they are older than their parents?

c. We experience time differently from the rigid way this definition suggests. When we are enjoying a situation, time flies. When we hate it, time drags. Something about this difference is universal and rings true, and an adequate definition of time ought to be able to take it into consideration without thereby making time so flexible that it is useless in scientific and everyday contexts.

3. For another definition of time, instead of time being a static measurement of known physical bodies moving in proximity to each other, it is preferable to think of it conceptually or logically. That is, time is the regular succession of events. An event is itself a transformation from future (defined as relatively open possibilities) to past (defined as absolutely closed possibilities) through the present (defined as the point of logical transformation). By definition, a closed possibility cannot change, which accounts for why we think that the past cannot be changed. A relatively open possibility can be changed,[1] which accounts for why we think that the future is changeable, not determined. There are certain aspects of the future which, assuming a constant space-time location, cannot be changed (if today is Thursday, then tomorrow cannot but be Friday), but there are other aspects of the future which can be (it is completely

possible that I might eat either a chicken or a tuna sandwich for lunch tomorrow; as of today, that is an open question). So time also may be defined as future (relatively open possibilities) moving to past (absolutely closed possibilities) through the present (the moment or instant of transformation).

If this is an acceptable definition of time, then God cannot know the future as traditionally thought. For God to know the future comprehensively and infallibly means that God cannot be wrong about the future, which is another way of saying that the future cannot be other than what God knows it to be. But if this is so, then the future is exhaustively full of absolutely closed possibilities, since it must occur exactly as God knows that it will occur. But this is a definitional mistake, since it is the past and not the future that is defined as absolutely closed possibilities.

Does this mean God does *not* know the future? No. Instead, God knows the future precisely as what it is, namely relatively open possibilities. Thus, God knows all of the various possibilities that might occur at 2:13 P.M., March 13, 24,991, but God does not know comprehensively and infallibly which one(s) will occur. This suggests a refinement of the traditional notion of omniscience. Instead of omniscience referring to God's comprehensive and infallible knowledge of the future as though it were the past, it should be taken instead to refer to God's comprehensive and infallible knowledge of everything *as it is when God knows it*. This small refinement is necessary in order to realign the notion of God's knowledge so that it reflects what we believe about the notion of knowledge itself and so that it does not make God's knowledge, or God's way of knowing, so different from our own that it no longer relates to ours in any religiously useful way.

In his book *A Brief History of Time: From the Big Bang to Black Holes*,[2] Stephen W. Hawking suggests three different "arrows" by which time could be measured:

> First, there is the thermodynamic arrow of time, the direction of time in which disorder or entropy increases. Then, there is the psychological arrow of time. This is the direction in which we feel time passes, the direction in which we remember the past but not the future. Finally, there is the cosmological arrow of time. This is the direction of time in which the universe is expanding rather than contracting.[3]

With reference to the first two arrows, Hawking says that the ultimate reason why time moves in only one direction is seated in the second law of thermodynamics, which reminds us that order always tends to degenerate into disorder in the universe. An ordered state always requires a higher energy input than a disordered one.

This condition is reflected in our memories, or what Hawking calls the psychological arrow of time. He claims that the psychological arrow not only reflects but is in fact determined by the thermodynamic arrow. Thoughts are more ordered states of affairs than non-thoughts, and so we would expect them to require more energy to acquire and to maintain than non-thoughts. And sure enough, if one calculates the energy required for the brain to function normally, the body converts far more calories into heat and dissipates them into the universe than the brain needs for its functions; that is, ordered energy (food) is converted into disordered energy (dissipated heat) with but a relatively minor amount of that energy going toward the support of brain functions. The second law of thermodynamics holds true, the single direction of the psychological arrow is affirmed, and time moves in one direction only. But if this is so, then things cannot be different for God from how they are for us, with the obvious exception of the extent and quality (the infallibility) of God's knowledge of what was, what is, and the possibilities that might yet be.[4]

B. *The argument from ethics* begins from the observation (or the presupposition) that human beings are morally responsible beings. This is not optional or arbitrary but is instead essential; it is inescapably a part of what it means to be human to be morally responsible. No other earthly being is responsible, so far as we know. And, excepting the kinds of cases that pose no *theoretical* difficulties, no human being is not.

But if this is the case, then it is just as inescapable that human beings exist in a condition of relative freedom, because responsibility always and inescapably entails freedom. (A better way to say this would be to say that freedom and responsibility mutually entail each other; wherever there is the one, there is the other as well.) True, we are not free to choose our gender or our nationality, for example, but it is just as true that we are not held responsible for being (e.g.) male Americans; instead, we are held responsible for what we *do* with our maleness and our Americanness. We are responsible for things about which we have options and choices, and to have options and choices means having freedom. Without freedom, there is no relevant option or choice; there is not both alternative A and alternative B but only one of them.

However, if it is the case that God knows the future infallibly and comprehensively, then God knows precisely what we will do when we arrive at (what looks to us like) a decision to be made in (what looks to us like) the future. We will think that there is a decision to be made, but that is a significant moral delusion if God knows infallibly, for example, that we are going to choose A and not B. And if that is the case, then it is surely the case that God cannot hold us responsible for what we choose since God knew all along what that choice would be and what it would not be.[5] But then we cannot be held responsible for that choice, and most particularly we cannot be held responsible by God for that choice, since we did not have at least two real alternatives to choose between so far as God is concerned. And this means that we are never held responsible for anything we choose, since (*ex hypothesi*) God knows all of our choices comprehensively and infallibly.

But this violates the core of Christian notions of human responsibility, sin, salvation, and the like, since all of them depend essentially on some form of responsibility that we have toward God and the world. Thus, it would appear to be anti-Christian to hold that God knows the future comprehensively and infallibly since such a notion collides directly with the well-grounded Christian belief that we are morally responsible beings and that ultimately our moral responsibility is grounded in God. This is where my earlier hypothesis concerning the discontinuity between Christian assertions and behaviors is usually closest to the surface.

The usual or "orthodox" response to the position I have outlined is that there is no incompatibility here at all, and thus no need to choose between freedom and responsibility on the one hand and God's infallible knowledge of the future on the other. God knows that we will choose A in the future, but since we do not know it, we are still responsible for the choice and thus exist within the conditions of freedom and responsibility.[6] I do not think that this objection is coherent; that is, I think that it so separates God from history that it is useless as an objection within a Christian consideration of the matter. However, it is very easy simply to sidestep this objection altogether by focusing on the responsibility we have to God and not to anything else. When we do this, then it is clear that there is an incompatibility between God's comprehensive and infallible knowledge of our future choices on the one hand and our moral responsibility to God on the other, precisely because we cannot be held responsible by God for doing something God knows we cannot avoid doing.[7]

C. *The argument from liturgy* reflects on the Christian habit of prayer, specifically the kind called petitionary prayer. An example of such a prayer is "Dear God, please help me on my exam tomorrow." This may not be an acceptable type of prayer to some believers, but to those who think that it is, then the following argument is relevant.

When we pray a petitionary prayer, we normally assume some kind of stance toward the future. (Note the relevance of this to my consideration of hope above.) And that stance indluces at least the two following possibilities: (1) that I will not do well on my exam tomorrow, and (2) that I will. thus, petitionary prayers show that the praying person thinks that the future is relatively open, since clearly the person thinks that (1) might occur but that it would be preferable if (2) did. Furthermore, petitionary prayers show that the praying person thinks that something can be done to influence that future; in this case, the something is more than likely some kind of a cooperative effort by God and the person herself or himself.

The significant aspect of this argument is the observation that petitionary prayer presupposes a relatively open (or influenceable) future. Think how stupid it would be to pray "Dear God, please make $2 + 2 = 5$ tomorrow." That is, we do not pray for things we know cannot be changed, but only for things that we believe can be. Those persons who pray such prayers, therefore, do not believe that God knows the future comprehensively and infallibly, even if they think that they do, as is evident from their continued habit of praying petitionary prayers. As with the ethical argument, then, here too it seems to be the case that it is not simply conceptually inadequate but in fact anti-Christian to think that God knows the future infallibly and comprehensively.

III. Conclusion: God and Impossibility

The usual objection to the approach suggested above is that it somehow limits God by claiming that God is unable to do certain things, in this case that God is unable to know the future. The rationale for this objection is that it contradicts all of the "omni-" attributes of God to claim that God cannot do a certain thing. For example, it appears to violate God's omnipotence to say that God cannot make a certain something, and thus we always want to say that God can make anything.

The best response to this objection is to recall that there are huge categories of things we believe that God cannot do. Typically, we lump them all together and call the class of such things impossibilities. These impossibilities are of different sorts, and I shall discuss three below (logical, chronological, and moral impossibilities). But it should be recalled that these differences simply reflect the different kinds of things being considered and thus fit within the larger category of impossibility.[8]

For example, if it is logically impossible to conceive of a square triangle, then it is impossible for one to exist. But if it is impossible for a square triangle to exist, then it is equally impossible for God to make one. But so what? Who goes to bed at night thinking that God is inferior simply because God is unable to make a square triangle?

Or similarly, if it is impossible for us to conceive of changing the past, then it is impossible for us to think of God changing it. But again, whose spiritual or religious life is upset by this?

And besides, let us say just for the sake of the argument that God did change the past from A (what we used to think happened in the past) to B (what God has now changed the past into). Then God would also have to change all of those memories we have of A into memories of B; otherwise, God's knowledge of the past and our knowledge of the past would be incompatible, and we would never be able to know which was the real past. But if God changes A into B and *also* changes all of our A memories into B memories, then when God is finished with all of those changes we have no more A memories left. But if we now have no more A memories, then we have no more memory of A but instead only of B. So in that case what has changed? If God has changed A into B and has changed all of our A memories into B memories, then A has completely disappeared as something that happened. So from our point of view, nothing has changed: the past was and always will be B.

Finally, if it is impossible for us to conceive of a morally justified murder (which is true by definition since *murder* means "unjustified taking of life"; if there is any justification for the death, then the category shifts to something like manslaughter, etc.), then it is impossible for us to conceive of God murdering someone. But so what? My guess is, in fact, that we are a great deal happier with this "restriction" on God's omnipotence than we would be if we discovered that God really could do anything at all, especially if it included murder.

The above three examples are restrictions on God's "omni-" attributes. That seems to be clear, especially if one assumes the traditional perspective. But if we are comfortable with any of these restrictions, much less with all of them, then what is different with the restriction concerning God's knowledge of the future (which, it appears, is simply another instance within the chronological category)? If, in fact, one defines the future as I did above, then it is impossible for God to know it in the traditional sense. But if it is not an offense to faith for God not to be able to do things that cannot be done, as the preceding three paragraphs show and, I would claim, with which we are all familiar and comfortable, then we need not lose sleep over this "restriction" either.

IV. Related Topic: Is God "In" Time?

Ninety percent of Christian believers and theologians believe that God is outside of time. I disagree. I think that God is "in" time. The traditional position has two general kinds of defense (A and B), to which I will respond (A.1 and B.1) and then enlarge with another line of argument altogether (B.2).

A. Time is a creation of God. The assumption here is that time was created by God at the point at which everything else was created, and thus for God to be "in" time would be unwarranted for the same reason that it is unwarranted to think of God as "in" history, "in" materiality, and the like. In specific christological terms, the error here seems to be similar to Arianism.

B. Time as a consequence of change. This is the specific objection of Aquinas, who thought that to be involved in time meant irreducibly that one was involved in change, either for the better or for the worse.[9] But if that is true, then for God to be in time would mean that God changed, too, either for the better or for the worse. But both are inappropriate with respect to God because of their implications: either that God is getting better, which means that God is inferior now, or else that God is getting worse, which is wrong on the surface. Since we do not want to say either of these about God, then it must be the case that God is beyond the category of change, and hence of time, altogether.

A.1. Ever since the notion of incarnation occurred to Christians, it is no longer possible to say simply that God cannot be involved "in" any part of creation. On the surface of it at least, surely it is more difficult to conceive of God being "in" materiality than it is to conceive of God being "in" time. The ease and regularity with which we do the former should make us think twice about refusing even to consider the latter.

B.1. Aquinas would be right by definition had he claimed only that to be involved in change is to be involved in time. But he claimed the opposite: to be involved in time is to be involved in change. That does not seem right. Surely we all know of things that are involved in time (e.g., the number 3) which are unchanging as well. More importantly, Aquinas seems to have overlooked the nature of human beings here (and others as well, but they do not interest me at the moment). With respect to human beings, who all insist are "in" time, there are two levels or spheres to discuss: that which changes over time and that which does not. Examples of the first are our physicality, our intellectual capacities and expressions, and the like. Examples of the latter are our spirit itself, our materiality itself (i.e., that we are material bodies, not the form and shape of those material bodies at any given instant), and the like. That is, my eight-year-old daughter and I have different capacities, physical sizes, and shapes, and lots of other things, many of which change over time. But we are both, and equally, and completely, human. She is no less human simply because she has not yet learned about quadratic equations and Chandresekhar's limit, and I am no more human because I have. Both of us are fully and equally human. Thus, there are things that exist in time and do change over time, and there are also things that exist in time but do not. So it is not the case that for God to be involved in time would necessarily entail that all aspects of God change for the better or for the worse, which is what Aquinas feared. Some aspects of God's divine nature might well change (e.g., God's actual love for me, which God by definition could not display a thousand years ago but which God does display today), whereas other aspects do not (e.g., God's trinitarian nature, God's promise to love and to save the world, etc.). Thus, this objection needs more nuance about what kinds of divine things do, and do not, change when considered from within time.

B.2. Finally, another type of objection altogether. I suggested earlier that time is the (logical) process whereby relatively open possibilities are transformed into absolutely closed ones. Thus, the claim that God is in time is equivalent to the claim that God is involved in the process whereby relatively open possibilities are transformed into absolutely closed ones. The way to examine the rightness of this claim is thus to examine whether there is at least one instance in which God has been involved in such a process. There is: incarnation.

Let the following diagram represent the following states of affairs. "SA1" represents God at a state of affairs prior to the incarnation, "I" is incarnation itself, and "SA2" represents God at a state of affairs after the incarnation. In this case, "the arrow of time" is moving from left to right.

SA1	I	SA2

time →

It seems to be pretty clear that at SA1, I has not yet occurred. But clearly it is possible at SA1 for I to occur; so at SA1, I can be said to be a relatively open possibility. That is, at SA1, I is in the future. And if we say that God exists, then for God at SA1, I is in the future.

However, at SA2, I has already occurred, and it is no longer possible for it not to have occurred since that would involve changing the past and we know that that is impossible. So, at SA2, I is an absolutely closed possibility; it is in the past. And that means that at SA2, I is an absolutely closed possibility so far as God is concerned.

What this tries to show is that God has been involved in a process of change that is identical in all respects to the process of time. That is, God has undergone the change from I being a relatively open possibility for

God (at SA1) to I being an absolutely closed possibility (at SA2). At SA1, God could have decided not to become incarnate, but at SA2, that decision is no longer a possibility.

This codicil has been either rapid or reckless, depending on one's prior stance toward the notion of God's knowledge of the future. At the very least, it suggests those related areas that a transcendentalist theology needs to consider in order to be consistent with its more central insights about God. But I trust that it has suggested as well that the reasons why one might continue to defend the traditional extent and character of divine knowledge are not overwhelming, either in their conceptual elegance or in their religious orthodoxy. Much remains to be done to fill in the gaps left herein, I would insist, but I think that the goal itself is worth it. The most religiously satisfying terms available to Christians when thinking of God are personal and relational, and the least satisfying, to my mind, are impersonal and philosophical. That should tell us something, especially if we continue to think of God as Father ("*abba*") of Jesus.

NOTES

Introduction

1. In saying this, I might be thought to be taking issue with what Avery Dulles suggests in response to the same question. In *Models of Revelation*, Dulles notes that specific and deliberate attention to the doctrine of revelation began in the seventeenth and eighteenth centuries in the controversies between traditional Christianity and deism. This implies that the primary context of revelational theology was apologetic rather than soteriological, if I may put it that way. I do not at all take issue with Dulles but instead would add the clarification that apologetics is always in service to soteriology. Anselm's famous definition of theology as "faith seeking understanding" reflects this same priority: the mind does not create objects of belief but instead reflects on that which is already believed. See Avery Dulles, *Models of Revelation* (New York: Image, 1985), p. 5.

This rephrases the ancient dictum "Whatever is received is received according to the mode of the receiver."

3. This and parallel examples are traditional among so-called transcendentalists. See, for example, John Honner, SJ, "Disclosed and Transcendental: Rahner and Ramsey on the Foundations of Theology," *Haythrop Journal* 22 (1981), pp. 149–61.

4. Such as, for example, the Bible, miracles, the death-and-resurrection of Jesus, covenant, the Gospel, and so on. This class of assertions will be addressed more fully in Chapter 1.

5. Michael Polanyi, *Personal Knowledge* (Chicago: University of Chicago Press, 1958), pp. 55–57.

6. This wording is peculiarly Protestant. The thought itself is also problematic, especially to more conservative Protestants, in that the Bible says nothing specific about the Trinity or about the boundaries of Scripture itself. The latter is especially discomforting since the very notion of the *sufficiency* of Scripture presupposes a divinely authorized disclosure concerning its boundaries which by definition only Scripture could give but

which it lacks. Both of these crucial problems are regularly overlooked, in my opinion, by those who continue to interpret *sola Scriptura* as though it were identical with the sufficiency of Scripture.

7. Carl F. H. Henry, *God, Revelation and Authority*, Vol. 2: *God Who Speaks and Shows* (Waco, Texas: Word, 1976), p. 10. I shall treat Henry in more detail in Chapter 1.

8. As an admittedly arbitrary representation, see Herman Hoeksema, *Reformed Dogmatics* (Grand Rapids, Mich.: Reformed Free Publishing Association, 1966), pp. 17–20. In summarizing his discussion of this distinction, Hoeksema says, "even [the] speech of God in creation and history cannot properly be understood except when it is heard and understood in connection with, and is interpreted by, the speech of God in Jesus Christ our Lord" (p. 20).

9. This gap should not be misunderstood as though it referred to an ontological gap; that is, I am not assuming that the function of revelation is to eradicate the difference between divinity and humanity, between God and persons. Instead, it is a religious gap in that it refers to the moral distance between what people naturally are and what God would have them become.

10. This type of work should not be devalued. On the contrary, we are extremely fortunate that a contemporary one is available: H. D. McDonald, *Theories of Revelation: An Historical Study 1700–1960* (Grand Rapids, Mich.: Baker, 1979). He says of this work: "we have sought to cover in an adequate manner the literature of the whole period [between 1700 and 1960]" (Vol. 2, p. 10).

11. *Oxford Dictionary of the Christian Church*, 2d edition, ed. by F. L. Cross and E. A. Livingston (Oxford: Oxford University Press, 1983), p. 1182.

12. I think that this is worse because it alleges a near complete independence of God and human beings, with the primary if not exclusive relationship between them being the cognitive data transmitted from One to the other which constitute the saving interpretation I just discussed.

13. One of the indicators of the backwardness of the so-called attributes-of-God approach to divine revelation may be seen in the furrowed brows of those who try to sort out the compatibility of some of those attributes (e.g., divine omniscience with respect to the future) with what we all assume to be true of human nature (e.g., our moral responsibility and freedom). The reason for the furrowed brows is precisely that no thought is given to the relationship between divine revelation and human freedom; the latter is simply defined as an ontological given with no transcendental grounding within the intentions of God. As I shall try to show later, though, once we assume that the purpose of divine revelation is soteriologi-

cal, to tell us about ourselves in a saving relation with God, "problems" such as this fall away. If the purpose of divine revelation is to disclose what is true of ourselves and then how that is grounded in God, intellectual ticklers such as this are ruled out of court, since reality itself cannot stand in substantial discontinuity with its own transcendent ground.

Chapter 1

1. Many persons have discussed this notion. I have also, in my *Evangelical Theories of Biblical Inspiration: A Review and Proposal* (New York: Oxford University Press, 1987), pp. 105-9.

2. William J. Abraham, *Divine Revelation and the Limits of Historical Criticism* (Oxford: Oxford University Press, 1982); and *The Divine Inspiration of Holy Scripture* (Oxford: Oxford University Press, 1981).

3. Abraham, *Divine Revelation*, p. 17.

4. Ibid.

5. Ibid., p. 18.

6. Ibid., p. 21.

7. As a clue to how I shall later construe the notion of revelation, note here the critical priority of "effect of speaking" over "mode of speaking." I shall refer back to this priority to substantiate my claim that revelation is only revelation once it has been received. Prior to that reception, it is just a datum or message or body of information, but it is not revelation. A baseball is not a "gift" until it is received.

8. Abraham, *Divine Revelation*, p. 22.

9. Ibid., citing the *Oxford English Dictionary* definition of *telepathy*. Interestingly enough, the etymology of *telepathy* reflected here suggests that its primary use was to refer to the communication of *pathos*, impressions of passions or emotions between or among agents. It would seem, though, that Abraham's argument requires something more akin to what we might call *telegnosis*, the communication of the type of notional information that is clearly at the heart of performative utterances.

10. Ibid., p. 20.

11. Ibid., p. 25.

12. Ibid., p. 29, citing John Locke, *The Reasonableness of Christianity*, ed. by I. T. Ramsey (London: Black, 1958), pp. 83-84.

13. The argument here and following is taken from Abraham, *Divine Revelation*, pp. 38-43.

14. One reason it is fatally weak, of course, is that Abraham has not yet said clearly what he thinks revelation itself is. Thus, to talk about the relationship between miracles and revelation at this stage is tricky at best

because we do not yet know what he means by revelation. At this point, he has only told us one of the two terms of the relationship.

15. Walter Kasper makes much the same point when he distinguishes between sign and miracle in the life and teachings of Jesus. Miracles are scientifically or historically problematic actions, whereas signs have "the aim of leading men to faith and can . . . only be recognized without ambiguity in faith as acts of God's sovereign power. They are above all signs of the coming kingdom of God. In them, God's kingdom is made proleptically present." Abraham's case here would have been strengthened had he defended the revelatory essence of signs rather than mere miracles. But signs by their very definition presuppose the prior agreement of sign maker and sign receiver regarding the nature of the message that the sign conveys from the one to the other, which is the point Abraham's text seems to overlook. See Walter Kasper, *An Introduction to Christian Faith* (New York: Paulist Press, 1980), pp. 47–8.

16. Abraham, *Divine Revelation*, pp. 59–66.

17. Ibid., p. 60.

18. Ibid., p. 57.

19. It is not by accident that I choose an example from John, because his is the New Testament book that most clearly portrays Jesus as God incarnate. In John, therefore, we would expect faith in Jesus to reflect an incarnational awareness of Him. What we find in this instance, though (John 4:16–42, especially 39), is a great number of Samaritans coming to faith in Jesus without any reference to incarnation at all. Two errors need to be avoided here: we must be careful not to interpret the ancient Samaritans as though they lived in our day, and we must be even more careful not to interpret ourselves as though we lived in theirs.

20. This is essentially the argument and the conclusion of James D. G. Dunn in *Christology in the Making: A New Testament Inquiry into the Origins of the Doctrine of the Incarnation* (Philadelphia: Westminster, 1980).

21. Abraham, *Divine Revelation*, p. 82, citing Maurice Wiles, *The Remaking of Christian Doctrine* (London: SCM, 1974), p. 57.

22. Abraham, *Divine Revelation*, p. 83.

23. Ibid., p. 187. This point is even more quickly established by inspecting Abraham's chapters, half of which include "Divine Intervention" as part of their titles.

24. Carl F. H. Henry, *Revelation*, Vol. 1: *Preliminary Considerations* (Waco, Texas: Word, 1976), p. 13.

25. Ibid.

26. Ibid.

27. Ibid., Vol. 2: *Fifteen Theses*, Part One, pp. 7, 8.

28. Note the twin and ordered emphases on what we have already discussed as general and specific revelation.

29. Henry, *Revelation*, Vol. 2, pp. 8–16.

30. It is not solely contemporary, however. Its roots lie in the scholastic distinction between sense and reference, or *modus significandi* and *res significata*. For a good introduction to this distinction and illustration of its usefulness, see David Burrell, *Exercises in Religious Understanding* (Notre Dame, Ind.: University of Notre Dame Press, 1974), pp. 127–29.

31. This is the crudest or most obvious form, not necessarily the form preferred by the majority of double-predestinarians.

32. Henry, *Revelation*, Vol. 2, p. 10.

33. It should not be assumed that the only function of theology is the grammatical one, however. Many persons have made what I would take to be this reductionist error. For example, in *The Nature of Doctrine* (Philadelphia: Westminster, 1984), George Lindbeck constructs a "postliberal way of conceiving religion and religious doctrine" which is "more concerned with how to think than with what to assert about matters of fact" because this way is "religiously neutral" (pp. 7, 9). I reject this approach as being far too abstract to be of service to the Christian community. In refusing to take the claims of Christian experience as the primary data to be understood, Lindbeck insulates his proposal from being useful to the widest community of Christian believers.

34. Henry, *Revelation*, Vol. 1, pp. 323–43.

35. Ibid., p. 322.

36. Ibid., pp. 335–43.

37. I shall return to knowing as an essentially human stance toward the world in my final chapters, relating it to other such stances in the effort to see how humans reflect, and thus reveal, the Trinitarian God.

38. Henry, *Revelation*, Vol. 1, p. 337.

39. By the "ultimate rationality of the universe" I do not mean that the universe is ultimately ideal as in Plato or Berkeley, but rather that it is susceptible to the rational understanding of the human mind. This is itself seen as the basic presupposition underlying all of the natural or bench sciences; inquiry into the natural world would be pointless and incoherent apart from the assumption that it could be understood.

40. Henry, *Revelation*, Vol. 1, p. 343.

41. Ibid., Vol. 2, pp. 124–42, "The Image of God in Man."

42. Ibid., pp. 138–42.

43. Henry cites Anderson, "Man's Dominion over Nature," Address to the American Theological Society, April 14, 1972, New York.

44. Henry, *Revelation*, Vol. 2, p. 141.

45. Norman Perrin and Dennis Duling, *The New Testament: An In-*

troduction, 2d ed. (New York: Harcourt Brace Jovanovich, 1982), pp. 56–60.

46. Henry, *Revelation*, Vol. 2, p. 142.

47. Hans Frei writes, "No more crucial event has taken place in modern Protestant theology than Karl Barth's break with liberalism. It was the most significant single impetus to the subsequent theological generation's conception of its task," in "The Doctrine of Revelation in the Thought of Karl Barth, 1909 to 1922: The Nature of Barth's Break with Liberalism," doctoral dissertation, Yale University, 1956, p. ii.

48. *The Epistle to the Romans*, ed. by Edwin C. Hoskyns (New York: Oxford University Press, 1972). "Evangelical Theology in the 19th Century" was originally delivered January 8, 1957, in Hannover, Germany, then titled "Panorama of a Century," reprinted in *The Humanity of God* (Richmond, Va.: John Knox, 1972), pp. 11–33. "The Humanity of God" (pp. 37–65) was originally delivered September 25, 1956, in Aarau, Switzerland.

49. This objection is raised in addition to the one noted in the discussion of Abraham above, namely that a scientifically anomalous event becomes "miraculous" only when the saving activity of God is identified within it. But since this is the case, then it is the prior decision (of faith) that sees God's presence in the event, and not the event itself, that is revelatory.

50. Frei notes that for this earlier Barth, "faith must negate itself, point away from itself; yet not in such a way as to dissolve the reality of the creaturely action that it is, since it is human, not divine activity." "Doctrine of Revelation," p. 519.

51. "The gospel itself is the criterion for its being understood. The knowledge of God as self-revelation is based on that self-revelation and not on any symmetry between that revelation and human capacity for spontaneous or free reception." Frei, "The Doctrine of Revelation," p. 506.

52. For an expanded discussion of this wording, see Richard P. McBrien, *Catholicism* (Minneapolis: Winston, 1981), chap. 2 and especially pp. 76–77.

53. See the discussion of Romans 1:22–32 in *The Epistle to the Romans*, pp. 48–54.

54. Frei, "The Doctrine of Revelation," p. 525.

55. Barth, "Humanity," p. 39.

56. Ibid., pp. 52–65.

57. Hans Küng noticed this in what was long taken to be the quintessential fighting ground between Catholicism and Protestantism, namely the meaning of justification by faith. Barth writes of his sense of startled shock in his letter to the author: "The positive conclusion of your critique is this: What I say about justification . . . does objectively concur on all points with the correctly understood teaching of the Roman Catholic Church. You

can imagine my considerable amazement at this bit of news; and I suppose that many Roman Catholic readers will at first be no less amazed." See Hans Küng, *Justification: The Doctrine of Karl Barth and a Catholic Reflection* (New York: Nelson and Sons, 1964), pp. xix–xx.

58. Barth, "Humanity," p. 60.

59. Ibid.

60. "For in him all the fullness of God was pleased to dwell, and through him to reconcile to himself all things, whether on earth or in heaven, making peace by the blood of his cross." Barth's reference should have included v. 20 as well as 19.

61. Ibid., pp. 61–62.

62. Karl Barth, *Evangelical Theology* (Garden City, N.Y.: Doubleday, 1964), pp. 13–14. This observation grounds my confidence in my own trinitarian theology of revelation outlined later in the book.

63. Ibid., p. 15. Barth here describes the covenant as the relationship in which "God is man's God and man is God's man."

64. In the same league, though, one would have to include B. B. Warfield, Carl Henry, Francis Schaeffer, and C. S. Lewis.

65. He is careful to deny, though, that he is a "fundamentalist," which he defines more in cognitive than in theological categories. He is quite willing to agree with fundamentalism insofar as it rejected nineteenth-century Protestant liberalism, but not insofar as it is characterized by "regrettable" features such as "distrust of reason, shoddy apologetics, cultural barrenness, eccentric individualism," [and] indifference to churchmanship." See his *"Fundamentalism" and the WORD OF GOD: Some Evangelical Principles* (Grand Rapids, Mich.: Eerdmans, 1980), pp. 29–40. His own approval of "evangelicalism" is culturally innocent, though, to the degree that he claims it is nothing other than "the oldest version of Christianity; [i.e.,] just apostolic Christianity itself" (p. 38).

66. My criticism of his use of a double standard is thus directed not at his pragmatic or perhaps tradition-authorized use of it as an authority but rather his unwillingness to admit that that is what he is doing. It is perfectly appropriate for a believer to say that the Bible is the primary critical location of God's self-revelation because the church has been able to function best with that belief, but once one says instead that it is because the Bible claims that about itself, then one is involved in the circular argument that I will consider in more detail shortly.

67. *Knowing God* (Downers Grove, Ill.: InterVarsity Press, 1973), pp. 13–19.

68. Ibid., pp. 17–19.

69. In the final chapters of this book, I will describe this enrichment as encountering the "saving character" of God.

70. If one follows the biblical habit of casting the God-human relationship as a marriage, this gets to the heart of what many have identified, or at least felt, as religiously uncomfortable in prenuptial agreements. Granted, engaged couples ought to do serious planning for the future, but it seems that such planning functions best, both relationally and theologically, when it outlines the minimum that each partner volunteeres to do for the enhancement of the beloved. The "theory" of prenuptial agreements seems conversely to point to the maximum that each person will do, or, worse yet, damage that each will accept from the other, before calling it quits. The theological perverseness of such an agreement is thus not its restriction upon spontaneity but rather its minimalistic contractual limitation of that which should be unlimited: our commitment to enhance our beloved's life, coupled with our grace in receiving grief when we attempt to do so.

71. Packer, *Knowing God*, p. 15.

72. Ibid.

73. Here is Packer's recitation of it: "Thou shalt not make unto thee any graven image, or any likeness of any thing that is in heaven above, or that is in the earth beneath, or that is in the water under the earth: thou shalt not bow down thyself to them, nor serve them: for I the Lord thy God am a jealous God." Ibid., p. 38. On the following page he calls the Ten Commandments "the ten basic principles of biblical religion."

74. Ibid., pp. 40, 41.

75. Ibid., p. 42.

76. Ibid., p. 44.

77. Ibid., pp. 40–41.

78. Bernhard W. Anderson, *Understanding the Old Testament*, 3d ed. (Englewood Cliffs, N.J.: Prentice-Hall, 1975), p. 54. See also the *Jewish Encyclopedia* VII (New York: Funk and Wagnall, 1904), p. 88.

79. Packer, *"Fundamentalism" and the WORD OF GOD*, p. 73. This work was originally published in 1958. Packer has remained consistent, though, in his identification of the Bible and God's message, and thus in his susceptibility to the criticism rendered here. See his chapter entitled "In Quest of Canonical Interpretation" in Robert K. Johnston, ed., *The Use of the Bible in Theology/Evangelical Options* (Atlanta: John Knox, 1985), pp. 35–55, especially p. 42, where he says, "by entering into the expressed mind of the inspired writers I do in fact apprehend God's own mind. What Scripture says, God says."

80. Clearly this is a circular argument, since the fundamental reason why anyone would call the Bible inspired in the first place is that it contains the self-revelation of God. However, this does not appear to be fatal; most of our ultimate values in life are grounded in similar circularities. My own understanding of divine revelation will quite intentionally reflect this same

circularity precisely because I do not believe that most of us succumb to the need to warrant our beliefs about God in syllogistic arguments, which by definition are noncircular. Instead, I think, we are justifiably convinced that we are dealing with God when we are in the presence of that which is ultimately and uniquely personal-relational, which I will discuss under the names of knowledge, love, hope, and community.

81. I need to add "in today's world" because it would not have been possible to ground the certainty of divine revelation in the inspiration of the Bible prior to its finalization in canonical form.

Chapter 2

1. We will encounter this thought in more detail when we consider Michael Polanyi below. Right now I am not concerned to specify a sufficient list of such presuppositions, if indeed that can even be done. With that qualification in mind, however, we might agree that the following are necessarily presupposed by the possibility of rhetorical argumentation: (1) that successful rhetoric is formally as well as materially structured, (2) that both the form and the content of successful rhetoric (somehow) reflect the real world, and (3) that both the form and the content of successful rhetoric affect the real world. Think of how different the possibility of criminal prosecution would be, for example, if any or all of these could not be taken for granted.

2. In this chapter and especially in succeeding ones, we shall see not only that the revelation of God cooperates with the natural but in fact that the natural presupposes such revelation. This results from two traditional Christian beliefs, first in the universality of revelation, and second in the dynamic moral responsibility of human beings. Apart from these beliefs, revelation could never be more than arbitrary and capricious.

3. This is similar to Dietrich Bonhoeffer's methodological and theological warning about the peripheralization of religion. John Macquarrie paraphrases it thus: "one may remember Bonhoeffer's insistence that faith is not for the extremities of life but for its center, and his rightful criticisms of preachers and others who would frighten men into religiosity." John Macquarrie, *Principles of Christian Theology*, 2d ed. (New York: Scribner's, 1977), p. 99, referring to Dietrich Bonhoeffer, *Letters and Papers from Prison* (New York: Macmillan, 1974), p. 165.

4. Avery Dulles, *Revelation Theology: A History* (New York: Herder and Herder, 1969), p. 182.

5. Avery Dulles, *Models of the Church* (Garden City, N.Y.: Image, 1978), p. x.

6. Avery Dulles, *Models of Revelation* (Garden City, N.Y.: Image, 1985), p. 3.

7. In addition to *Revelation Theology* and *Models of Revelation*, see *Revelation and the Quest for Unity* (Washington, D.C., and Cleveland: Corpus Books, 1968).

8. Dulles, *Quest*, p. 60.

9. Dulles, *Revelation Theology*, pp. 27–28.

10. Ibid., pp. 171–77.

11. Ibid., pp. 177–78. Note the similarity in tasks, if not in content, between this and Bernard Lonergan's project to identify various types of differentiated consciousnesses, which are the glasses or filters through which we experience the world but which are so naïve and nonconscious to us that we do not often understand that they are "a" way to experience the world rather than "the" way. See Bernard Lonergan, *Method in Theology* (New York: Seabury, 1979), esp. chap. 12, and also *Doctrinal Pluralism* (Milwaukee: Marquette University Press, 1971), for a more succinct discussion of this topic.

12. Dulles, *Models of Revelation*, pp. 16–17.

13. Ibid., pp. 27–28. Each of these models is given extensive treatment further on in the book.

14. Ibid., pp. 267–69.

15. Ibid., p. 278. These three functions are discussed more fully below.

16. Thus, "the catholic tradition" includes Anglicanism and some branches of Protestantism.

17. Dulles, *Quest*, pp. 20–46; and *Models of Revelation*, pp. 131–54.

18. Dulles, *Models of Revelation*, p. 132.

19. Ibid.

20. Lest it be thought that I am overly hasty in rejecting the reduction of language to its referential mode, think of its implausibility with respect to "the exact and precise lexical meaning" just mentioned. Which lexicon will we use? Who compiled it? When and where was it compiled? Language is evolutionary, and its permutations over time are made by human beings in the effort to render it more expressive of and for their own experience. Thus, there simply is no "exact and precise lexical meaning" in the sense necessary to undergird this restriction.

21. Dulles, *Models of Revelation*, p. 132.

22. Ibid., pp. 132–34.

23. Ibid., p. 136.

24. Ibid., pp. 136–37.

25. Ibid., p. 137.

26. This is not to say that it is not gracious, however, as we shall see below.

27. John Macquarrie, *Principles of Christian Theology*, 2d ed. (New York: Scribner's, 1977). Well along in his consideration of divine revelation, he tells us why this would be useless: revelation is always conveyed or disclosed in particular, concrete events of history, never in abstract or universal categories. He cites Karl Barth to the effect that "the Bible does not permit us to set up the general thought of a being furnished with divine attributes but 'concentrates our attention and thoughts upon one single point and what is to be known at that point.' This insistence on concreteness and particularity is acceptable, provided it is not arbitrarily restricted to the biblical revelation. . . . [One] can hardly speak of a 'general' revelation, though there is a universal possibility of revelation" (p. 89, citing Barth, *Church Dogmatics*, II, 2 [Edinburgh: T. and T. Clark, 1964], p. 52).

28. Macquarrie, *Principles*, p. 39. The succeeding two divisions cover what he calls the symbolic and applied aspects of a Christian systematic theology.

29. Macquarrie's "Diagram Showing Religious Types from a Christian Perspective" on p. 167 of *Principles* is quite useful in this context.

30. Macquarrie, *Principles*, pp. 62–68. Elsewhere he summarizes this state of affairs by calling it "man's synoptic awareness of his being, in its authentic possibility and its actual disorder" (p. 103).

31. Ibid., p. 87.

32. More precisely, truth is a penultimate intention. What is ultimate is God. I will account for how I understand the relationship between God and truth in Chapters 3 and 4 of this book.

33. Macquarrie is careful to note that this account of revelation is both reductionistic and overly intellectualistic. Neither particularly bothers him, the former because philosophical theology is by definition universalistic and thus reductionistic, and the latter precisely because he is trying to render a given phenomenon understandable. Making revelation understandable is not the same thing as making understanding revelation.

34. Macquarrie, *Principles*, pp. 113, 115. There are a great variety of ways to differentiate the theories of this chapter from those of Chapter 1. Here we have another one: discontinuist theories generally invite us to think of revelation as brand new knowledge about overcoming sin and its effects, with God as source of that knowledge, whereas continuist theories invite us to think of revelation as a new stance toward reality, with God as both essence and goal of the stance.

35. Ibid., p. 115.

36. This is not to say dogmatically that nonhuman animals do not participate in the dynamic of self-transcendence, and thus in that dynamic that existential-ontological theism identifies as the clearest location of divine-human participation. It is only to say that human beings have no

access to such a location for nonhuman beings, and thus that we cannot speak about it.

37. It is true that humans have and fulfill the capacity for other types of self-transcendence, such as the physiological self-transcendence that evolution has shown us. But by definition this is not a distinctly human dynamic and thus does not specifically help us in the present task.

38. The reason for this is that other sorts of beings are female, intelligent, healthy, and so on. The additional feature of *human* being, namely that we are intentionally self-transcending, is what calls for and in fact demands an additional accounting.

39. Macquarrie, *Principles*, p. 88.

40. Ibid., p. 103. It could not be incontrovertibly from God, since that would move the entire matter from the realm of faith to the realm of certitude and thus remove it from the specific interests of religion.

41. Here again I can be more accurate by saying that the critical test for the former is primarily truth and secondarily love, while that for the latter is primarily love and secondarily truth. Putting it this way helps to preserve our experience of truth and love as integrally related, rather than disparate, sorts of things.

42. Karl Rahner, SJ, a "transcendentalist" like Macquarrie and in fact a theologian whom Macquarrie calls "most helpful . . . [and] outstanding" (*Principles*, p. vii), has often been accused of collapsing theology into psychology—that is, of paying relatively little attention to the communitarian and social implications of transcendentalist thought about God. I do not happen to agree with this accusation, but in any event my own attempt in this book will take the community into deliberate regard. I have just said how and where: the community is the outer pole of that which is constitutively and essentially human, namely moral capacity.

43. Most traditional Christian understandings of revelation, for instance, simply stipulate the identification of the Bible, or of Jesus, as the prime moment of divine revelation, ignoring or at best bypassing the critical usefulness of the notion of God as *universal* creator.

44. A recent doctoral dissertation attempts to distill order from the clutter of this discipline (Randy L. Maddox, *Toward an Ecumenical Fundamental Theology* [Chico, Calif.: Scholars Press, 1984]), clutter that may be attributed to two factors. First, until quite recently fundamental theology has been taken to be a specifically Catholic enterprise, in light of both the traditional Catholic openness to natural law reasoning and the equally traditional Protestant suspicions of it. Second, not all Catholic fundamental theologians themselves agreed on the nature, much less the content, of their task. Maddox cites Joseph Cahill's discovery that "after investigating thirty-two fundamental theologies, . . . there was no general Catholic con-

sensus as to the nature and properties of the discipline." He goes on wryly to note that "the Catholic fundamental theologian Josef Schmitz recently characterized his discipline as having a sign hung over its door that read 'Temporarily Closed due to Total Reconstruction.'" See Maddox, *Ecumenical Fundamental Theology*, p. 5. Notwithstanding this mess, Maddox suggests that the proper scope of fundamental theology is "a discipline which deals with questions both of the responsible justification of Christian faith (apologetics) and the methodological justification of Christian theology" (p. 2).

45. To be more precise, it is not so much a matter of debate whether these humane disciplines should be included in fundamental theology, as how they should be. This question is a type of pre-fundamental theology, or perhaps a meta-fundamental theology, whose canons and criteria are even more fuzzy than fundamental theology considered by itself. If this were a book on fundamental theology, we would have to work through these critical issues. Since it is not, we can simply report on what faces such theologians and not have to worry about facing it ourselves.

46. Gerald O'Collins, *Fundamental Theology* (New York: Paulist Press, 1981), p. 2.

47. "Origin" in the sense of where we begin our study of revelation, not where the content of revelation itself begins, which is in God's love of the world.

48. O'Collins, *Fundamental Theology*, pp. 32–52.

49. It is difficult to know which word to use here since the distinction at issue is that between the *rational* and the *experiential*.

50. By "breadth or holism," I mean to include "all aspects of our personal existence: the imagination, the emotions, the mind, the will, the memory and our other (spiritual and bodily) powers." O'Collins, *Fundamental Theology*, p. 35. In particular, O'Collins here insists that experience always includes a certain kind of knowledge even when it is not conscious or deliberate knowledge: "There is always at least a minimal cognitive dimension to experience." The negative value of this insistence is to account for the involvement of the human subject in experiencing. Experiences are not things that occur to, or work on, utterly passive persons. Instead, they are grasped and embraced, however minimally, in the ways here suggested.

51. O'Collins is here speaking about historical experience, although he has not yet introduced the distinction between them and transcendental ones.

52. That is, experience is the time-bound vehicle that carries us forward from present into future or, more accurately, brings the future into the present.

53. Nor does it matter whether any two or more persons agree on their evaluations of a given experience. What matters here is not the results of an evaluation but rather and much more fundamentally the possibility of one in the first place.

54. This is not to say, of course, that our world is morally *good*. That is a historical evaluation that cannot be made on a priori or transcendentalist grounds alone. We shall soon get to the relevant distinction between historical and transcendental.

55. Note the relationship between this categorization and Richard P. McBrien's fundamental categorization of the discipline of theology into "faith, theology, belief and tradition." Both operate with the same cognitive and experiential dynamic: from first-order to second-order experience, thence to critical and public articulation, and finally to gathering and passing along. See Richard P. McBrien, *Catholicism* (Minneapolis: Winston, 1981), pp. 23–77, especially the summary on pp. 76–77.

56. For example, he cites various OT and NT passages in defense of the claim that multiple criteria are used to separate wheatlike and chafflike experiences: obedience to the divine will, doing good, demonstrable pastoral and other "social" concerns, previous historical experience such as Paul's vision on the road, and the like. "The process of discernment will normally need to invoke some signs establishing authenticity" (O'Collins, *Fundamental Theology*, p. 43). True enough, but circular, since these criteria are supposed to help us differentiate between authentic and inauthentic experiences and thus cannot themselves depend on a prior distinction between them.

57. Karl Rahner, *Foundations of Christian Faith* (New York: Seabury, 1978). O'Collins cites materials selectively drawn from Part I ("The Hearer of the Message," pp. 24–43) and Part II ("Man in the Presence of Absolute Mystery," pp. 44–89).

58. O'Collins, *Fundamental Theology*, p. 49. That this horizon is hidden, of course, does not make it any less real. An analogy might be the difference between historically experiencing pain when a brick drops onto one's foot and transcendentally experiencing gravity as the condition within which objects exert certain kinds of attractive forces upon each other. Both pain and gravity are differently experienced as soon as one cries "Ouch!" and starts hopping around.

59. Ibid.

60. Ibid.

61. I will add a significant nuance to this idea later on, when I discuss how the love of God "prompted" the creative moment of what is not-God, the universe, as that which God could love even more concretely and expressively than God's own self-love, the love by the First Person of the

Second Person. The only point being made here, though, is that both of these moments of divine love, inner and outer, are expressions of an intrinsic part of God's character, and which Christians affirm in the traditional "God is love."

62. I am well aware that this is a contestable claim, and since this is a book about divine revelation rather than epistemology, I will simply note this complication and move on. I will return to the subject, though, or at least come close to it, when considering Ian T. Ramsey in the next section. Interestingly enough, this is the criterion around which Augustine's celebrated conversion from Manicheeism to Christianity occurred. Reflecting back on this conversion which he had made when he was twenty-nine, he later says, "I had read a great many scientific books which were still alive in my memory. When I compared them with the tedious tales of the Manichees, it seemed to me that, of the two, the theories of the scientists were the more likely to be true. . . . The reason and understanding by which [the scientists] investigate these things are gifts they have from [God, whereas] all of [the teaching of Manes is] extremely incoherent" (Augustine, *Confessions* V, 3).

63. O'Collins, *Fundamental Theology*, p. 55.

64. Ibid., p. 57.

65. Ibid., pp. 127–29.

66. The reason I found this latter insistence surprising is that it would seem much more ecumenically hopeful to search out other religions for evidences of their transcendental grounding in the Trinitarian God rather than merely look for instances of triads, triangles, and threes. This approach seems to neutralize the very usefulness of the distinction between categorical and transcendental: a given religion may be authentically rooted in the transcendent God even if its historical expression does not readily yield three-sided concepts that call the Trinity immediately to mind. This is why I shall look for trinitarian reverberations (vestiges?) in the nature of human beings themselves in Chapter 3.

67. O'Collins, *Fundamental Theology*, pp. 134–37.

68. Ibid., p. 134.

69. Ibid., p. 136.

70. Ibid.

71. Ibid., p. 137.

72. It must be both, I believe (that is, both ontological and critical), in order to avoid the charge of circularity, a charge I shall shortly make of O'Collins himself.

73. O'Collins, *Fundamental Theology*, pp. 114–29.

74. Ibid., p. 124.

75. To oversimplify, but in ways that I hope are of relevance to the task at hand, philosophy is interested in proving the existence of God. Theology

is not. It rather presumes that question, asking instead what *kind* of God it is that exists. These two questions ought not be confused. To anticipate the discussion of Chapters 3 and 4 somewhat, there I shall try to show how God is transcendent Goodness and Love, and how concrete experience of goodness and love by human beings *is* God's self-revelation. If that is the case, though, then at best it is superfluous to prove the existence of a God who might be neither, and at worst it is injurious to the possibility of saving faith. The question of "whether God is" is theologically useless until the question of "who God is" has been settled, but once it has been, then the question of "whether God is" is moot.

76. William B. Williamson, *Ian T. Ramsey* (Waco, Texas: Word, 1982), p. 19.

77. Ian T. Ramsey, "Contemporary Empiricism," *Christian Scholar* (Fall 1960), p. 181, cited in Edward Cell, *Language, Existence, and God* (Atlantic Highlands, N.J.: Humanities, 1978), pp. 320–21.

78. That is, the overall intention that is of interest to us.

79. Donald Evans, "Ian Ramsey on Talk about God," *Religious Studies* 7, nos. 2, 3 (June and September 1971), p. 127. This occurs in the midst of Evans's helpful catalogue of the many examples of the "more" of empirical language that Ramsey scattered throughout his various works. He presents these examples in the following order: awareness of *I*; personal encounter or awareness of others; moral claims; aesthetic wonder; whole and part; scientific models, infinite mathematical series; and (what seems to be a summary of all of the above) concrete and particular.

80. Karl Rahner, SJ, "Thomas Aquinas on the Incomprehensibility of God," *Journal of Religion* 58 (1978 supp.), pp. S107–25. Evans notes this same dynamic nature of the "more" in Ramsey when he says that his "'more' is a form of *activity* rather than a mere happening. . . ." See Evans, "Ian Ramsey," pp. 127–28.

81. Williamson, *Ramsey*, pp. 120–21.

82. Ian T. Ramsey and Ruth Porter, eds., *Personality and Science* (London: Churchill Livingstone, 1971), pp. 128–29.

83. Were I more interested in philosophy per se, this would be the place where the epistemological question would be taken up, the process of justifying the existence of the subject "beyond" the level of the observations themselves. Here Ramsey's celebrated insights concerning the illuminating usefulness of models would help, especially what he calls the disclosure models whose twin purposes echo the two ways by which we come to understand the existence of the self itself. The two purposes for which disclosure models are pressed into service are (1) to reproduce the structure of the thing being modeled rather than merely its form or shape, and (2) to elicit or generate further experiences of the thing being modeled, what

Ramsey called "evoking new disclosures." Ian T. Ramsey, *Models and Mystery* (London: Oxford, 1964), p. 3.

84. Terrence W. Tilley, *Talking of God* (New York: Paulist Press, 1978), p. 81.

85. Ian T. Ramsey, *Religious Language: An Empirical Placing of Theological Phrases* (London: SCM, 1967), p. 38.

86. What was noted in the earlier footnote concerning the different intentions of philosophy and theology with respect to the question of God needs to be recalled here. The following reflections presume the existence of God and thus cannot be taken as though they intend to prove it. Instead, they intend to outline the means by which we are licensed in certain situations to ask how certain experiences of the cosmos are "empirically personal."

87. For those more familiar with Ramsey than necessary for my purposes here, these rhetorical questions functioned as negative qualifying models, which "[fix] on mutable or passible features of perceptual situations, and then . . . apply the qualifier 'not,' progressively obliterating these features. . . . [Such models] are designed to give a kind of technique for meditation, in order to bring about that discernment which is the basis for talking about God." Ramsey, *Religious Language*, p. 53.

88. In particular, it lacks the feature of absolute or ultimate commitment that Ramsey said was reflective of the ultimacy of the God who evoked it, although I suppose that my subsequent attitudes toward church evaders might be construed as a sort of modified commitment resulting from it. This is not fatal, though, since neither then nor now did I need to have God's existence proved to me. Husbands and wives may still be ultimately committed to each other even if all of their marital experiences are not honeymoonlike in either intensity or enjoyment.

89. Interestingly enough, even the latter responses would negatively illustrate the personalness of the experience itself, since typically we are estranged or terrorized more by persons than by things.

90. If it does not actually fail, it at least limps significantly. Tilley is somewhat more optimistic about this possibility when he summarizes Ramsey's justification of such experiences as experiences of *God*: "The argument [Ramsey] offered for the non-illusory character of these experiences was that just as a personal response to a real person underlies personal response to a fake person, so personal response to a real personal God underlies personal response to a fake god, i.e., to our projections, or hopes, or our delusions. But just as a response to a fake person is dependent upon the possibility of responding to a genuine person, so the response to a fake god depends upon the possibility of response to a genuine God. Thus finally construing all cosmic disclosures as responses to fake

gods is precluded since response to a fake god depends upon the response to a real one." Tilley, *Talking*, pp. 90–91.

91. Michael Polanyi, *Personal Knowledge: Towards a Post-Critical Philosophy* (Chicago: University of Chicago Press, 1958, rev. 1962), pp. 56, 57.

92. Even less, of course, can we depend on the external world itself to do the discriminating work for us, as though it itself possessed some kind of critical capacity. This might sound obvious, but it does not seem to have occurred to the early logical positivists who thought that human knowledge simply and merely reflected what was already in the external world.

93. Polanyi, *Personal Knowledge*, p. 95.

94. Ibid.

95. Polanyi does not much care for this extreme. Toward the end of the book, he thinks back about its major purpose: "Its aim is to re-equip men with the faculties which centuries of critical thought have taught them to distrust. The reader has been invited to use these faculties and contemplate thus a picture of things restored to their fairly obvious nature. This is all the book was meant to do. For once men have been made to realize the crippling mutilations imposed by an objectivist framework—once the veil of ambiguities covering up these mutilations has been definitively dissolved—many fresh minds will turn to the task of reinterpreting the world as it is, and as it then once more will be seen to be." Ibid., p. 381.

96. This is, I think, a nice way to think about Aquinas's discussion of the simpleness and oneness of God in the *Summa Theologiae* I, qq. 3, 11. They may be likened to the dynamic process of the growth of knowledge: whenever we come to know a fact or feature of the world, it thereby becomes integrated within the previously existing unity of our prior knowledge of it, forming a larger whole or unity from which we intend, at least optimally, to excise all contradictions and gaps. Simpleness and unity are thus not opposed to complexity and division, but especially with respect to God are to be seen instead as wholeness. See David Burrell's discussions of the early methodological questions of the *Summa Theologiae* in his *Exercises in Religious Understanding* (Notre Dame, Ind.: University of Notre Dame Press, 1974), pp. 91–122, and his *Aquinas: God and Act* (Notre Dame, Inc.: University of Notre Dame Press, 1979), pp. 17–41.

97. Polanyi, *Personal Knowledge*, pp. 308, 309. Earlier he had written: "[The] act of knowing includes an appraisal; and this personal coefficient, which shapes all factual knowledge, bridges in doing so the disjunction between subjectivity and objectivity. It implies the claim that man can transcend his own subjectivity by striving passionately to fulfill his personal obligations to universal standards" (p. 17).

98. I say "subjectivistically" rather than "subjectively" here because all knowledge, whether ultimately determined to be true or false, is by defini-

tion subjective. Here, then, I simply mean to rule out the subjectivistic or solipsistic extreme discussed earlier.

99. This is not an epistemological claim, of course, but rather a metaphysical one. That is, the observation that fiduciary commitments ground all acts of knowing does not commit us to a given method of describing how knowing itself works. That is a different matter, where legitimate diversity can and will occur.

100. Polanyi distinguishes between subjective and objective knowing. The former is defined as passive, and to that degree is shared by many animals in the world. Only humans, though, so far as we know, are capable of objective knowing; "only knowing that bears on reality is active, personal, and rightly to be called objective" (*Personal Knowledge*, p. 403). These are not two different and unrelated kinds of knowing. Instead, they are different points along the same spectrum, distinguished by degrees of intentionality and representing the striving of the material universe to emerge into conscious self-awareness and self-expression—that is, personal knowledge.

101. So, for example, we do not have fixed and inflexible ecological responsibilities to the environment per se, independent of any consideration of its present and future personal inhabitants. That ignores the fact that the environment itself changes so that, over time, it is most congenial to the possibility of material reality coming to self-awareness and self-expression, which itself is best conceivable if divine self-communication is seen as the eliciting pole of such an awakening. The ecological and environmental responsibilities we do have, then, are duties to those persons who today or tomorrow will be affected by what we do in that environment. That is precisely why we must take such responsibilities with urgency.

102. Polanyi, *Personal Knowledge*, p. 405.

103. See Carl J. Peter, "A Shift to the Human Subject in Roman Catholic Theology," *Communio* (U.S.) 6, no. 1 (1979), pp. 56–72; and David B. Burrell, CSC, "Theology and the Linguistic Turn" *Communio* (U.S.) 6, no. 1 (1979), pp. 95–112, for careful analyses of the roots and the meaning of this shift.

104. I shall not consider angels as part of this analysis. Their mere existence is extremely problematic, and that in itself is sufficient to disqualify them from consideration in a work that already has enough difficulties. In addition, if one takes the usual descriptions and functions of angels as adequate, then they neither exist within the need of God's self-disclosure nor possess any longer the relevant decisional faculties parallel to the ones *we* need in order to express our stance toward God. Thus, even if we could get around the problems associated with their existence, we would still discover, I think, that angels are moot with respect to helping us better understand God's self-revelation.

Chapter 3

1. See Stephen C. Pepper, *World Hypotheses: A Study in Evidence* (Berkeley: University of California, 1942).

2. In a lecture at the University of Notre Dame ("The Bible and the Church," June 29, 1988), Jerome Murphy-O'Connor summarized the thought of St. Paul on this topic. Framing the discussion in the terms of Cyprian's dictum ("outside the church there is no salvation"), Murphy-O'Connor noted that Paul would have come to precisely the oppsite conclusion ("outside the church there is no damnation"). Why? Because for Paul damnation presupposes culpability, culpability presupposes responsibility, and responsibility presupposes revelation. But if those outside the church are characterized *ex hypothesi* as existing beyond revelation, then they are also beyond responsibility, culpability, and damnation. I would object. This may or may not be true for Paul, but *we* should not think that it is, both because it proposes a two-level hierarchy of humanity and because salvation is always salvation *from* damnation. But if there is no damnation, then there is no salvation either, and God's relationship with those "outside" is severed altogether, both in principle and in reality.

3. They are materially gratuitous, of course, a point that should not be overlooked here.

4. Polanyi is emphatic that we cannot completely eliminate what he calls our "self-set standards," those critical operations and goals that we presuppose every time we act critically. For the same reason, neither can we warrant or justify them; we can only use them and hence justify them by "dwelling" in them. "When we accept a certain set of pre-suppositions and use them as our interpretative framework, we may be said to dwell in them as we do in our own body. Their uncritical acceptance for the time being consists in a process of assimilation by which we identify ourselves with them. They are not asserted and cannot be asserted, for assertion can be made only *within* a framework with which we have identified ourselves for the time being; as they are themselves our ultimate framework, they are essentially inarticulable." Michael Polanyi, *Personal Knowledge: Towards a Post-Critical Philosophy* (Chicago: University of Chicago Press, 1958), p. 60. See also p. 315 for his suggestion that commitment "circumscribes the hazards of belief."

5. This is not to imply that the world has reached its final stage of evolutionary development. No given epoch or species is ever able to say that with confidence. If there are beings in the future of our world who advance over our own stage, though, it will be their responsibility to frame these questions and answers in ways that make sense of their time and context.

6. See "Augustine: On the Trinity," in Maurice Wiles and Mark Santer,

eds., *Documents in Early Christian Thought* (Cambridge: Cambridge University Press, 1975), pp. 36–42.

7. A conceptual argument against this restriction is that if we were to restrict the meaning of *moral* to *moral goodness*, then we would not have an ethical yardstick or criterion by which to criticize and condemn those who were evil. If good and evil resided on two yardsticks rather than on opposite ends of the same one, then we could never condemn the latter by the former without some algorithm or formula by which to relate the two yardsticks. But then this algorithm would logically antedate the two yardsticks and would thus claim logical superiority over both of them. This is one of the two reasons why Augustine eventually rejected Manicheeism (see his *Confessions*, VII, 2): our minds cannot achieve critical security in the presence of ultimate dualisms.

8. I considered this briefly at the very end of my book on biblical inspiration, *Evangelical Theories of Biblical Inspiration: A Review and Proposal* (New York: Oxford University Press, 1987), pp. 107–9.

9. This implies that one can know something that is not true, which at first glance seems odd. It does not seem so odd to me, though, for precisely the reason that I am here developing: both knowing and believing are actions of the mind and not of the external world. Perhaps the matter would be clearer if it were put both negatively and epistemologically. *Knowledge* refers to the degree of mental certainty we have when we do not possess any reason for doubting what our minds think, whereas *belief* refers to the degree of certainty we have when we do possess some reasons for doubt but not so much as to warrant an overall change in what we think. Therefore, both knowledge and belief are in principle subject to revision; we may be wrong about either. The relevant distinction is that *now* I possess no reason to revise what I *know*, whereas *now* I do possess some reason to revise what I *believe*, although in fact I might not revise it until I have more such reasons.

10. This is a somewhat imprecise way of putting the matter. Greater precision demands that I say that truth is *presupposed* by the attainment of Point S, since the latter is a strictly psychological phenomenon whereas truth is that plus more. Thus, this way of putting it risks confusing a given criterion of truth with truth itself, epistemology with reality. This point is especially worth insisting upon within a transcendentalist methodological framework. I am not entirely unhappy with this imprecision, though, for reasons that I trust are becoming clearer to the reader. Our perspective, that of finite and historically conditioned human beings in the real world, is the only one within which we can operate. From within that perspective, the attainment of truth (Point S) is psychologically indistinguishable from truth itself, which follows from my earlier discussion concerning the no-

tions of knowing and believing. Things are relevantly different when approached from the transcendental methodological perspective from how they are when approached from the psychological.

11. Although this might appear to be too simplistic an answer, there are not many alternatives. For example, if one were to say that the relaxation itself was deliberate and not instinctual on our part, then one would have to inquire about the roots of this deliberateness, and then how *it* relaxed when it became satisfied by the attainment of *its* Point S, which reduces to the analysis I have suggested here.

12. Although this sounds formally similar to Augustine's "Our hearts are not at rest until they find their rest in Thee," I do not mean to imply here an acceptance of the outmoded and quiescent emmanationist epistemology according to which dynamic human knowing arises from "the fall" and will thus be rendered moot in Paradise. As a transcendentalist, I am rather persuaded that it is essential to the notion of human beings that we continually grow and develop in our knowledge of the world; in a nutshell, that is what Karl Rahner's transcendental subjectivism is all about. Were I to use Augustine's dictum above, therefore, I would interpret the "rest" not in epistemological or critical categories, but instead in spiritual ones: heavenly "rest" will occur when we fully realize and commit ourselves to the goals of the Kingdom of God rather than to those that serve our own selfish intentions.

13. Hence the sentence could also employ the word *evil* or any synonym thereof, since according to the scheme discussed above, evil is the opposite and not the absence of good. Note that all identity predications thus fall within this scheme since they report on our judgments that this X is Y and not Z. And the great bulk of our sentences are, in one form or another, identity predications.

14. Although not of experiencing the world, which we saw Ramsey discuss above.

15. Special exceptions such as mental illnesses do not disrupt this conclusion.

16. Without being tendentious, however, I would still say that each of these instances embodies a reciprocal structure, although admittedly not an equivalently balanced one. Parents of infants might think that they give and do not receive, especially at the three A.M. feeding, but that is truncated and somewhat selfish. After all, we are not parents at all until we have children; quite literally, they bestow parental status upon us, and we are dependent upon them to do that. Much the same can be said for nurses and comatose patients, and for God and the world, too, although the specific reciprocity of this latter relationship needs the greater attention I will give it in my discussion of christology below.

17. Eberhard Jüngel, *God as the Mystery of the World* (Grand Rapids, Mich.: Eerdmans, 1983), pp. 314–30.

18. Ibid., p. 318.

19. Ibid., pp. 319–20.

20. In saying that this movement is from one state of existence to another, I am deliberately vague. This is because subjective self-transcendence occurs in all of the realms in which the human person exists, what I earlier referred to as the psychological, intellectual, spiritual, and physiological realms.

21. That is, time is not something that moves inexorably from future to past. More precisely, it is a dynamic that is in part activated by human decisions and intentions (the present) that reach into the realm of possibilities (the future) and render some of them into actualities (the past). Its inexorability reflects the conditions of existence over which we have no influence, in this case the logical structure of open possibilities transforming to closed ones. Within those conditions, though, we have a relatively large degree of influence.

22. Of course, it might in actuality turn out not to be better, but given usual or healthy psychological conditions, this results from unexpected and unplanned influencing factors. The point is that we do not deliberately intend the bad but instead the good. Even evil persons identify their own (bad) intentions as good ones in order to justify the effort required to progress toward them. No one consciously identifies an intention as bad and pursues it precisely *as* bad; instead, they call it good and pursue it as such. That is precisely what is evil about them.

23. There is an enormous body of literature that presents this same analysis, which usually goes under the names of "transcendental subjectivism" (Rahner) or "intentionality analysis" (Lonergan), and thus what is presented here represents only a summary of it.

24. Here I have moved from using the "other" as my object of transcendental inquiry, to using "I" as that object. That is an appropriate move whether one's ultimate interest is ethics on the one hand or theology on the other. And with respect to the latter, which is my interest here, we can recall Ian T. Ramsey's axiom: "'I' will never cease to be a useful guide for us when we are confronted with puzzles about 'God.'" Ian T. Ramsey, *Religious Language: An Empirical Placing of Theological Phrases* (London: SCM, 1967), p. 38.

25. We can and must learn more carefully how to circumscribe it, however, lest its native vigor be mistaken for, or in fact become, selfishness.

26. We will see why God's goodness is "graciously" present within the universe when we consider christology below.

27. Alves's groundbreaking work, now a classic, is *A Theology of Hope*

(Washington, D.C.: Corpus, 1969). Others that plowed the same ground are Carl Braaten, *The Future of God: The Revolutionary Dynamics of Hope* (New York: Harper and Row, 1969), and Rosemary Ruether's two works, *Liberation Theology: Human Hope Confronts Christian History and American Power* (New York: Paulist Press, 1972) and *The Radical Kingdom: The Western Experience of Messianic Hope* (New York: Harper and Row, 1970). Douglas Meeks summarizes the recent history of the theology of hope in his *Origins of the Theology of Hope* (Philadelphia: Fortress, 1974).

28. At least I think that its shape is cosmic or universal. Some would no doubt disagree with this, either because they reject the specific shape I shall describe or because there are insufficient data to consider with respect to other parts of the universe than ours, or both. At the very least, then, it will be a metaphysical context.

29. The complications of "good" and "bad" memories, as well as of the distinction between short-term and long-term memory, do not detract from the overall point being discussed here. For my purposes, I can simply stipulate a memory that collects all of the features of a given set of experiences and can serve up the relevant ones on demand.

30. Collection and storage is not a merely passive function, even if we limit the discussion to the collection of sensory impressions. Jacob Bronowski discusses the critical or discriminating operations of sight itself: our sense of vision does not perceive the world "as it truly is" but instead as it is reconfigured in such a way as to aid in comprehension and in everyday pragmatic functions. For example, even though the physical and molecular edge of a desk is quite ragged or jagged, our eyes "see" the edge as sharp and distinct so that we do not miss where it is and perhaps hurt ourselves on it. Things are similar with our auditory sense: human beings do not need to hear in the ranges that other animals do and thus have lost the capacity to do so. This, too, is a pragmatic and thus critical feature at work in the mere functioning of our five senses. See Jacob Bronowski, *The Origins of Knowledge and Imagination* (New Haven, Conn.: Yale University Press, 1978), pp. 15–17.

31. By "stored data" I mean nothing other than the stuff of memory, such as knowledge, beliefs, concepts, images, and the like.

32. In my discussion above, I used the word *knowledge* rather than *cognition*, since I was then concerned with the relationship between the dynamic mind and *present* data of information. Here it would be illicit to use *knowledge*, since we are considering *future* data, to which by definition our minds cannot be as firmly and indubitably related.

33. Once again, it matters materially and historically whether or not we are morally justified in hoping for these intentions rather than those, but it

does not matter formally and conceptually if we are. The point discussed here remains the same in either case, provided only that the person honestly intends to bring about a "good" state of affairs.

34. The reason why I use "belief" rather than "knowledge" here is that we must always bear in mind that we might be wrong in identifying a certain intention as a "good" one. Sin and idiosyncratic selfishness lurk nearby at all times.

35. This is a logical point. Even the deliberate and existential decision to abstain from taking a stand toward the future is itself a stand taken toward it.

36. It is, of course, the case that many persons are psychologically pessimistic rather than optimistic. This does not affect the transcendental analysis just made, though, because pessimism reflects the same critical *shape* as optimism: a certain evaluation of the present, and of the future, and one's commitment to act in concert with those expectations. The difference between these stances is not formal but rather material and at root, I think, spiritual as well; pessimism reflects one's belief that goodness and its opposite are dualistically balanced and thus that the moral shape of the future is a toss-up, whereas optimism reflects one's belief that goodness is ultimate, both abstractly and eventually historically as well.

37. I mean "rather than" in a weak sense here since obviously communities are communities *of* individuals. I simply mean to distance the present theory of revelation from any that locates it strictly within individuals per se. It will be recalled that I criticized William Abraham's "telepathy" model of revelation on precisely these grounds.

38. Lest I be misunderstood here, I am not saying that these things are *non*-revelatory. By now it should be clear that there are relatively few things that are *non*-revelatory, if by *things* we mean phenomena contained within or else implied by the dynamic relationships of knowing, loving, and hoping. Once again, though, in this study I am trying to uncover the abstract and thus universally identifiable content of divine revelation rather than the actual expressions of such revelation as received and enunciated within concrete communities or persons in history.

39. Bernard Lonergan, *Method in Theology* (New York: Seabury, 1979), p. 42.

40. Once again, I should emphasize that I am not equating "the possibility of moralness" with "concretely good acts," although the foregoing discussion might tend to blur the distinction. In depending on the concretely good contributions of others to our present acts of knowing, we thus disclose our even more fundamental belief that they are able to be good, and it is *this* ability that I have argued is distinctive of human beings.

41. The dynamic imbalance pictured here is the reason why persons are never static in their love for each other; instead, love either intensifies or

recedes. The concrete responsibility of the donor is to donate that which is enriching or enhancing to the beloved. The concrete responsibility of the beloved, though, is twofold. First, the person must concretely demonstrate willingness to receive from the other, and, second, she or he must reciprocate. When the possibility of this reciprocation is contemplated, the donor must indicate his or her willingness to be enhanced, thus authorizing the specific exchange of love. The lover and the beloved thus oscillate as to their asymmetrical responsibilities, which is why there will always be a growth curve, whether positive or negative, in the relationship of love.

42. One can, of course, hope for a better life for Spot or Fifi, so it cannot be said with analytic rigidity that the intentionality of hope always and everywhere designates a human person, which is something that we do want to say about the intentionality of love. We never intend hope with respect to other kinds of things, though; I do not "hope" that my bicycle has a good existence, for example, or that this building will enjoy its bricks and corridors. That is one of the ways I know that bicycles and buildings are not personal. There are two things we can do with this observation concerning the relationship between personal expressions and personal objects. Either we can grant that our stance toward animals disclosed by the appropriateness of hoping for them is simply anomalous, or we can contemplate whether in fact animals are perhaps closer to being "persons" than we typically think. For a representation of the latter, see Andrew Linzey, *Christianity and the Rights of Animals* (New York: Crossroad, 1987), which includes a list of sixteen ecclesial statements on the rights of animals published between 1956 and 1986. See also Tom Regan and Peter Singer, eds., *Animal Rights and Human Obligations* (Englewood Cliffs, N.J.: Prentice-Hall, 1976). On the other side, however, see Nicholas Wolterstorff's "Why Animals Don't Speak," *Faith and Philosophy* 4, 4 (October 1987), pp. 463–85). His response, materially similar to mine here, is that speaking is a normative act: "to perform an illocutionary action is to acquire a certain normative standing, or status" (p. 463). He goes on to clarify this: speaking does not so much *acquire* normative standing as it *presupposes* it: "To perform a speech action is to acquire a certain *normative standing* in one's society, a standing constituted in part by a certain complex of rights and/or responsibilities" (p. 471). He goes on to discuss how the possibility of understanding between any two persons presupposes a certain "fit [in] the moral relation between the two," a relation I have portrayed above as Point S. What Wolterstorff discusses here in the specific category of speech acts, I would expand to include other experiences of moralness as well.

43. Richard P. McBrien, *Catholicism* (Minneapolis: Winston, 1981), p. 1257.

Chapter 4

1. Gerald O'Collins, *Fundamental Theology* (New York: Paulist Press, 1981), p. 54.

2. For example, if revelation is simply identified with christology, such that learning about the significance of Jesus Christ is stipulated *as* being disclosed-to by God, an option we saw presented in various ways in the first two chapters of this book, then the need to discuss the present question in addition to the christological one is clouded. In such cases it could become unclouded, such as by asking why one identifies christology with revelation, but this can be an arduous task if for no other reason than that the question itself is usually regarded as contentious, skeptical, heretical, or the like.

3. It will be recalled here that I speak as a theologian and not a philosopher. Clearly it is possible to conceive of God apart from the aspect of divine self-revelation, but I would argue that all such attempts to do so are a-Christian, at least in classically Christian categories, precisely insofar as they attempt to identify a God whose existence is exclusively self-directed rather than hetero-directed. But a God who is so directed has only an ancillary interest (if that) in human salvation. No such God could qualify to be the Father of Jesus, and it is *this* God in whom the Church believes.

4. This is not mere ungrounded optimism. Quite to the contrary, it is essential to the possibility of science, law, medicine, and the whole array of other disciplines of thought. Seen from the other way around, that a particular conundrum might remain unresolved is demonstration of the more basic assumption that it should not.

5. Suppose, for example, a person alleged to know everything that could be known. This person would still need to answer the question "What can be done with all of this knowledge?" not as a rhetorical question but instead as a quite real one. It would thus constitute a still-existing limitation to his or her knowledge calling for self-transcendence.

6. In a sense, this statement is self-referentially inconsistent, since by definition we cannot know "the nature and definition" of the unknowable. But as I shall try to show, that it is unknowable means we cannot make any ultimately positive or categorical propositional statements about it. We can, however, further refine what the unknowable must be by paring away from it everything it could not possibly be. Aquinas began his extended treatment of "The One God" by noting this very point: "Now we cannot know how God is, but only how he is not; we must therefore consider the ways in which God does not exist, rather than the ways in which he does. . . . The ways in which God does not exist will become apparent if we rule

out from [the consideration of] him everything inappropriate [to him]."
Summa Theologiae, I, 3, Introduction.

7. I do not hesitate to give the impression of personifying this unknown because my intention is theological. I intend to show how it is reasonable even if not necessary to refer to Unknowable Mystery as God.

8. Karl Rahner, "The Concept of Mystery in Catholic Theology," *Theological Investigations* IV (New York: Crossroad, 1982), p. 51.

9. Another way to make this same point is to recall the fact that the first generation of believers in Jesus did not invent the category of divine revelation in order to account for how they experienced Jesus as the Messiah, the Word of God, and so on. In fact, things were the other way around. They were confident that Jesus was the Messiah, Word of God, and so on, precisely because in Him they experienced a fuller and clearer revelation of God. But this presupposes that they already possessed a "leaner and hazier" revelation of God, a presupposition confirmed in their earliest sermons with respect to both Jews (Acts 13:13–43) and non-Jews (Acts 17:22–34). It is my intention in this study to repeat that approach.

10. To say that this discussion approaches divine revelation from the outside or considers it in the abstract is not to propose a generic notion of revelation fully and completely discoverable, say, within a History of Religions context and thus constituting a lowest-common-denominator approach. Although I go on in this section to discuss this in greater clarity, here I can defend my approach by saying that it is always possible to reflect back upon a specific event in history (here, the specific revelation of God in Christ) and see both in it and through it the "larger" event intended by God. I believe that Jesus is the fullest revelation of God, but that does not mean He is either the first or the final one; surely the Christian community since the first century has discovered more about the whole reality that revelation seeks to illuminate than that which the first-century community knew. That Jesus is the "fullest" revelation of God means instead that whatever we learn about God ever since His disclosure of God must be evaluated back against that disclosure itself. Thus, the confession "Jesus is the revelation (or Word) of God" functions more like a critical guide than a mere historical observation or predication.

11. In my earlier book, *Evangelical Theories of Biblical Inspiration* (New York: Oxford University Press, 1987), I proposed a description of evangelicalism that includes what I then called transdenominationalism or pluralism, and what I have here called ecumenism. Although not all are happy with pluralism thus built in as a constituent element within the very notion of evangelicalism, I continue to think now as I did then: "evangelicalism discloses a greater implicit emphasis upon the experience of salvation in Jesus than upon [denominational] articulations of this experience. . . .

Thus, considered ecclesiologically, evangelicalism is Protestantism's clearest attempt to recapture the pluralistic nature of the early church" (p. 4).

12. To those who balk at the claim that "God is love" is interchangeable with "Love is God," there are two basic avenues of response. I shall take up the more directly theological one in my discussion of the Holy Spirit below. (The insight we shall explore there is that the love by which the Father loves the Son and vice versa is itself both personal and divine.)

The second or "grammatical" approach is brought to light by David Burrell, who elaborates on St. Thomas's discussion of some essential attributes of God in his *Exercises in Religious Understanding*. When talking of God, says Thomas, we must recall that our usual grammatical constructs do not work, for they reflect the compositeness of the world in (for example) the logical distinction between subject and object in sentences, whereas the Jewish-Christian insight into God has insisted that God is noncomposite or "simple." Thus, the only sentence that is similarly interpretable when used *in divinis* and otherwise is "God is" or "To be God is to be." All attempts to predicate differentiations between God and God's various attributes, says Burrell, are inappropriate with respect to the "first cause of all things." From this perspective, then, too, we can see that the grammatical inappropriateness of the identity between "God is love" and "Love is God" resides in the fact that love is identical with nothing else in the world. But if, in fact, the insight that "God is love" is valid for Christian faith, then the reverse predication must be as well precisely as the best way of showing *how* God is love.

13. At least, it is not what is at stake in most christological discussions. To the degree that there is an ethical intention to christological discussions, it is important to say something about the quality of the human life that Jesus lived. And in terms of His faithfulness to God, I am fully convinced that His life provides the model or paradigm for ours. But it is precisely because Jesus models faithfulness before *God* that the ultimate point of christology remains soteriology rather than ethics.

14. This is the thesis of James D. G. Dunn's *Christology in the Making: A New Testament Inquiry into the Origins of the Doctrine of the Incarnation* (Philadelphia: Westminster, 1980). The underlying dynamic that became progressively clearer throughout the first century was Judaism's intention to portray God's immanence without thereby nullifying God's transcendence. In Christ, Dunn claims on behalf of the early Christians, these converge.

15. For a very helpful account of the spectrum of alternatives that stretches between these two extremes, see J. Peter Schineller's "Christ and Church: A Spectrum of Views," *Theological Studies* 37 (1976), pp. 545–66. Schineller identifies the two extremes as an "ecclesiological universe with

an exclusive Christology" on the one hand and a "theocentric universe with a nonnormative Christology" on the other.

16. In more classical christological terms, we shall first do christology "from below," showing how Jesus was able to be the real presence of God on earth while remaining fully human. Then we shall take up a christology "from above," showing how God could become other than what God was and is precisely and only because God is love. Or, in more systematic terms, we shall first consider theological anthropology and then move to theological soteriology.

17. This "formal nature of the cosmos itself" is not uninteresting for our purposes, since it, too, calls for an accounting that, for Christians, finally terminates in God ("We believe in God . . . the creator of heaven and earth, and of all things visible and invisible . . ."). But since my specific focus here is on divine revelation and hence on the *moral* sphere of cosmic reality, this point may be noted and then passed over.

18. The significance of this statement is not in how it designates humans as somehow "unique" in the cosmos, as though their specialness lay only in that uniqueness. As a matter of fact, I think that if we were to discover other beings in the universe capable of intentional events of self-transcendence who were not otherwise recognizably human, the following account would be even more decisively confirmed. See Francine Patterson, "Conversations with a Gorilla," *National Geographic*, October (1978), pp. 438–65; and Joyce Dudney Fleming, "The State of the Apes," *Psychology Today* 7 (1974), pp. 31–38.

19. For example, it is precisely because we are material beings that we cannot do certain kinds of things, such as run a mile in one minute. Even these "far extremes," however, are flexible, and thus the *cannot* of the previous sentence is historically rather than logically bound. We discover this anew each and every time the existing world-record time for the mile is lowered by another tiny increment of time, for example. As mind-boggling as it is to think of right now, it is a brave person indeed who would insist that what is a physical impossibility at our moment of history is in fact a conceptual impossibility per se and thus eternally. Twenty thousand years from now, a one-minute mile might well be routine for folks who in all other respects look rather like us. This illustration could be expanded to reflect the particularities of the other realms of human existence identified earlier, namely the intellectual, psychological, and spiritual realms. At present we may be comfortable in our beliefs that there are certain borders or boundaries that will not be surpassed by human beings. But we must carefully guard against equating this (historical) comfortability too casually with (transcendental) impossibility, lest someday we need to reconceive our history books rather than merely add chapters to them.

Karl Rahner makes this same point when he describes the notion of concupiscence as the inevitable tension between "person" and "nature." The latter refers to those concrete and limiting features of human life that are the collective expression of historical life, such as gender, race, intelligence, nationality, subjectivity to sin, and so on. The former refers to how we as self-transcending subjects grasp those features of ours, interpreting them not as ultimate and pessimistic limitations but rather as constituting the foundation and framework within which we are called by God to be faithful and which we are empowered by grace to transcend. It is true that our nature will never be neutralized and disabled altogether, but it is also true that our person is always free to transcend whatever natural limitations intrude upon our calling to be faithful to God. It is in this sense, then, that the freedom grace empowers is "more" ultimate than the natural features within which freedom operates. See Karl Rahner, "The Theological Concept of Concupiscentia," *Theological Investigations* I (Baltimore: Helicon, 1961), pp. 347–82.

20. This should not be surprising to read in a study that attempts to articulate the distinctively moral nature of human life and thus of divine revelation which constitutes the moral possibilities of that human life. This arises from the age-old realization that morality and freedom mutually imply each other. If this is so in the historical or concrete or *a posteriori* realm of existence, then it is also true in the transcendental or universal or *a priori* realm as well.

21. In spite of what was said in note 19 above, there are theoretical limits beyond which humans as historically conceived will not pass. For example, it would not be not possible to think of a being as human if, when considered in its spiritual dimension, it had "passed through" the moral boundary of knowing that murder is wrong and became morally comfortable with gratuitous killing.

22. Catholics and Orthodox, for example, typically assert this about Mary but are not thereby tempted to worship Mary as God incarnate.

23. I have omitted the title *Lord* from this list because it is more difficult for us to interpret as a genitive; "Jesus is the Lord of God" rolls less smoothly off the confessing tongue than, for example, "Jesus is the Word of God." This is not at all to say, though, that those who first used *Lord* in their response to Jesus used it in the same way as we do today, and so in *this* sense the word functions in the same way as the titles I have listed here. James D. G. Dunn outlines what he calls the "spectrum of dignity" attaching to this word in *Unity and Diversity in the New Testament* (Philadelphia: Westminster, 1977): "What role or status does [Lord] attribute to Jesus or recognize as belonging to Jesus? The answers of earliest Christianity vary and we cannot always be sure if we are hearing them correctly. The

problem is that 'lord' can denote a whole range of dignity—from a respectful form of address as to a teacher or judge to a full title for God. Where do the early Christian references to the lordship of Jesus come within this spectrum? The answer seems to be that over the first few decades of Christianity the confession of Jesus as 'Lord' moved in overt significance from the lower end of this 'spectrum of dignity' towards the upper end steadily gathering to itself increasing overtones of deity" (p. 50).

24. Colossians 2:9, 10. Note how the author "warrants" his christological claim by behavioral or experiential recourse: if his readers could not reflect upon the fullness of life that characterized their lives "now" as over against "before," then the statement itself would be meaningless to them. But because they are able to chart that change, they are able likewise both to understand and to affirm the claim about God's presence in Christ. Note, too, that this is not an incarnational claim.

25. That is, it presupposes relative human freedom.

26. I need to add "under normal circumstances" here because it might well be the case that we hope for something in our beloved's life that we are somehow precluded from helping to effect but yet which is effected anyhow in the ways we had hoped. One thinks here of parents who hope for their infant child's medical health yet cannot directly affect it because they are not physicians. As common as this might be, let us simply call it an exception to the "normal" rule and return to the situation where we both intend and help to effect a transformation in our beloved's life.

27. We need to remind ourselves again at this point that this analysis intends to reflect the usual and not the exceptional in human relationships. That is, I am aware that hope and love are genuinely present in a parent's love for a severely mentally handicapped child, for example, or in a nurse's love for Alzheimer's patients. But again, I would interpret these instances as exceptions that can be viewed *as* love precisely in view of the inability of the beloved to respond and reciprocate in the ways we more usually identify as disclosing the presence of love.

28. See William J. Hill, *The Three-Personed God: The Trinity as a Mystery of Salvation* (Washington, D.C.: Catholic University of America Press, 1982), as well as the aforementioned Eberhard Jüngel, *God as the Mystery of the World* (Grand Rapids, Mich.: Eerdmans, 1983), especially "On the Humanity of God," pp. 299–396.

29. For a summary of this evolution, see Dunn, *Christology*, pp. 258–68.

30. The best accessible survey of alternative trinitarianisms in Christian history is found in Hill's *The Three-Personed God.*

31. This is how David Burrell translates Thomas Aquinas's preferred description of God as "*ipse esse.*" Burrell notes that there are two senses in which Thomas uses the affirmative *to be* with respect to God, the definitive

and the affirmative. Only the former is used by Thomas, though, when he wishes to discuss God, because the kind of knowledge requisite for the latter is unavailable to human beings. Thus, the sentence "God is" means not that "God exists" but instead that "To be God is to be." "[It] is one of those crucial tautologies defining the logical space of God-talk." See David Burrell, *Aquinas: God and Act* (Notre Dame: University of Notre Dame Press, 1979), p. 8.

32. Hill, *Three-Personed God*, p. 293, citing Thomas, I *Sent.*, d. 14, q. 1, a. 1, sol.

33. Note the methodological identity between this statement (unveil, communicate, commit) and the structure and claims of the present book (know, love, hope).

34. Hill, *Three-Personed God*, pp. 296–97.

35. See what was said earlier about the close relationship between hope and political (or liberation) theology, above, p. 130.

36. I am aware that "the Trinity" is a dogma and not simply a doctrine. This distinction is most comfortable within a Catholic context, though, a context I would hope the present book includes but is not limited to. Thus, and in deference to Protestant audiences, I shall refer to it as a doctrine without prejudice to the essential centrality of the notion itself within the Christian understanding of God. For a concise introduction to this distinction, see Richard P. McBrien, *Catholicism* (study edition) (San Francisco: Harper and Row, 1986), pp. 67–74, 77.

37. At first blush, this seems to ignore or reverse the age-old distinction in trinitarian discussions between the Trinity considered *in se* and *ad extra*. In specific, it seems to do so by claiming that the Trinity *in se* acts within history. I am not unaware of the controversy that lies within this discussion, especially the controversy over whether God exists in time or in eternity. Most parties to this discussion claim that God exists in eternity and thus that trinitarian acts *in se* are by definition outside of time and history. I am rather of the belief that God exists in time and thus that all divine acts, whether we distinguish them for our own convenience as *in se* or as *ad extra*, are performed within time and history. I shall consider this in some more detail in the appendix, although not so much as to constitute a comprehensive critical review.

38. See Maurice Wiles and Mark Santer, eds., *Documents in Early Christian Thought* (Cambridge: Cambridge University Press, 1975), p. 24, citing the *Library of Christian Classics* 3, 437–40 (trans. by Henry Chadwick).

39. Hill's *Three-Personed God* is an excellent resource for those wishing to embark upon such a process.

40. Romans 5:5 and 8:16.

Appendix

1. This is rhetorically clear but logically imprecise. The open possibility itself cannot change, of course, but only the event that eventually instantiates either it or else other open possibilities. To say that the future is changeable logically implies that it is determined except to whatever degree it is changeable, which I would also contest. It is better logic to say that the future is "open" than to say that it is "changeable." However, for the sake of rhetoric, I shall continue to use these phrases interchangeably.

2. Stephen W. Hawking, *A Brief History of Time: From the Big Bang to Black Holes* (New York: Bantam, 1988), pp. 143–53.

3. Ibid., p. 145.

4. Hawking's discussion of this point uses the analogy of the energy required to maintain computer memory rather than cranial: "It is rather difficult to talk about human memory because we do not know how the brain works in detail. We do, however, know all about how computer memories work. . . . I think that it is reasonable to assume that the arrow for computers is the same as that for humans. If it were not, one could make a killing on the stock exchange by having a computer that would remember tomorrow's prices!" Ibid., pp. 146–47.

5. The related question of whether or not God is thereby responsible for what we "choose" is irrelevant in this discussion, for here I am only interested in whether the traditional notion of divine omniscience is compatible with the freedom and responsibility that are a fundamental and inescapable part of how we stand in and toward the world.

6. This is often referred to as the liberty of spontaneity, which is the liberty to do what we want regardless of whether those wants themselves are determined or not. The alternative to this is the liberty of indifference, which is the liberty to do something or not to do it, as determined only by whether the thing is doable at all. Not surprisingly, I am arguing on behalf of liberty in the stronger sense of indifference.

7. Another usual feature of the response to my argument here comes from Boethius, who was the first to have said that God's knowledge of event X does not in fact "cause" it any more than my knowledge that Jane murdered John makes me guilty of murder. This is true but irrelevant. The reason is that it gratuitously ignores that God's omniscient knowledge is also infallible; that is, whatever God knows is known without the possibility of being false. Boethius's claim does not need to be attached to omnipotence (which it usually is because most participants are interested in the ultimate reasons why human beings do things) in order to be seen as irrelevant. Instead, all that is needed is to notice that God cannot be wrong in God's knowledge of anything, regardless of whether God caused that

thing directly or indirectly, primarily or secondarily. If God knows that I will choose alternative A and that knowledge is infallible, then my future is determined even if not by God. And correlatively, I cannot be held responsible for it. See Boethius, *The Consolation of Philosophy*, trans. by V. E. Watts (London: Penguin, 1969), Book 5, Chapter 6.

8. William Rowe makes much the same point with respect to the divine attribute of omnipotence, which means for him that "God can do anything that is an absolute possibility" (i.e., is logically possible) *and not inconsistent with any of his basic attributes.*" *Philosophy of Religion* (Encino, Calif.: Dickenson, 1978), p. 9, cited in Ronald H. Nash, *The Concept of God: An Exploration of Contemporary Difficulties with the Attributes of God* (Grand Rapids, Mich.: Zondervan, 1983), p. 50.

9. Aquinas, *Summa Contra Gentiles*, I.16.1, 2.

BIBLIOGRAPHY

Abraham, William J. *The Divine Inspiration of Holy Scripture*. Oxford: Oxford University Press, 1981.

———. *Divine Revelation and the Limits of Historical Criticism*. Oxford: Oxford University Press, 1982.

Alves, Rubem. *A Theology of Hope*. Washington, D.C.: Corpus, 1969.

Anderson, Bernhard W. *Understanding the Old Testament*, 3rd ed. Englewood Cliffs, N.J.: Prentice-Hall, 1975.

Bainton, Roland. *Yesterday, Today and What Next? Reflections on History and Hope*. Minneapolis: Augsburg, 1978.

Barth, Karl. *Church Dogmatics*, II, 2. Edinburgh: T. and T. Clark, 1964.

———. *The Epistle to the Romans*. New York: Oxford University Press, 1972.

———. *Evangelical Theology*. Garden City, N.Y.: Doubleday, 1964.

———. *The Humanity of God*. Richmond, Va.: John Knox, 1972.

Berkouwer, B. C. *General Revelation*. Grand Rapids, Mich.: Eerdmans, 1955.

Boff, Leonardo. *Trinity and Society*. Maryknoll, N.Y.: Orbis, 1988.

Braaten, Carl. *The Future of God: The Revolutionary Dynamics of Hope*. New York: Harper and Row, 1969.

Bronowski, Jacob. *The Origins of Knowledge and Imagination*. New Haven, Conn.: Yale University Press, 1978.

Brueggemann, Walter. *Hope within History*. Atlanta: John Knox, 1987.

Burrell, David B. *Aquinas: God and Act*. Notre Dame, Ind.: University of Notre Dame Press, 1979.

———. *Exercises in Religious Understanding*. Notre Dame, Ind.: University of Notre Dame Press, 1974.

Cell, Edward. *Language, Existence, and God*. Atlantic Highlands, N.J.: Humanities, 1978.

Dickie, Edgar P. *Revelation and Response*. Edinburgh: T. and T. Clark, 1938.

Dulles, Avery. *Models of the Church*. Garden City, N.Y.: Image, 1978.

——. *Models of Revelation*. Garden City, N.Y.: Image, 1985.

——. *Revelation and the Quest for Unity*. Washington, D.C., and Cleveland: Corpus, 1968.

——. *Revelation Theory: A History*. New York: Herder and Herder, 1969.

Dunn, James D. G. *Christology in the Making: A New Testament Inquiry into the Origins of the Doctrine of the Incarnation*. Philadelphia: Westminster, 1980.

Dunne, Tad. *Lonergan and Spirituality: Towards a Spiritual Integration*. Chicago: Loyola University Press, 1985.

Eiseley, Loren. *The Immense Journey*. New York: Random House, 1957.

Fleming, Joyce Dudney. "The State of the Ape." *Psychology Today* 7 (1974), pp. 31–38.

Frei, Hans. *The Doctrine of Revelation in the Thought of Karl Barth, 1909 to 1922: The Nature of Barth's Break with Liberalism*. Doctoral dissertation, Yale University, 1956.

Hawking, Stephen W. *A Brief History of Time: From the Big Bang to Black Holes*. New York: Bantam, 1988.

Henry, Carl F. H. *God, Revelation and Authority*. Waco, Tex.: Word, 1976.

Hill, William J. *The Three-Personed God: The Trinity as a Mystery of Salvation*. Washington, D.C.: Catholic University of America Press, 1982.

Hoeksema, Herman. *Reformed Dogmatics*. Grand Rapids, Mich.: Reformed Free Publishing Association, 1966.

Honner, John. "Disclosed and Transcendental: Rahner and Ramsey on the Foundations of Theology." *Haythrop Journal* 22 (1981), pp. 149–61.

Johnston, Robert K., ed. *The Use of the Bible in Theology/Evangelical Options*. Atlanta: John Knox, 1985.

Jüngel, Eberhard. *God as the Mystery of the World: On the Foundation of the Theology of the Crucified One in the Dispute between Theism and Atheism*. Grand Rapids, Mich.: Eerdmans, 1983.

Kasper, Walter. *An Introduction to Christian Faith*. New York: Paulist Press, 1980.

Küng, Hans. *Justification: The Doctrine of Karl Barth and a Catholic Reflection*. New York: Nelson and Sons, 1964.

Lash, Nicholas. *Easter in Ordinary: Reflections on Human Experience and the Knowledge of God*. Charlottesville, Va.: University Press of Virginia, 1988.

Latourelle, René. *Theology of Revelation*. Staten Island, N.Y.: Alba House, 1966.

Latourelle, René, and Gerald O'Collins, eds. *Problems and Perspectives of Fundamental Theology*. Mahwah, N.J.: Paulist Press, 1982.

Lindbeck, George. *The Nature of Doctrine*. Philadelphia: Westminster, 1984.

Linzey, Andrew. *Christianity and the Rights of Animals*. New York: Crossroad, 1987.

Lonergan, Bernard. *Doctrinal Pluralism*. Milwaukee: Marquette University Press, 1971.

———. *Method in Theology*. New York: Seabury, 1979.

McBrien, Richard P. *Catholicism*. Minneapolis: Winston, 1981.

McClendon, James W., and James M. Smith. *Understanding Religious Convictions*. Notre Dame, Ind.: University of Notre Dame Press, 1975.

McDonald, H. D. *Theories of Revelation: An Historical Study 1700-1960*. Grand Rapids, Mich.: Baker, 1979.

Macquarrie, John. *Principles of Christian Theology*, 2d ed. New York: Scribner's, 1977.

Maddox, Randy L. *Toward an Ecumenical Fundamental Theology*. American Academy of Religion Series, Number 47. Chico, Calif.: Scholars Press, 1984.

Man as Man and Believer. Concilium Series, Vol. 21: *Dogma*. New York: Paulist Press, 1967.

Marty, Martin. *Protestantism*. Garden City, N.Y.: Image, 1974.

Meeks, Douglas. *Origins of the Theology of Hope*. Philadelphia: Fortress, 1974.

Nash, Ronald H. *The Concept of God: An Exploration of Contemporary Difficulties with the Attributes of God*. Grand Rapids, Mich.: Zondervan, 1983.

O'Collins, Gerald. *Fundamental Theology*. New York: Paulist Press, 1981.

O'Meara, Thomas F. "Toward a Subjective Theology of Revelation," *Theological Studies* 36 (1975), pp. 401-27.

Packer, James I. *"Fundamentalism" and the WORD OF GOD, Some Evangelical Principles*. Grand Rapids, Mich.: Eerdmans, 1980.

———. *Knowing God*. Downers Grove, Ill.: InterVarsity, 1973.

Patterson, Francine. "Conversations with a Gorilla." *National Geographic* (October 1978), pp. 438-65.

Pepper, Stephen C. *World Hypotheses: A Study in Evidence*. Berkeley, Calif.: University of California Press, 1942.

Perrin, Norman, and Dennis Duling. *The New Testament: An Introduction*, 2d ed. New York: Harcourt Barce Jovanovich, 1982.

Peter, Carl J. "A Shift to the Human Subject in Roman Catholic Theology." *Communio* (U.S.) 6, no. 1 (1979), pp. 56-72.

Polanyi, Michael. *Personal Knowledge: Towards a Post-Critical Philosophy*. Chicago: University of Chicago Press, 1958; corrected edition 1962.

Preller, Victor. *Divine Science and the Science of God: A Reformulation of Thomas Aquinas.* Princeton, N.J.: Princeton University Press, 1967.

Rahner, Karl. "The Concept of Mystery in Catholic Theology." *Theological Investigations* IV. New York: Crossroad, 1982, pp. 36–73.

———. *Foundations of Christian Faith: An Introduction to the Idea of Christianity.* New York: Seabury, 1978.

———. "Thomas Aquinas on the Incomprehensibility of God." *Journal of Religion* 58 (1978 supp.), pp. S107–25.

Rahner, Karl, and Joseph Ratzinger. *Revelation and Tradition.* New York: Herder and Herder, 1966.

Ramsey, Ian T. *Christian Discourse.* London: Oxford University Press, 1965.

———. *Christian Empiricism* (ed. by Jerry Gill). Grand Rapids, Mich.: Eerdmans, 1974.

———. *Models and Mystery.* London: Oxford University Press, 1964.

———. *On Being Sure in Religion.* London: Athlone, 1963.

———. *Religious Language: An Empirical Placing of Theological Phrases.* London: SCM, 1957.

Ramsey, Ian T., ed. *Words about God: The Philosophy of Religion.* New York: Harper and Row, 1971.

Ramsey, Ian T., and Ruth Porter, eds. *Personality and Science.* London: Churchill Livingstone, 1971.

Regan, Tom, and Peter Singer, eds. *Animal Rights and Human Obligations.* Englewood Cliffs, N.J.: Prentice-Hall, 1976.

Reuther, Rosemary. *Liberation Theology: Human Hope Confronts Christian History and American Power.* New York: Paulist Press, 1972.

———. *The Radical Kingdom: The Western Experience of Messianic Hope.* New York: Harper and Row, 1970.

Schillebeeckx, Edward. *Christ: The Experience of Jesus as Lord.* New York: Crossroad, 1980.

———. *Jesus: An Experiment in Christology.* New York: Crossroad, 1981.

———. *Revelation and Theology.* New York: Sheed and Ward, 1967.

Schillebeeckx, Edward, and Bas van Iersel, eds. *Revelation and Experience.* New York: Seabury, 1979.

Schineller, J. Peter. "Christ and Church: A Spectrum of Views." *Theological Studies* 37 (1976), pp. 545–66.

Shorter, Aylward. *Revelation and Its Interpretation.* London: Geoffrey Chapman, 1983.

Tilley, Terrence W. *Talking of God.* New York: Paulist Press, 1978.

Torrance, Thomas F. *Reality and Evangelical Theology: A Fresh and Challenging Approach to Christian Revelation.* Philadelphia: Westminster, 1982.

Trembath, Kern R. *Evangelical Theories of Biblical Inspiration: A Review and Proposal.* New York: Oxford University Press, 1987.

Viladesau, Richard. *The Reason for Our Hope: A Theological Anthropology.* New York: Paulist Press, 1984.

Wiles, Maurice. *The Remaking of Christian Doctrine.* London: SCM, 1974.

Wiles, Maurice, and Mark Santer, eds. *Documents in Early Christian Thought.* Cambridge: Cambridge University Press, 1975.

Williamson, William B. *Ian T. Ramsey.* Waco, Tex.: Word, 1982.

Woltersdorff, Nicholas. "Why Animals Don't Speak." *Faith and Philosophy* 4, no. 4 (October 1987), pp. 463–85.

Zimmerman, Laura L. *God and Time.* Doctoral dissertation, University of Notre Dame, 1983.

SUBJECT INDEX

NAME INDEX

229